Cultural Political Economy

The global political economy is inescapably cultural. Whether we talk about the economic dimensions of the 'war on terror', the sub-prime crisis and its aftermath, or the ways in which new information technology has altered practices of production and consumption, it has become increasingly clear that these processes cannot be fully captured by the hyper-rational analysis of economists or the slogans of class conflict. This book argues that culture is a concept that can be used to develop more subtle and fruitful analyses of the dynamics and problems of the global political economy.

Rediscovering the unacknowledged role of culture in the writings of classical political economists, the contributors to this volume reveal its central place in the historical evolution of post-war capitalism and explore its continued role in contemporary economic processes that range from the commercialization of security practices to the development of ethical tourism. The book shows that culture plays a role in both constituting different forms of economic life and in shaping the diverse ways that capitalism has developed historically – from its earliest moments to its most recent challenges.

Providing valuable insights to a wide range of disciplines, this volume will be of vital interest to students and scholars of international political economy, cultural and economic geography and sociology, and international relations.

Jacqueline Best is Associate Professor in the School of Political Studies at the University of Ottawa, Canada.

Matthew Paterson is Professor in the School of Political Studies at the University of Ottawa, Canada.

RIPE series in global political economy

Series editors: Louise Amoore (*University of Durham, UK*), Jacqueline Best (*University of Ottawa, Canada*), Paul Langley (*Northumbria University, UK*) and Leonard Seabrooke (*Copenhagen Business School, Denmark*).

Formerly edited by Randall Germain (*Carleton University, Canada*), Rorden Wilkinson (*University of Manchester, UK*), Otto Holman (*University of Amsterdam*), Marianne Marchand (*Universidad de las Américas-Puebla*), Henk Overbeek (*Free University, Amsterdam*) and Marianne Franklin (*Goldsmiths, University of London, UK*).

The RIPE series editorial board are:

Mathias Albert (*Bielefeld University, Germany*), Mark Beeson (*University of Birmingham, UK*), A. Claire Cutler (*University of Victoria, Canada*), Marianne Franklin (*Goldsmiths, University of London, UK*), Randall Germain (*Carleton University, Canada*) Stephen Gill (*York University, Canada*), Jeffrey Hart (*Indiana University, USA*), Eric Helleiner (*Trent University, Canada*), Otto Holman (*University of Amsterdam, the Netherlands*), Marianne H. Marchand *(Universidad de las Américas-Puebla, Mexico)*, Craig N. Murphy (*Wellesley College, USA*), Robert O'Brien (*McMaster University, Canada*), Henk Overbeek (*Vrije Universiteit, the Netherlands*), Anthony Payne (*University of Sheffield, UK*), V. Spike Peterson (*University of Arizona, USA*) and Rorden Wilkinson (*University of Manchester, UK*).

This series, published in association with the *Review of International Political Economy*, provides a forum for current and interdisciplinary debates in international political economy. The series aims to advance understanding of the key issues in the global political economy, and to present innovative analyses of emerging topics. The titles in the series focus on three broad themes:

- the structures, processes and actors of contemporary global transformations;
- the changing forms taken by governance, at scales from the local and everyday to the global and systemic;
- the inseparability of economic from political, social and cultural questions, including resistance, dissent and social movements.

The series comprises two strands:

The *RIPE Series in Global Political Economy* aims to address the needs of students and teachers, and the titles will be published in hardback and paperback. Titles include:

Transnational Classes and International Relations
Kees van der Pijl

Gender and Global Restructuring:
Sightings, sites and resistances
Edited by Marianne H. Marchand and Anne Sisson Runyan

Global Political Economy
Contemporary theories
Edited by Ronen Palan

Ideologies of Globalization
Contending visions of a new world order
Mark Rupert

The Clash within Civilisations
Coming to terms with cultural conflicts
Dieter Senghaas

Global Unions?
Theory and strategies of organized labour in the global political economy
Edited by Jeffrey Harrod and Robert O'Brien

Political Economy of a Plural World
Critical reflections on power, morals and civilizations
Robert Cox with Michael Schechter

A Critical Rewriting of Global Political Economy
Integrating reproductive, productive and virtual economies
V. Spike Peterson

Contesting Globalization
Space and place in the world economy
André C. Drainville

Global Institutions and Development
Framing the world?
Edited by Morten Bøås and Desmond McNeill

Global institutions, marginalization, and development
Craig N. Murphy

Critical Theories, International Relations and 'the Anti-Globalisation Movement'
The politics of global resistance
Edited by Catherine Eschle and Bice Maiguashca

Globalization, Governmentality, and Global Politics
Regulation for the rest of us?
Ronnie D. Lipschutz, with James K. Rowe

Critical Perspectives on Global Governance
Rights and regulation in governing regimes
Jean Grugel and Nicola Piper

Beyond States and Markets
The challenges of social reproduction
Edited by Isabella Bakker and Rachel Silvey

The Industrial Vagina
The political economy of the global sex trade
Sheila Jeffreys

Routledge/RIPE Studies in Global Political Economy is a forum for innovative new research intended for a high-level specialist readership, and the titles will be available in hardback only. Titles include:

*Also available in paperback

Cultural Political Economy

**Edited by Jacqueline Best
and Matthew Paterson**

Routledge
Taylor & Francis Group

LONDON AND NEW YORK

First published 2010
by Routledge
2 Park Square, Milton Park, Abingdon, Oxon, OX14 4RN

Simultaneously published in the USA and Canada
by Routledge
711 Third Avenue, New York, NY 10017

Routledge is an imprint of the Taylor & Francis Group, an informa business

© 2010 Jacqueline Best and Matthew Paterson
selection and editorial matter; individual contributors, their contributions

Typeset in Times New Roman by Keyword Group Ltd

British Library Cataloguing in Publication Data
A catalogue record for this book is available from the British Library

Library of Congress Cataloging in Publication Data
Includes bibliographical references and index.
1. International economic relations–Social aspects. 2. Capitalism–Social aspects. 3. Economics–Sociological aspects. 4. Politics and culture.
I. Best, Jacqueline, 1970- II. Paterson, Matthew, 1967-
HF1359.C846 2009
306.3–dc22   2009029331

ISBN 10: 0-415-48931-8 (hbk)
ISBN 10: 0-415-48932-6 (pbk)
ISBN 10: 0-203-86139-6 (ebk)

ISBN 13: 978-0-415-48931-7 (hbk)
ISBN 13: 978-0-415-48932-4 (pbk)
ISBN 13: 978-0-203-86139-4 (ebk)

Contents

Figures

Preface

This book started life as a series of conversations – in the hallway, at lunch, over a beer. We discovered that although we came from somewhat different intellectual traditions and focused our research on different kinds of empirical objects, we both saw ourselves struggling with a similar set of problems – which we came to understand as needing something that we have come to call cultural political economy.

This intuition had both empirical and theoretical aspects. As we first began to discuss the idea of cultural political economy, we were both involved in research projects – on automobile politics and on the 'ethical turn' in IMF rhetoric, respectively – in which the cultural character of political-economic practices seemed to be increasingly obvious. We were also struck by the resonance between these more formal manifestations of cultural politics and the diverse everyday practices that we saw around us – the cult of homeownership, changing experiences of security at the border, in shopping malls or at the workplace, ever-changing technological fetishes from iPhones to Twitter, projects to 'clean the streets' of the homeless or of drug users, and so on. To make sense of these concrete practices seemed to require a richer, more complex way of linking their economic, cultural and political dimensions.

Our motivation for putting this book together was also linked to our theoretical preoccupations. As scholars, we had both always been theoretically eclectic and disciplinarily open in our reading. While we both worked in international political economy, we had been significantly influenced by the cultural turn in international relations. We had also drawn inspiration from the cultural economy literature in sociology, anthropology and geography. We could both see connections among these different kinds of scholarship that had not yet been fully recognized – connections that linked the economic, the cultural and the political in new and important ways.

We also knew that we were not the only ones to have identified these connections and asked these sorts of questions. In fact, part of our interest in the project came from our recognition that there were a growing number of scholars who were beginning to do so. We therefore set out to organize a workshop in June 2007 that brought together a diverse group of scholars to discuss what it might mean in theoretical and empirical terms to invoke the phrase 'cultural political economy' – to explore the cultural dimensions of the economy, the economic aspects of culture, and the political character of both. Our aim was to open up a series of conversations through which we might all clarify our understanding of these relationships both through a set of theoretical debates and in diverse empirical contexts. That workshop was succeeded by a panel at the International Studies Association 2008 meeting in San Francisco. And so, this book did not only begin as a conversation, but has continued to evolve through a series of ever-wider conversations. With luck, of course, this book will only be the beginning of that process.

Jacqueline Best and Matthew Paterson
Ottawa, April 2009

Acknowledgements

A number of people have helped to make this book possible. First, are those who have worked hard for us behind the scenes. Much of the final quality of the text was made possible by fabulous editing work by Natalie Britton. The book would have taken a lot longer, and the process would have been a lot more stressful without her. The book was based on a series of papers given at a workshop in Ottawa in June 2007, and Andreas (Res) Krebs, Gail Pétrin, Anick Mineault and Céline Widmer all provided excellent logistical and organizational support which enabled us to concentrate on the substance of the papers and discussions. The workshop was also supported financially by the Social Sciences and Humanities Research Council, as well as the University of Ottawa, and we thank them for making it possible. We thank in particular François Houle and Marcel Mérette in the Faculty of Social Sciences for their support of the project.

   This book is a product of a wider set of conversations than those articulated within these pages. We therefore heartily thank those who contributed to those discussions, chief among them the other scholars who presented at the workshop, or at a follow-up panel at the International Studies Association meeting in March 2008 – William Biebuyck, Randy Germain, Adam Harmes, Paul Langley, Mark Salter and Deborah Sick. Thanks also to Len Seabrooke and Mlada Bukovansky who provided excellent feedback on the project in their capacity as discussants at the ISA meeting panel. A number of other colleagues and graduate students from the University of Ottawa and elsewhere participated in our discussions at the workshop; thanks in particular to Paul Saurette, Kathy Trevenen, Dalie Giroux, Kevin McMillan, Heather McKeen-Edwards and David Grondin.

   We thank the various people and organizations who have given us permission to reproduce images in the book: Henrik Knudson c/o Burnham Riker for the HSBC advertisements produced in the Introduction; BBC News Online, The Protection Project, the *Arizona Daily Star*, ICMPD, and hackitectura for the maps reproduced in Chapter 5, and Intel Corporation for the Intel advertisement reproduced in Chapter 8. We also thank Christian Borch, editor of *Distinktion: Scandinavian Journal of Social Theory* for permission to reproduce Chapter 9 which first appeared in that journal, and Cambridge University Press for permission to reproduce extracts from Eric Helleiner, 'Central bankers as good neighbours: US money doctors in Latin America during the 1940s', *Financial History Review*, 16, 1: 5–25, which appear in Chapter 4.

Finally, the authors have provided us with great chapters, responded wonderfully to feedback and kept the process ticking along nicely. Rarely has a process of putting together an edited volume gone so smoothly. Lucy Dunne and Heidi Bagtazo at Routledge have also been very supportive in helping us put the book together.

Jacqueline Best and Matthew Paterson

Contributors

Rob Aitken teaches International Political Economy and International Relations in the Department of Political Science at the University of Alberta. His research interests lie at the intersection of IPE and cultural studies and focus on the everyday cultures of global finance, governmentality and the role of culture in the making of economic space.

Louise Amoore is Reader in Geography at the University of Durham. Her research focuses on three key areas: global geopolitics and the governance of worker and migrant bodies; the politics and practices of risk management (with specific reference to the rise of risk consulting as a technology of governing); and political and social theories of resistance and dissent. Her publications include *Globalisation Contested: An International Political Economy of Work* (Manchester University Press 2002), and (edited) *The Global Resistance Reader* (Routledge 2005).

Jacqueline Best is Associate Professor in the School of Political Studies at the University of Ottawa. Her work combines an interest in international political economy, international relations and political theory, with an empirical focus on international economic governance issues. Her first book, *The Limits of Transparency: Ambiguity and the History of International Finance*, was published by Cornell University Press in 2005. She is currently working on a book, Governing the Margins, which examines the changing character of authority in global economic governance.

David L. Blaney is Professor of Political Science, Macalester College, St Paul, Minnesota. His research focuses on the political and social theory of international relations, culture and identity and IR/IPE, political economic thought, and democratic theory. With Naeem Inayatullah, he has written *International Relations and the Problem of Difference* (Routledge 2004). A second book with Naeem, *Savage Economics: Wealth, Poverty and the Temporal Walls of Capitalism* (Routledge), focuses on the image of the savage in the construction of political economy as theory and practice. It should be published in 2010.

Matt Davies is a lecturer in International Political Economy at Newcastle University, Newcastle-upon-Tyne. His published work includes *International Political Economy And Mass Communication In Chile: National Intellectuals And Transnational Hegemony* (St Martins Press and Macmillan) and he co-edited, with Magnus Ryner, *Poverty and the Production of World Politics: Unprotected Workers in the Global Political Economy* (Palgrave Macmillan). His research interests are focused on work and everyday life, in particular the critique of everyday life as a critique of global political economy, and on popular culture and global politics.

Marieke de Goede is Senior Lecturer in the Department of European Studies, University of Amsterdam. Her current research focuses on the themes of the war on terrorist finance, poststructuralist approaches to International Political Economy, and the 'carnival of money'. Her principal publications are *Virtue, Fortune and Faith: A Genealogy of Finance* (University of Minnesota Press 2005), and the edited volume *International Political Economy and Poststructural Politics* (Palgrave 2006).

Eric Helleiner is CIGI Chair in International Political Economy at the Balsillie School of International Affairs, and Professor, Department of Political Science, University of Waterloo. He is author of *States and the Reemergence of Global Finance* (Cornell 1994), *The Making of National Money* (Cornell 2003) and *Towards North American Monetary Union?* (McGill-Queen's 2006). He has also co-edited *Nation-States and Money* (Routledge 1999), *Economic Nationalism in a Globalizing World* (Cornell 2005) and *The Future of the Dollar* (Cornell 2009). He is co-editor of the book series Cornell Studies in Money and is presently a Trudeau Fellow.

Naeem Inayatullah is Associate Professor of Politics at Ithaca College. His research focuses on the political and social theory of international relations, culture and identity and IR/IPE, political economic thought, and aspects of popular culture. With David Blaney, he has written *International Relations and the Problem of Difference* (Routledge 2004) and with Robin Riley he is co-editor of *Interrogating Imperialism* (Palgrave 2006). A second book with David, *Savage Economics: Wealth, Poverty and the Temporal Walls of Capitalism* (Routledge), focuses on the image of the savage in the construction of political economy as theory and practice. It should be published in 2010.

Debbie Lisle is a senior lecturer in the School of Politics, International Studies and Philosophy at Queen's University Belfast. Her research addresses questions of travel and tourism within International Relations, and more generally, how cultural products operate in the global realm (especially film, museums, photography and popular writing). Along with her book *The Global Politics of Contemporary Travel Writing* (Cambridge 2006), her work has been published in *Alternatives*, *Cultural Research*, *Millennium*, *Review of International Studies* and *Security Dialogue*. She is currently working on a book about the relationship between tourism, war and visuality.

Maxime Ouellet is a postdoctoral researcher with the Canada Research Chair in *Mondialisation, Citoyenneté et Démocratie* at the Université du Québec à *Montréal*. He has recently completed his PhD in political studies at the University of Ottawa. His research interests combine international political economy, cultural studies and political theory. His thesis was on the topic of the so-called 'global information society' focusing on a cultural perspective of international political economy.

Matthew Paterson is Professor of Political Science at the University of Ottawa. His research focuses on the political economy of global environmental change. In addition to a book developing a general theoretical approach out of these interests, he has developed them in relation to global climate change and the politics of the automobile. His publications include *Global Warming and Global Politics* (Routledge 1996), *Understanding Global Environmental Politics: Domination, Accumulation, Resistance*, (Palgrave 2000) and *Automobile Politics: Ecology and Cultural Political Economy* (Cambridge University Press 2007). He is currently co-writing a book with Peter Newell (University of East Anglia, UK) provisionally entitled *Climate Capitalism*, as well as a series of articles on the political economy of climate change governance, especially its 'market-led' character.

Nigel Thrift is the Vice-Chancellor of the University of Warwick. Prior to this he was the Pro-Vice-Chancellor for Research at the University of Oxford. His current research focuses in particular on international finance, in the history of time, urban space and politics, and in non-representational theory. He has been central to the emergence of a cultural economy literature. His recent books include: *Non-representational theory: Space, Politics, Affect* (Routledge 2007); *Knowing Capitalism* (Sage 2005); and (co-edited with Ash Amin) *The Blackwell Cultural Economy Reader* (Blackwell 2003).

R.B.J. Walker is Professor of Political Science at the University of Victoria, where he teaches in the graduate programme in Cultural, Social and Political Thought. He has written widely on the implications of contemporary global/local transformations for modern accounts of sovereignty, subjectivity and the spatiotemporal articulation of political practice. His best-known work is *Inside/Outside: International Relations as Political Theory* (Cambridge 1993), while his most recent is *After the Globe, Before the World* (Routledge 2009). He has recently been involved in collective research projects on the relationship between liberty and security in Europe, on postcolonial understandings of the relationship between centre and periphery, and on the political implications of Kantian accounts of critique. He is editor of the journals *Alternatives: Global, Local, Political* and *International Political Sociology*.

William Walters is Professor in the Department of Sociology and Anthropology and the Department of Political Science at Carleton University. His research explores the geopolitical sociology of borders, migration and security, mostly in Europe. His recent publications include *Global Governmentality* (co-edited with Wendy Larner) (Routledge 2004) and *Governing Europe* (co-authored with Jens Henrik Haahr) (Routledge 2005).

Introduction

Understanding cultural political economy

Jacqueline Best and Matthew Paterson

How do we explain the World Bank's increasing emphasis on the social underpinnings of economic development? Or the ways that the social consequences of the tourism industry have recently been contested and 'ethical tourism' has emerged in response? Or the shift in the meaning of home ownership from a dwelling to an investment with consequent effects on consumer debt, home improvement spending, and asset prices? Or the way the pursuit of the 'war on terror' relies on a set of profiling technologies that have been borrowed from techniques developed in consumer marketing? Or the limited effects huge oil price increases have on demand for high-consumption cars, despite rhetoric of rational consumer behaviour? The list of such questions could go on. All of these are political-economic questions. Yet, traditional modes of political-economic analysis seem to miss one essential aspect of these different practices: their cultural dimension.

Contemporary debates about developments in the global economy reinforce the sense, given in our rhetorical questions above, that culture is somehow important to political economy. For example, if we look at the debates about the increasing role of consumption in shaping growth and legitimation in contemporary economies, asking questions about the cultures within which consumption makes sense, immediately become pertinent (Lash and Urry 1994). If we look at the parallel rise of finance in the global economy, it is becoming apparent that underneath the spectacle of 'global finance' lies a set of daily practices of borrowers and savers, and the reshaping of individuals as 'investing subjects' (e.g. Harmes 2001; Aitken 2005). If we look at the political shift to neoliberalism, it is increasingly clear that this shift has operated through a series of cultural conflicts, not least the deployment of consumerism to undermine the power of labour and legitimize the neoliberal project (Gamble 1988; Hall and Jacques 1989; Frank 2001).

As we will elaborate later on, these three shifts – to consumption, to financialization, and to neoliberalism – have been central to making the global economy work the way it currently does. In our reading of these changes, there are distinct limits to understanding them narrowly through the categories provided by political economy, conventionally understood. These shifts cannot be reduced to the 'rational pursuit of self-interest', given that their complex cultural underpinnings reveal that what counts as 'self-interest' and 'rationality' is itself being constantly redefined. Although the language of class might be invoked to understand the political strategies of neoliberal politicians, such an analytic approach quickly reaches its limits in understanding these phenomena. A focus on institutions, as common in institutionalist economics and rationalist political economy, might be able to describe these as processes of institutional change but would struggle to get to grips with the power of the intangibles entailed in the desires that produced, for example, the fragmentation of consumer markets. Political economy, as conventionally understood, whether in neoclassical, public choice, institutionalist, statist or Marxist terms, thus fails to fully explain its object because it abstracts political economy from its cultural constitution. Whatever culture might mean (and we attempt to elaborate our sense of this below), the contributors to this volume share a conviction that thinking about it will help us to better understand political-economic processes. At the same time, of course, incorporating culture will in all likelihood transform our understanding of what political economy itself *is*.

Why cultural political economy?

Our contention in this book is that to understand the phenomena described above, and many more, we need a conceptual category and analytic approach that we are calling 'cultural political economy'. The need to combine culture with political economy is by no means an entirely novel claim, and has been recognized in many different contexts. In several academic disciplines – notably anthropology, geography and sociology – as well as in many concrete political situations, our attention has recently been drawn to the cultural dimensions of the economy, the economic aspects of culture, and the political character of both. This attention reminds us that modern societies – and the disciplines that attempt to understand them – have been founded precisely on the rhetorical *separation* of these aspects of social life.

Karl Polanyi's well-known narrative of the 'disembedding' of markets is a classic account of this separation. For Polanyi (1944: ch. 4), before the advent of market society, economic practices were closely connected to social norms, organized around the principles of reciprocity, redistribution and subsistence production. For the self-regulating market economy to be born, such traditional practices had to be uprooted and social relations subjected to the logic of the market. As Albert Hirschman (1978) has demonstrated, this was morally as well as socially disruptive, as religious constraints on charging interest had to be overcome, and notions of a 'just price' replaced with a concept of market value. The free market economy that was the ultimate product of this slow and painful process – our own contemporary economy – is a disembedded one, in which the economic sphere confronts the social, political and cultural realms as an autonomous and self-regulating entity. At least in theory, in such an economy, prices are not determined based on a complex web of social relations but are instead set through the automatic play of supply and demand, as buyers and sellers each seek to pursue their own rational self-interest and in doing so unwittingly produce a coherent and self-regulating economic system.

To maintain this careful distinction between culture, politics and economics, enormous effort is expended to purify each – by insisting on the acultural character of the economy, for example. At the same time, this effort is constantly destabilized in practice, for example through the invocation of cultural themes – such as family values, a particular work ethic or gender norms – in support of various political-economic projects. This process occurs not only in academic debates; politicians, business managers, World Bank presidents and NGO activists are themselves engaged in this complicated process of purification and destabilization of the boundary between economy, culture and politics. In a very real sense, then, Polanyi was simply wrong. The 'disembedding' of markets never in fact detached markets from culture, they rather reconstituted the content of that culture. The idea of a 'free market economy' may serve certain ideological purposes, but it is never in fact able to realise its utopia of a culture-free economy.

The legacy of this problem of separation and the destabilization of the boundaries that result from it can be seen in the three specific academic debates we take as points of departure for the book, and whose weaknesses we aim to address throughout the volume. These can be crudely summarised as a lack of politics in cultural economy debates, a lack of economy in culturally inflected international/political theory and a lack of culture in international political economy.

At the most general level, we are motivated by a desire to contribute to the revitalization of political economy itself. We are not alone in observing the detour taken from the 1890s onwards by the discipline of economics, and in regretting that discipline's rejection of important elements of the classical political economy of Smith, Ricardo and Marx. Rediscovering the cultural component of political economy is one means of trying to enrich debates about the central practices of contemporary life that have been deadened by the insistence that 'the economy' can be analysed without reference to the specific sorts of people which inhabit and produce it (its cultures), the forms of power embedded in it (its politics) and the normative questions which animate both it 'in itself' and reactions to it.

One specific and prominent attempt to revive political economy can be seen in the emerging sociological and geographical literature on 'cultural economy' (Ray and Sayer 1999; du Gay and Pryke 2002; Amin and Thrift 2004; MacKenzie 2006). These scholars share both a belief in the crucial significance of economic life in determining differential life chances of people across the globe, and a rejection of the ability of orthodox models of economic life to fully capture the nature and dynamics of the economy. They also insist that various aspects of culture – in its broad sense of the meanings that we give social life and material objects, and the concrete practices that they enable and depend on for their sustenance – are important determinants of concrete economic forms of life. As du Gay and Pryke put it, 'this particular understanding of economics as "culture" focuses attention on the practical ways in which "economically relevant activity" is performed and enacted' (2002: 5). This body of literature has produced an extremely rich set of analyses of how cultural forms constitute what the economy is (as in Callon's example of the creation of strawberry markets outlined below), and how cultural forms shape the operation of the economy in a number of concrete ways, from the gendered character of financial markets (McDowell 1997) to the evolving character of the work ethic (Heelas 2002).

Part of our goal is therefore simply to contribute both theoretically and empirically to this literature. But we also have two specific objectives in relation to it. One comes from a sense that this literature underplays the *political* in cultural political economy. There are clearly specific sorts of politics in many of these analyses, often drawn from Foucault's notion of governmentality (e.g. Miller and Rose 1990), and also often defined in relation to a specific 'left' politics, but we would contend that there is not a systematic account of the place of politics – questions of authority and power, and the way they are sustained and contested – in this cultural economy literature. The typology of themes in cultural economy analyses given by Amin and Thrift in the introduction to their cultural economy reader confirms this; political analyses are seriously underrepresented (Amin and Thrift 2004: xix). Second, and perhaps ironically given the centrality of writers from similar backgrounds to earlier debates about 'globalization' (Appadurai 1990; Robertson 1992), we would also suggest that this literature underplays the specifically *global* dimensions to contemporary political-economic life. For example, the du Gay and Pryke (2002) volume draws almost exclusively on analyses from the UK. To be sure, this in part arises out of an insistence that all cultures are first and foremost local, and certainly there is much in these analyses that either highlights processes which are global in scope or that points to the multicultural character of local cultural economies, due to patterns of global migration. But, as the HSBC ads we discuss below show powerfully, the cultural character of contemporary political economy is decidedly global, both in that there are a set of shared meanings across the globe which enable similar marketing strategies to operate everywhere (even while those strategies highlight cultural difference as a particular marketing ploy) and that specific management cultures become globalized through the strategies of a firm like HSBC.

This emphasis on the political and the global clearly comes from the disciplinary background of most contributors to this volume. However, debates in political science, in particular within international relations (IR) and international political economy (IPE), have largely failed to engage this emerging cultural economy literature. Over the past years, IR has witnessed a 'cultural turn', involving a focus on identity (Connolly 1991; Walker 1993; Campbell 1998; Albert *et al.* 2001), ideas (Kratochwil 1995; Onuf 1998), or governmentality (Rose 1993, 1996; Hindess 1997; Dean 1999; Larner and Walters 2004; Sending and Neumann 2006). Where this culturally inflected IR has focused on empirical questions, it has tended to emphasize the security domain. The growing literature on securitization, for example, explores the role of language and identity in constituting particular kinds of problems as security threats (Buzan, 1983; Waever, 1993; Huysmans, 2006). Only rarely (e.g. Shapiro 1993; Rosow *et al.* 1994; Murphy and Rojas 1995;

de Goede 2005, 2006) does this cultural turn in IR extend to the economic dimensions of global politics. This project therefore seeks to both engage with this literature and to push it in new directions by working to develop a coherent conception of the cultural constitution of the political economy. In doing so, we hope not only to encourage cultural IR scholars to extend their analyses to the economic dimensions of global politics, but also to reflect on the ways in which the economic is already implicated in other aspects of international life – to consider, for example, how practices of securitization both depend on and obscure the economic conditions of their production, as Amoore and de Goede point out in their chapter.

Conversely, there is a rich and sophisticated critical literature in IPE that has yet to engage fully with the question of culture in relation to its problems, concepts and analyses. For example, constructivists in IPE (McNamara 1998; Blyth 2002) have usefully extended constructivist IR to the economic realm but have tended to rely on a narrow notion of 'culture' as 'ideas' or 'norms'. There also exists a growing literature on the role of 'organizational culture' in explaining international organizations' adoption and diffusion of ideas and norms (Barnett and Finnemore 2004; Weaver and Leiteritz 2005; Park 2006). Although these studies provide useful ethnographic studies of institutions like the IMF and World Bank, they still focus primarily on norms and ideas, ignoring the role of habits and practices; moreover, although they provide useful insights into the culture of economic institutions, they do not take the next crucial step and examine the cultural constitution of the economy more broadly.

Our emphasis on the ways in which culture is implicated in everyday economic practices also clearly contributes to a growing literature on the everyday politics of international political economy (Harmes 2001; Hobson and Seabrooke 2007; Langley 2008). At the same time, by emphasizing the cultural character of these day-to-day practices, we also hope to deepen the theoretical foundations of such analyses. Finally, neo-Gramscians and other Marxists (Cox 1987; Gill 1995; Jessop and Sum 2001) have invoked the notion of hegemony in global politics, opening up some space to talk about the cultural conditions of capitalism. Yet, their continued emphasis on class has tended to reduce the question of culture to one of the means by which capitalist domination is reproduced and resisted; this remains one possible answer to the questions of cultural political economy, but we would want to leave open the possibility of more open-ended interrogations of the phenomenon.

By developing the concept of cultural political economy, the ambition of this project is to bring the culturally inflected IR and critically attuned IPE literatures into conversation with each other and with the cultural economy literature, to fill the gaps in each, and to develop a more robust conception of the cultural dynamics of the global political economy. While we have said so far a lot about what we think focusing on culture can add to this understanding, it remains the case that culture is a notoriously polysemic term and we should attempt to pin down the sorts of meanings it has for us in this book.

Theorizing culture

In a prominent, globally organized marketing campaign over the last few years, HSBC has self-consciously presented itself as 'the world's local bank'. Invoking a discourse that globalization means firms must 'be local everywhere', HSBC's strategy relies on the assumption that the success of its banking operations depends on its capacity to adapt to a range of local and global cultures. The portrayal of this strategy in HSBC ads is inevitably individualistic and consumerist, interpellating the reader as someone able to use HSBC for their own purposes. However, that individualism is also embedded in a broader moral and cultural context: the campaign plays expressly with questions of cultural difference, suggesting variously that 'everyone looks at the world from a different point of view'; 'the world would be a dull place if everyone agreed on everything'; 'who knows what you'll see when you see someone else's point of view'; and 'an open mind is the best way to look at the world'.[1] Thus the reader of the ads is exhorted to participate in a celebration of diversity and difference through their association with HSBC, avoiding the trap of allowing the process of globalization to produce homogeneity and dullness.

There are of course limits to what one can say from one set of ads, as well as clear dangers in suggesting that 'culture' is really (only) about these sorts of images and thus particular sphere of social life. We accept these limits and dangers, but want however to suggest that there is something worthwhile in exploring this particular marketing strategy by HSBC. Our interest in these ads is not based on HSBC's use of graphic cultural images in the service of its business interests, but rather on the ways in which the campaign displays bankers' own understanding that they require cultural knowledge in order to do business well. In the examples shown here, the assumption is that the person reading the ad will think that HSBC is a better bank because it can tailor its investments according to the cultures of those it invests in. The ad works because it makes assumptions about the cultural significance the reader of the ad ascribes to values such as diversity and difference. So culture is not defined here as a specific sphere of social life, but rather as integral to all social practices. Fundamental to HSBC's strategy is an understanding that the economy must be read culturally. Because the values that people ascribe to different objects and experiences work to condition how they will act economically, a bank needs to be sensitive to those varying meanings in order to operate effectively.

Crucial here also is that the HSBC ads operate in a politically contested field where HSBC is both itself highly privileged – a large transnational bank – and able to constitute all sorts of other forms of privilege and exclusion. That the most famous ads appear exclusively in large hub airports is a clue here. More precisely, as we show below, the ads frequently operate in a register where difference is merely something to be understood, celebrated, adapted to. At the same time an underlying hierarchy is at least implicitly acknowledged – in the various dyads, the reader is presumed to be on one side, with the privilege to judge difference from *their* 'point of view'. So the deployment of culture by economic actors is always at the same time political.

By examining the logic and assumptions underlying HSBC's campaign, we can begin to delineate some of the ways in which we can conceptualize culture for the purposes of this volume.

Culture as identity and difference

Many of the ads in this campaign, notably displayed at the world's major airports such as Heathrow, involve the juxtaposition of two images, each reproduced twice, with a pair of judgments reversed each time. These contrasted images work precisely because of the way that they simultaneously exploit and complicate traditional assumptions about cultural difference.

In the wise/old ad (see Figure 0.1), commonplace judgments about age are overlaid with orientalist imagery. The ads rely on a series of common but contradictory prejudices: assumptions about the general wisdom of elders as well their decrepitude are combined with beliefs that East Asians are wise or backward, as well as similar judgements about Europeans. The ad also invokes a notion of progress, as the two figures can be understood as figures of modernity and backwardness. As such this ad illustrates David Blaney and Naeem Inayatullah's argument (Chapter 1, this volume) that classical political economy is founded on a hierarchical conception of time and space, in which the Third World is constructed as temporally backward and spatially distant. The relation in the ad is not simply a play on stereotypes about age and particular cultures. There is no 'equal but different' here; the presumed reader of the ad is the European in the ad itself. Other ads in the series similarly play with the notion of progress and contrast it to colonial imagery, such as the 'traditional/trendy' ad that explores the cultural meanings of tattoos, and the 'scary/reassuring' ad that examines different images of scariness (see Figures 0.2 and 0.3).

These ads reveal the ways in which culture is simultaneously homogenizing – as one means by which people in specific settings come to develop a sense of shared identity through common interpretations of similar phenomena – and differentiating – as a means of distinguishing different cultures through the meanings they attribute to different things. The ads simultaneously reinforce notions of cultural difference and deny them: they point out the strangeness of other conceptions of wisdom, beauty or scariness at the same time as they work to undercut those differences by suggesting that the two juxtaposed images are equivalent and interchangeable. And they simultaneously present cultural difference as about relations between equals even while depending on hierarchy and exclusion for their performative effect.

Many of the contributors to this book draw on a similar conception of culture as a force for reinforcing relations of identity and for defining lines of difference. William Walters (Chapter 5) shows how discourses of cultural difference serve at times to depoliticize migration politics by making it a matter of technical management of those who are 'different' or 'outsiders'. Rob Aitken (Chapter 3) illustrates the use of film to construct a sense of common identity as part of the British Empire, and thus to shape consumption patterns. And Eric Helleiner

Figure 0.1 HSBC wise/old ad.

(Chapter 4) demonstrates the ways in which the shifts in North–South international monetary relations between 1920s and the 1940s were enabled by a changing set of cultural assumptions about the lines of identity and difference that defined the developed and the developing world, as the paternalistic conceptions of Latin America that had characterized the *laissez-faire* years became complicated by an emerging sense of economic solidarity in the New Deal era.

Culture as webs of meaning

The forms of relationship between identity and difference that the HSBC ads articulate are specific expressions of the semiotic character of social life – the various meanings that we ascribe to the world around us. Clifford Geertz provides us with another way of understanding culture in his classic definition of culture as the 'webs of significance', or systems of meaning, through which social life is both interpreted and organized (1973: 5).[2] Culture is what gives meaning to a variety of phenomena, including practices, devices, techniques, bodies, conduct, experiences and relationships. A focus on culture thus presumes and attempts to demonstrate that these phenomena cannot be usefully understood separately from the meanings that people collectively give to them. The phrase 'collectively' here is important: culture cannot be reduced to ideas and values that can be adopted or espoused individually, but rather implies that the means by which individuals come to espouse such values or ideas are themselves culturally constituted by broader webs of significance.

One of Geertz's best known examples of cultural practices is the wink – a physical movement whose distinction from an involuntary tick depends entirely on a set of cultural conventions: 'Contracting your eyelids on purpose when there exists a public code in which so doing counts as a conspiratorial signal *is* winking. That's all there is to it: a speck of behavior, a fleck of culture, and – *voilà!* – a gesture' (Geertz 1973: 6).

The HSBC ads play up the ambiguity of gestures and the importance of cultural conventions for interpreting them. In one of the television ads (not reproduced on the website, but shown at least in Canada and the UK in recent years), a series of hand gestures is displayed each in two different national contexts: in the first country the signal is friendly whereas in the second it is rude or offensive. Similarly, in the print and airport campaigns, various ads make distinctions between the cultural meanings ascribed to different modes of dress, tattoos, masks and toys.

Culture understood as webs of meaning plays an important role in both the contemporary and historical evolution of political-economic practices. As Maxime Ouellet (Chapter 8) demonstrates, new information technologies have succeeded in redefining the structure and patterns of the global economy in large measure because of the power of the new imaginary that they have advanced – one that gains legitimacy through its efforts to combine democratic and market ideals. The historical analyses of Rob Aitken (Chapter 3) and Eric Helleiner (Chapter 4) reveal the form and global scope of this imaginary. Thrift's chapter (Chapter 9) expressly understands culture as about the semiotic sphere of life, in his case focusing on the emergence and consequences of an obsession with 'talent' in economic life. Lisle's chapter (Chapter 6) can be understood as about the interpretation of the complex and contested meanings of tourist practices.

Culture as material

Yet culture is not purely about meaning or language. It is also sedimented in routines and rituals, and embodied in living practices. The HSBC ad 'traditional/trendy' provides us with a very concrete example of the materiality of culture by focusing on the way in which we sometimes choose to mark out cultural identity on our very bodies through tattooing (see Figure 0.2).

As several of the chapters in this book point out, culture is also about the everyday activities through which we live our lives. It is as much about the 'low' culture of workplace norms and consumer desires as it is about the 'high' culture of great art and philosophy (Davies, Chapter 2). Culture can be articulated and reproduced through the mundane activities of 'money doctors' as they work amongst themselves and with bankers and policy makers abroad, learning from and advising them on monetary reforms (Helleiner, Chapter 4). Culture is thus not simply the thing that draws tourists to new destinations, but is also embodied in the very practices of the tourists themselves – whether they fit the image of the boorish foreigner or the sensitive eco-tourist (Lisle, Chapter 6).

Isn't it better to be open to other
people's points of view?

yourpointofview.com

Figure 0.2 HSBC traditional/trendy ad.

The notion of culture thus refuses a clear separation between the ideal and the material. Culture gives meaning to and becomes embodied in concrete institutions, practices and rituals but cannot be reduced to those material effects. Hence, on the one hand, we cannot understand a wink, or explain its effects on its audience, by simply observing the behaviour of an individual who closes one eye; if we focus only on behaviour, we could well assume that the individual is suffering from an eye spasm. On the other hand, although culture is clearly about meaning, it cannot be reduced to ideas. The wink as a cultural phenomena is simultaneously material and ideal; the practice, the action, the bodily gesture are all as essential as the social conventions that give it meaning. An attention to culture therefore forces us to consider the mutual implication of the ideal and the material in a way that a focus on ideas does not. It also encourages us to focus on the concrete and particular ways in which cultural meanings inform our every day practices, rather than focusing on the big ideas generated by major thinkers and policymakers.

Culture and the limits of rationality

Although culture is not irrational – even if colonial and post-colonial narratives have sometimes portrayed it as such (Blaney and Inayatullah, Chapter 1) – as a concept, it does lead us to recognize both the limits of rationality and the cultural constitution of the boundary of the rational/irrational. The elements that make up a culture and our identification with it include affective, spiritual and aesthetic responses. Culture as a concept must therefore be separated from ideas, not simply because of its inherent materiality, but also because it exceeds the cognitive or linguistic.

The HSBC ads tap into this aspect of culture. The 'scary/reassuring' ad (Figure 0.3) reminds us of the cultural constitution of our emotional reactions.

Figure 0.3 HSBC scary/reassuring ad.

Our fears are not culturally determined, but they are refracted through the lens of cultural convention. Moreover, as recent volatility in the financial markets has reminded us, fear and hope can play crucial and even self-fulfilling roles in the global economy. And what market actors decide is scary can shift rapidly from one day to the next, as changing economic sentiments can change the way in which a similar set of economic data is interpreted (Best 2005: ch. 2). Moreover, as Nigel Thrift (Chapter 9) argues, global firms have come increasingly to rely on the affective and the visceral layers of human subjectivity in their efforts to increase their profitability: now, more than ever, he suggests, consumers' and workers' capacities for intuition and imagination are being cultivated and exploited by global capital. The HSBC ads appear to be doing precisely that. Crucial here is *whose* fear, of *what* phenomena, gets to count. In this ad, the hierarchal relation between the 'primitivist' mask and the soft cuddly toy is again obscured by their apparent interchangeability. But while one becomes scary through an intertext with a comedy horror film (*Gremlins*), as well as perhaps a particular sort of fear of random overconsumption, the other operates through a connection to a long colonialist history involving tales of cannibalism, voodoo and animism. Fear, in this instance, is the fear by the privileged and the dominant precisely of those they dominate and construct as backward and 'irrational' to legitimize their dominance. The focus on various forms of visuality or imagination in a number of chapters (Amoore and de Goede, Chapter 7; Walters, Chapter 5; Aitken, Chapter 3), deploy this conception of culture (see Figure 0.3).

Culture as ethical

If culture is in part about relations of identity and difference, or about meaning and interpretation, then it is also inherently about ethics. Cultural differences are articulated in some measure as particular and sometimes conflicting values and conceptions of the good life, while interpretation is always simultaneously empirical ('what is this thing like?') and moral ('is this thing a good thing?'). The HSBC ads explore this dimension of culture in an ad in this series where the framing is 'good/bad'. The two images are of a papaya and a piece of chocolate cake. Although the ad shies away from more political and contested conceptions of the good by focusing on dessert, it does nonetheless point to the relativity of our judgments and desires. Our notions of what constitutes 'good' food are wrapped up in feelings of temptation and guilt. Patterns of consumption – like tourism (Lisle, Chapter 6) – depend on a particular kind of moral culture organized around pleasure and self-denial. And like Lisle's example of tourism, this ad again has the trace of images that cannot be successfully expunged of their politics. The two foods here are contrasted where the 'good/bad' dyad could be coupled with 'healthy/unhealthy', 'pure (or fresh, or natural)/artificial', while for 'bad/good' we could substitute 'boring/tasty' or 'weird/familiar'. Where papaya is good, it is because of its purity, its 'primitive' or 'natural' character, while where it is bad, it is due to its 'exotic' origins. We are back here to the hierarchic character of the difference underpinning the meaning of HSBC's ads.

Such moral cultures run much deeper than our next trip to the supermarket, however, and are instead central to the ways in which we relate across lines of difference. A cultural ethos can be insular or open to difference; it can seek to learn from and negotiate with the other or can work to dominate or assimilate it (Inayatullah and Blaney 1999). As Aitken and Helleiner (Chapters 3 and 4) suggest, part of what defines the different eras of global economic evolution are their different orientations towards difference. Moreover, as Debbie Lisle (Chapter 6) points out and as we will discuss further below, the way in which one negotiates such ethical questions is itself highly political. As Amoore and de Goede (Chapter 7) suggest, contemporary security practices frequently operate through ways of sorting 'good' from the 'bad' people, even while the technologies deployed attempt to obscure this ethical judgment.

The notion of culture is thus a particularly slippery one. Rather than presenting a singular coherent 'consensus definition' of culture, this volume therefore proposes a number of different ways of introducing the idea of culture to contemporary debates on political economy. In part this is because part of the value of culture is precisely its messiness, its refusal to be fixed down neatly. In part it is because many of the analyses effectively focus on the question of what is done politically in the name of culture, so what culture is depends on how it is articulated in specific contexts. The book itself, in fact, is organized around a narrative that explores not so much what culture *is* but rather what it *does* in the economy and what is *done* in its name.

What culture does

What then does culture do in political economy? We can break down the role of culture in the market economy into two different levels of analysis. At the most basic or *constitutive* level, cultural processes work to produce the basic actors and objects in the economy and to define their relationships with one another. Culture also plays a secondary *contingent* role, intersecting with other social, economic and political processes to help to determine a particular economic outcome. Different contributions to this project emphasize one or both of these particular roles of culture in the economy.

Culture as constitutive: the invention of the market

For a market economy to function, there must exist particular kinds of economic actors who relate to one another and to the objects that they produce and exchange in specific ways. These individuals must be able to calculate not only the relevant information about the objects that they are buying and selling, but also determine their own best interests. They must therefore be capable of a particular kind of calculation (Miller 2004). These individuals must also structure their relationships in specific ways: they must come together and relate to one another in the market at the moment of exchange, but must not retain ongoing relationships that might compromise the automaticity of the price mechanism. At the same time, the boundaries of the economic realm must be carefully demarcated from the non-economic, in order to ensure that the market actors do not muddy their economic calculations with political or personal motives. To use Michel Callon's language, these individuals must be both entangled with one another and their objects in particular ways and simultaneously disentangled from them in other ways in order to ensure that the market functions (Callon 1998: 4–6, 16–17).

> To construct a market transaction, that is to say, to transform something into a commodity, and two agents into a seller and a consumer, it is necessary to cut the ties between the thing and the other objects or human beings one by one. It must be decontextualized, dissociated and detached.
>
> (Callon 1998: 19)

To illustrate the complex construction of this market relationship – its artificial rather than natural production – Callon describes a study by Marie-France Garcia of the transformation of the market for strawberries in the Sologne region of France in the early 1980s (Callon 1998: 19–22). Up to that point, strawberries had been bought and sold through a complex network of individual relationships between buyers and farmers. Through the initiative of the regional chamber of agriculture, this more entangled set of economic and social relationships was replaced by a classically Walrasian market: the strawberries were all delivered to a warehouse and data sheets produced on each batch setting out their relative quality. Buyers and sellers were kept separately from one another, with their exchanges mediated through an auctioneer. Thus the pre-existing social relationships were broken down and the economic agents given the tools for carefully calculating their exchanges. In effect, by creating this new set of practices for buying and selling strawberries, the regional agricultural council was able to produce a culture of calculation. Why was this a cultural as well as an economic change? Because not only the practices changed, but the relationships among the individuals involved and their perception of the strawberries did too; in the process, the meanings attributed to the economic practices also underwent a transformation. The disembedded market is as much an artefact of culture as the embedded one. The cultural practices that sustain each may differ, but the centrality of culture does not. As suggested above, Polanyi was mistaken that disembedding separates economy from culture in any serious sense. Similar processes involved in the creation of markets can be seen in the work of MacKenzie (2006) on financial markets, or perhaps most obviously at present in the construction of a whole series of 'carbon markets' in response to climate change (MacKenzie 2007; Paterson and Stripple 2007).

The creation of such 'free market' economies on a grander scale similarly entails cultural work to produce the sorts of people and institutions that can sustain such economies. Much recent work on the World Bank- and IMF-imposed reforms across the global South has emphasized this dimension of their efforts. The structural adjustment of the 1980s has been replaced by an emphasis on institutions and capacity building, much of which is about the creation of the cultural conditions under which market economies can come into being and reproduce themselves. In particular, it has entailed efforts to actively create 'rational economic man' (Williams 1999). The use of micro-credit systems by the World Bank depends expressly on specific cultural institutions – family forms, gender relations and identities – for its success (Weber 2002). More recently, practices in the two institutions have become more reflexively cultural, as in for example the World Bank's emphasis on the importance of social capital for economic performance. The World Bank's website defines social capital as 'the norms and networks that enable collective action' and suggests that 'increasing evidence shows that social cohesion – social capital – is critical for poverty alleviation and sustainable human and economic development' (World Bank 2004).[3] These international financial institutions have begun to recognize that cultural relations play a crucial role in sustaining the trust that is key to economic transactions. Culture is thus *constitutive* of political economy; it plays an important part in constituting what the practices we recognize as within that 'domain' *are*.

Political economy in this account is in effect an assemblage: a loose collection of objects, subjects, practices and institutions which are then reified into appearing like something much more solid. But just as culture constitutes a set of particular practices into 'an economy', it also works to define the things that it excludes as non-economic. Culture thus works to constitute the boundary between what is inside and outside the economy. In fact, as Walters (Chapter 5) shows, culture works as a very powerful negative force – defining certain domains as 'merely cultural' and therefore as neither economic nor political. Drawing on Andrew Barry (2002), Walters describes the ways in which this 'anti-political economy' works to define migratory flows (and efforts to contain them) as neither political nor economic. Similarly, in Lisle's chapter (Chapter 6), we see attempts by those promoting ethical tourism to present it as 'apolitical' – as simply a moral act – as well as efforts by critics of the industry to present tourism as profoundly political. In Ouellet's chapter, the 'new economic imaginary' of the information economy precisely serves to depoliticize it – to present it as of universal appeal and benefit. In each of these contexts, the politics of culture rests in part in its strategic deployment to obscure the political and economic stakes of contemporary practices.

Culture as contingent: the historical production of contemporary economies

For the most part, we do not recognize this cultural constitution of our basic economic activities because they have been internalized as habits. One might therefore reasonably ask the question of whether the cultural constitution of these economic identities and practices is worthy of much attention: if our economic habits are so stable, and taken for granted, then do we need to focus on their cultural nature? There are two reasons why we need to do so: because economic cultures are plural and because they are dynamic. It is not only possible to identify an overarching cultural logic to the market (the general constitution of the market by culture), as we have just done, but also to locate a variety of specific and smaller-scale cultures within the market economy – in other words to identify the *contingent* dependence of economic practices on various *specific* cultures which change over time and across space. Economic cultures are also dynamic; they are historically constituted, as Polanyi's analysis of the disembedding of the economy reveals. We may no longer be experiencing the kind of dramatic cultural change that accompanied the invention of the modern market economy, but transformations are nonetheless still ongoing.

The HSBC ads shown above provide us with a clue to the character of the cultural economic transformation currently underway. They point to the way that particular cultures and more precisely inter-cultural symbolic exchanges are appropriated for corporate purposes, something that is temporally and spatially specific; these ads would not have resonated the way they do today if they had been run 20 years ago. The historical context within which these HSBC ads make sense reveals the role culture plays in contemporary political-economic transformations. Globalization, however understood, plays an obvious role here, but it is more instructive to read the practices espoused by HSBC in terms of the emergence of the individual as an investing subject, as alluded to above. This new *homo economicus*, we argue here, is both part of and the outcome of a long process that can be traced back through a series of cultural-political-economic transformations. Specifically, one can highlight three interrelated processes at work: the shifts in economic identity from work to consumption, the (re)financialization of the economy, and the neoliberal assault on social democracy and Keynesianism.

It is commonplace to assert that economic identities in the West have gradually shifted from work to consumption (Lash and Urry 1994). Part of the brilliance of the post-war compromise was to provide workers with the benefits of mass consumption, which both defused worker militancy and helped to create a sustained period of growth by redistributing wealth (Aglietta 1979; Harvey 1989). The logic of consumption both works towards individualization and towards flexibilization, tending over time to create pressures to personalize and flexibilize the products being produced.[4] The result is a 'postmodernization' of consumption: its increased organization through niche markets rather than neatly hierarchized ones and its increased dependence on branding and other processes which in Thrift's nice phrase 'charging up the semiotic sphere' (Chapter 10). At the same time, the consumer has become increasingly identified in political discourse as the privileged economic subject.[5] The sphere of personal consumption has also progressively expanded as more and more arenas of life have been privatized: from the sale of council-housing in the UK to the privatization of pension benefits in the US, we are increasingly told to take ownership of our economic lives and learn to be savvy consumers.

A second historical transition, also well known, is the re-financialization of the global economy during the 1970s and 1980s (Helleiner 1994; Leyshon and Thrift 1997). The macro-economic dynamics of this transformation are relatively well known, and include the emergence of the Eurodollar market, the collapse of the fixed exchange rate system and the progressive liberalization of financial markets. But this macro process of financialization is closely connected to smaller-scale, individual and institutional changes that are clearly culturally constituted.[6] Specifically, the expansion of global financial markets has in part been underpinned by the growth in the West, especially in the Anglo-American economies, of private pensions, life insurance and mutual funds. These now tie the futures of millions of individual investors into the performance of such markets (e.g. Harmes 2001).

The liberalization and expansion of global finance has also enabled the massive expansion of consumer credit, which began in the early 1980s. This credit explosion, in turn, is an effect of the intertwining of financialization with the shift in economic identities towards consumption. As people become consumers, they thus become financial subjects; in order to support our growing desire to consume, we also need to learn to manage credit cards, lines of credit and mortgages. In order to prepare ourselves for an uncertain retirement, we also need to become informed investors, whether in mutual funds, in equity markets or in our own houses (Aitken 2005). The liberalization of global finance therefore has both cultural roots and cultural consequences (Thrift 2001), as well of course as the possibility for profound political and social destabilization, as is evidenced by the recent sub-prime mortgage crisis, among others (Langley 2008: ch. 10).

A third transition has been the more overtly political one of the shift from Keynesian management to neoliberalism. Financialization was expressly pursued in the leading neoliberal countries under Thatcher and Reagan through the deregulation of financial markets and the expansion of consumer credit. This credit expansion provided the kind of economic stimulus that had, in the Keynesian era, been provided by public expenditure. At the same time, as governments attempted to adopt monetarism, they sought to manage growth cycles through interest rates rather than through demand management. This strategy was closely associated with goals of undermining organized labour and also subordinated manufacturing to financial interests and power. At the same time, the shifts in identity to consumption played a part in legitimizing this political-economic shift. The Thatcher–Reagan governments, followed since by neoliberal governments the world over, actively promoted their policy package in terms of consumer freedom: crushing trade unions would minimise disruption to consumers; expanded credit would enable a broadening of the range of consumption possibilities; privatization would enable the emergence of a 'shareholder democracy', and in the case of sales of public housing, a 'householder democracy'. The shift to neoliberalism thus has both benefited from the shift to consumer identities and shaped its course through expansion of consumer credit, while the shift to consumerism has itself played an important part in stabilizing this political form in the last two decades.[7]

These three shifts – to consumption, to financialization, to neoliberalism – thus are the cultural political-economic conditions under which marketing strategies like those of HSBC are literally intelligible. The ads are primarily aimed at affluent Western investors who have become used to thinking about their lives in terms of investment opportunities, managing their life as a portfolio and operating in a 'global marketplace'. These ads reveal that the active management of investors' lives in this manner is a key part of the reproduction of the global economy. They naturalize and obscure the hierarchical relations involved between the various people figured in the ads themselves, and between the reader of the ad and any of the subjects portrayed. In short, they reveal the work done by culture, and in culture's name, in shaping contemporary political economy.

The narrative of the book

Through the chapters that follow, we attempt to tell a story to establish the importance and the character of cultural political economy, beginning from its theoretical foundations, tracing its historical evolution, considering its political implications, exploring its future tendencies, and finally returning to – and questioning – its foundational assumptions.

Interrogating the classics

The first section of the book explores the cultural character of the economy through an interrogation of classics in both political economy and cultural theory. In part this serves to reveal the traces of culture that persist in a discipline, which, as illustrated in the discussion of Polanyi above, has attempted to purify itself from such phenomena. Thus, the economy came to be seen a separate sphere of action from politics and culture, just as economic, political, and cultural theory were separated into distinct disciplines.

Naeem Inayatullah and David Blaney (Chapter 1) show the limits of this tradition of thought, by revealing the cultural underpinnings of the long tradition of classical political economy, specifically in relation to Hayek, Smith, Hegel and Marx. They challenge the commonplace assumption that classical political economy is acultural, in particular by showing how those classic writers espouse an ambivalent ethics in relation to capitalism and what Blaney and Inayatullah call its 'wound of wealth'. Significantly complicating Polanyi's suggestion that culture was largely expunged from theory and practice in political economy, Blaney and Inayatullah argue that culture was never in fact expelled, and that we instead remain in an uneasy relationship as political economy attempts to pretend that it has done so, while living with the consequences of having in fact failed. Matt Davies' chapter (Chapter 2) then provides an engagement with different classics, using key texts in the founding of cultural theory, specifically Raymond Williams and Henri Lefebvre, in order to demonstrate their importance for conceptions of political economy. This is achieved in part through an elaboration of the utility of Lefebvre's notion of everyday life, and of Williams' insistence that 'culture is ordinary'. If political economy is always already cultural, as is shown in the preceding chapter, Davies builds on this by outlining some of the theoretical resources which might re-integrate the two.

The cultural constitution of economic history

After this interrogation of traditions of thought in political economy and cultural theory, the book turns to the way that culture constitutes political economy by showing how an attention to culture can reframe our understanding of economic history. As with a history of ideas, so with economic history; we find here again a more interesting and complex history than would be found by insisting on or presuming the separation of these two dimensions of life. Rob Aitken (Chapter 3) reinterprets the post-war embedded liberal economic order by demonstrating the role of marketing films in constituting new kinds of economic citizen whose practices would sustain the evolving economic order. Eric Helleiner (Chapter 4) focuses on the ways that US 'money doctors' providing advice to Latin American governments, from the 1940s onwards, operated in a spirit of intercultural dialogue rather than through imposition of American economic orthodoxy. He thus shows how cultural shifts both amongst US economic elites and in US society more broadly provided the conditions for novel forms of economic diplomacy.

These two specific chapters illustrate particular instances of a more general claim made by cultural political economy, outlined above in relation to the work of Michel Callon: that the forms of calculative practice necessary for contemporary economic activity are themselves cultural and historical products. The analyses of Helleiner and of Aitken serve to underscore this point about the cultural construction of political economy: Helleiner focusing on the sorts of subjects involved in shaping economic policy, and the sorts of inter-state negotiation of such policies; Aitken elaborating the construction of certain types of consumer subjectivities as central both to the maintenance of an Imperial identity by Britain in the 1930s and of a form of 'embedded liberalism' in the 1940s and beyond.

Depoliticizing and concealing the economic

As suggested above, the constitutive character of culture in relation to political economy also entails constituting what the practices we recognize as within that 'domain' *are*. It can thus work to *conceal* the political and economic character of particular phenomena. In effect, the process of defining what counts as political and/or economic is simultaneously a process of defining what is excluded from that label – what is 'merely' cultural. The political effects of this process are to constrain the scope of debate by defining certain subjects as apolitical; ironically, appeals to culture can therefore work much the same way as appeals to technical expertise – as a way of depoliticizing certain crucial questions.

These processes are the subject of the third part of the book. William Walters (Chapter 5) explores this form of 'anti-political economy' in relation to the use of maps to portray migration as a cultural threat rather than as an effect of economic forces or as a profoundly political problem. At the same time, critics of such migration politics deploy maps both to repoliticize migration and to subvert dominant images of the 'swamping' of European or North American societies by various 'others'. Culture operates here both to refer to the medium of maps and cartography, but also to the questions of identity and difference that are deployed to de- or re-politicize migration and to conceal its economic character. Debbie Lisle (Chapter 6) then explores the contemporary contestations of tourism through the emergence of practices of 'ethical tourism', showing how they have origins in nineteenth-century moral discourse about pleasure. This recurrent moralization of pleasure operates precisely as a boundary around what sorts of 'economic activity' are culturally and politically acceptable; by promising to supersede politics and overcome economic inequalities, ethical tourism conceals its complicity in reproducing problematic forms of both. As in Walters' analysis, therefore, culture here operates to obscure the political character of the phenomena at hand: the discourse of ethical tourism obscures the power relations involved in its practices through its framing of the question in terms of individual morality and the relationship between morality and pleasure.

Imagining futures

Although the intersection of culture, politics and economics is longstanding, it has begun to take new and more self-conscious forms in recent years. Part 4 of the book turns to immediate contemporary debates to examine how culture, politics and economy are currently shaping each other, and to articulate a vision of their future. Louise Amoore and Marieke de Goede (Chapter 7) seek to reinvigorate security studies by bringing a cultural political economy perspective to bear on the 'war on terror'. They consider the ways in which the recasting of terrorism as the 'dark side' of globalization has also reconfigured its 'bright side'. They focus on the development of new data analysis techniques, suggesting that they are best understood as cultural practices of visualizing the identities of potential threatening individuals – practices that not only rely on techniques developed in the field of consumer marketing, but that also feed into a growing industry of private security providers. Maxime Ouellet (Chapter 8) analyses the hype about a new information-driven economy, focusing on how the rise of information technology is driven by a new kind of culturally mediated politics in which individuals are celebrated for their creative participation in what he calls a 'brand' new world. Nigel Thrift (Chapter 9) takes the analysis of the 'new economy' one stage further by focusing on the contemporary obsession in business discourse with 'talent' – a culturally constituted aptitude which business is attempting to cultivate and exploit in both workers and consumers. Together, these three chapters trace some of the outlines of our future, pointing to the increasingly intimate interconnection of cultural, political and economic practices.

In spite of their emphasis on the centrality of cultural processes to contemporary changes in political-economic practices, none of these analyses depend on the thesis that political economy is becoming increasingly 'culturalized'. Some scholars claim that we have over the last 30 years experienced an increased 'culturalization' of the economy – through the expansion of consumer culture, the emergence of specific discourses of management culture, and the expansion of 'the culture industries', including the 'cultural' component to new information technologies (see various contributions to du Gay and Pryke [2002], which, despite the intentions of the editors, follow such a 'culturalization' theme). Following others (e.g. du Gay and Pryke 2002: 6–12), we are unconvinced of this thesis, and would certainly place more emphasis on a claim that political economy has always been cultural.

To the extent that there is a shift underway, it is that discourse and practice in the global economy has become increasingly reflexively *understood as cultural* (Thrift 1997); the HSBC ads and the strategy underpinning it are thus not evidence that the economy is becoming more determined by 'cultural factors' but that actors such as HSBC are simply becoming more aware of the role that culture has always played, despite the rhetoric of economics that suggests the abstract, depersonalized (and thus deculturalized) character of 'modern' economies. Analyses of other dimensions of the culturalization of the economy, from studies of governmentality that emphasize the cultural character of power in contemporary economies (as subjects self-monitor rather than have control externally imposed), to analyses of corporate 'business culture', or advertising, or to studies of the professional cultures produced by MBA programmes, for example, are also best understood in this sense. That is, they testify to a trend towards recognizing that 'culture', however understood, has always been important to business success, national economic performance, class politics, employment chances, or any other dimension of political economy, rather than suggesting that culture is itself becoming more important to those phenomena. The various 'cultural futures' outlined by Amoore and de Goede, Ouellet and Thrift should be understood in this light; the processes they describe involve actors who themselves understand their economic and political practices as *cultural*.

Conclusions and provocations

We do not pretend to have resolved the many conceptual, theoretical and practical questions thrown up by the attempt to articulate a conception of cultural political economy. By way of conclusion, R. B. J. Walker provides a commentary on the notion of cultural political economy, and on how it is invoked across the chapters in the book. Walker argues provocatively that a notion of cultural political economy is simultaneously essential and impossible. Essential for the reasons we have already attempted to illustrate – those phenomena we conventionally understand as in the domain of political economy are always at the same time cultural. But impossible because, in Walker's words, 'each of these terms already imply versions of the others', and at the same time because 'these terms imply claims about value which are in profound contradiction with the others'. The attempt to combine them thus inevitably stumbles on problems of either basic contradictions between the values prioritized by one or other term and the others, and/or the choice of a particular version of one, in effect deciding what the other two look like. The chapter provides a critical reflection on the enterprise of the book as a whole.

Contributions

Despite Walker's provocations (or perhaps because of them), we do want to claim in this book that an attention to the concrete cultural constitution of the political economy has significant intellectual and practical advantages. We can, first, better understand the 'economic' in political economy. By recognizing the mutual implication of culture and economy, we can develop a richer understanding of significant economic phenomena, not only in the various specific instances discussed in the volume but also in terms of the overall character of the global political economy. Here we discuss diverse practices varying from ethical tourism, to the war on terror, to the search for talent, to the history of money doctoring. Our claim is nevertheless broader – while there will be many nuances in the stories which can be told in specific contexts, we do argue that the overall shape of the global economy, from the practices of multilateral agencies, global financial actors or multinational firms, and the manifold relations among them, can be better understood by insisting on and then interrogating their cultural character.

Second, we want also to claim that by focusing on culture, we can also better understand the 'politics' in political economy. In part this consists of a deepening of a claim about 'ideology'. Standard critiques of dominant practices might focus on the ideological character of the 'cultures' associated with them. The chapters here suggest that such a notion of ideology is often rather thin; it is more fruitful to take seriously the network of relations between particular ideas and the daily practices and desires to which those ideas give expression and shape. Thus one might imagine critiques of the chapter by Thrift that the notion of 'talent' is merely one more way to exploit labour; or that the maps in Walters' chapter simply reflect the instrumental deployment of cultural fears about migrants for particular purposes; or that the various imaginings in the chapter by Amoore and de Goede are constructs designed to 'keep people afraid' while serving specific corporate interests. Our reaction to this criticism is however to say that such understandings can certainly be brought to bear on these phenomena, but that they in turn exceed the parameters of the critique. 'Talent' can work ideologically precisely because it articulates with complicated patterns of desire which are difficult to completely reduce to effects of capitalist power; migration maps work because of their existence in a network of significations about migration which are difficult to simply disregard as racist simplifications; what is interesting about imaginations of terrorist attacks is precisely the complexities of the imaginations, which do not have specific political projects associated with them, or if they do, exceed the limits of those projects. And so on.

So certainly, culture can be strategically deployed, but it does not follow that that is the only question we can ask of it. It need not be strategically deployed, for example, for it to have significant effects on power relations. In fact, culture is perhaps at its most powerful when it is simply taken for granted as one of the markers of identity, privilege or appropriate behaviour, or when it produces the infrastructure of the economy and daily life. As the HSBC ads demonstrate, culture is a force that works to demarcate divisions between self and other – distinctions between identity and difference that can easily translate into logics of inclusion and exclusion, good and evil, powerful and powerless. Although the ads seek to unsettle such easy assumptions, and thus to embrace difference, they also work to reinforce their implicit hierarchies, and thus play into the logics of inclusion and exclusion that culture enables.

In short, a focus on cultural political economy not only enables us to better understand new patterns of activity and to attend to different sites of economic importance, but also contributes to our understanding of the core questions of political economy: the nature of production, trade and finance, the global patterns of distribution and inequality, and the power relations that sustain and constrain them all.

Notes

1 These ads can be viewed and downloaded at: http://www.yourpointofview.com/hsbcads_tv.aspx# (accessed 18 August 2008).
2 This broad definition has the advantage of avoiding reification, since culture in this reading does not need to become a thing, like 'British culture', but remains instead a fluid object of study. It also provides broad parameters within which more specific conceptions of culture can be organized. For similar classic statements concerning the conceptualisation of culture, see Bhabha (1994), or Hall (1980). See also the discussion by Matt Davies (Chapter 2) of Raymond Williams.
3 For some excellent critical analyses of the depoliticizing logic of the World Bank's concept of social capital, see Fine (2001) and Walters (2002). On similar practices in the IMF, see Best (2007).
4 See for example Gartman (2004) or Paterson (2007: ch. 4) on the car sector, crucial in this period of history and to this particular process.
5 In fact, the identity of the consumer has begun to infiltrate even 'non-economic' realms, as universities, local and national governments and non-profit agencies are all encouraged to develop an ethos of customer-service. This process simultaneously reveals the cultural constitution of the boundaries of the economic itself; why should certain spheres of social life be subjected to economic logics and others not?
6 That the money markets are themselves cultural phenomena is also well analysed, for example by Leyshon and Thrift (1997: ch. 4) or McDowell (1997).
7 This brief and highly selective review of neoliberal politics draws, among others, on Gamble (1988), Frank (2001) and Hall and Jacques (1989).

Bibliography

Aglietta, Michel (1979) *A Theory of Capitalist Regulation*, London: New Left Books.

Aitken, Rob (2005) ' "A direct personal stake": Cultural economy, mass investment and the New York Stock Exchange', *Review of International Political Economy*, 12(2): 334–65.

Albert, Mathias, David Jacobson and Yosef Lapid (eds) (2001) *Identities, Borders, Orders: Rethinking International Relations Theory*, Minneapolis, MN: University of Minnesota Press.

Amin, Ash and Nigel Thrift (eds) (2004) *The Blackwell Cultural Economy Reader*, Oxford: Blackwell.

Appadurai, Arjun (1990) 'Disjuncture and difference in the global cultural economy', in Mike Featherstone (ed.) *Global Culture: Nationalism, Globalization and Modernity*, London: Sage, pp. 295–310.

Barnett, Michael and Martha Finnemore (2004) *Rules for the World: International Organizations in Global Politics*, Ithaca, NY: Cornell University Press.

Barry, Andrew (2002) 'The Anti-Political Economy', *Economy and Society*, 31(2): 268–84.

Best, Jacqueline (2005) *The Limits of Transparency: Ambiguity and the History of International Finance*, Ithaca, NY: Cornell University Press.

—— (2007) 'Legitimacy dilemmas: the IMF's pursuit of country ownership', *Third World Quarterly*, 28(3): 469–88.

Bhabha, Homi (1994) *The Location of Culture*, London: Routledge.

Blyth, Mark (2002) *Great Transformations: Economic Ideas and Institutional Change in the Twentieth Century*, Cambridge: Cambridge University Press.

Buzan, Barry (1983) *People, States and Fear: the National Security Problem in International Relations*, Chapel Hill, NC: University of North Carolina Press.

Callon, Michel (1998) *The Laws of the Markets*, Oxford: Blackwell.

Campbell, David (1998) *Writing Security: United States Foreign Policy and the Politics of Identity* (second ed.), Minneapolis, MN: University of Minnesota Press.

Connolly, William E. (1991) *Identity/Difference: Democratic Negotiations of Political Paradox*, Ithaca, NY: Cornell University Press.

Cox, Robert W. (1987) *Production, Power and World Order*, New York: Columbia University Press.

de Goede, Marieke (2005) 'Carnival of money: Politics of dissent in an era of globalizing finance', in Louise Amoore (ed.) *The Global Resistance Reader*, New York: Routledge, pp. 379–91.

—— (2006) *International Political Economy and Poststructural Politics*, London: Palgrave.

du Gay, Paul and Michael Pryke (eds) (2002) *Cultural Economy*, London: Sage.

Dean, Mitchell (1999) *Governmentality: Power and Rule in Modern Society*, Thousand Oaks, CA: Sage.

Fine, Ben (2001) *Social Capital versus Social Theory: Political Economy and Social Science at the Turn of the Millennium*, London: Routledge.

Frank, Thomas (2001) *One Market Under God: Extreme Capitalism, Market Populism and the End of Economic Democracy*, London: Secker and Warburg.

Gamble, Andrew (1988) *The Free Economy and the Strong State: the Politics of Thatcherism*, London: Macmillan.

Gartman, David (2004) 'Three ages of the automobile: the cultural logics of the car', *Theory, Culture and Society*, 21(4–5): 169–95.

Geertz, Clifford (1973) *The Interpretation of Cultures*, New York: Basic Books.

Gill, Stephen (1995) 'The global panopticon? The neoliberal state, economic life and democratic surveillance', *Alternatives*, 20(1): 1–49.

Hall, Stuart (1980) 'Cultural studies: two paradigms', *Media, Culture and Society*, 2(1): 58–72.

Hall, Stuart and Martin Jacques (eds) (1989) *New Times the Changing Face of Politics in the 1990s*, London: Lawrence and Wishart.

Harmes, Adam (2001) 'Mass investment culture?', *New Left Review*, 9 (May/June): 103–24.

Harvey, David (1989), *The Condition of Postmodernity*, Oxford: Blackwell.

Heelas, Paul, (2002), 'Work ethics, soft capitalism and the "turn to life" ', in Paul Du Gay and Michael Pryke (eds) *Cultural Economy*, London: Sage, pp. 78–96.

Helleiner, Eric (1994) *States and the Reemergence of Global Finance: From Bretton Woods to the 1990s*, Ithaca, NY: Cornell University Press.

Hindess, Barry (1997) 'Politics and governmentality', *Economy and Society*, 26(2): 257–72.

Hirschman, Albert (1978) *The Passions and the Interests: Political Arguments for Capitalism before Its Triumph*, Princeton, NJ: Princeton University Press.

Hobson, John and Leonard Seabrooke (eds) (2007) *The Everyday Politics of the World Economy*, Cambridge: Cambridge University Press.

Huysmans, Jef (2006) *The Politics of Insecurity: Fear, Migration and Asylum in the EU*, London: Routledge.

Inayatullah, Naeem and David L. Blaney (1999) 'Towards an ethnological IPE: Karl Polanyi's double critique of capitalism', *Millenium* 28(2): 311–40.

Jessop, Bob and Ngai-Lin Sum (2001) 'Pre-disciplinary and post-disciplinary perspectives', *New Political Economy*, 6(1): 89–10.

Kratochwil, Friedrich (1995) *Rules, Norms and Decisions: On the Conditions of Practical and Legal Reasoning in International Relations and Domestic Affairs*, Cambridge: Cambridge University Press.

Langley, Paul (2008) *The Everyday World of Global Finance: Saving and Borrowing in Anglo-America*, Oxford: Oxford University Press.

Larner, Wendy and William Walters (eds) (2004) *Global Governmentality: Governing International Spaces*, London: Routledge.

Lash, Scott and John Urry (1994) *Economies of Signs and Space*, London: Sage.

Leyshon, Andrew and Nigel Thrift (1997) *Money/Space: Geographies of Monetary Transformation*, London: Routledge.

MacKenzie, Donald (2006) *An Engine, Not a Camera: How Financial Models Shape Financial Markets*, Cambridge, MA: MIT Press.

—— (2007) 'Making things the same: gases, emissions rights and the politics of carbon markets', paper presented to the seminar on Carbon Markets in Social Science Perspective, Durham University, 7 November 2007.

McDowell, Linda (1997) *Capital culture*, Oxford: Blackwell.

McNamara, Kathleen R. (1998) *The Currency of Ideas: Monetary Politics in the European Union*, Ithaca, NY: Cornell University Press.

Miller, Peter (2004) 'Governing by numbers: why calculative practices matter', in Ash Amin and Nigel Thrift (eds) *The Blackwell Cultural Economy Reader*, Oxford: Blackwell, pp. 179–90.

Miller, Peter and Nikolas Rose (1990), 'Governing economic life', *Economy and Society*, 19(1): 1–31.

Murphy, Craig and Cristina Rojas de Ferro (1995) 'Introduction: the power of representation in international political economy', *Review of International Political Economy*, 2(1): 63–69.

Onuf, Nicholas (1998) 'Constructivism: a user's manual', in V. Kubálková, N. Onuf and P. Kowert (eds), *International Relations in a Constructed World*, Armonk, NY: M.E. Sharpe, pp. 58–78.

Park, Susan (2006) 'Theorizing norm diffusion within international organizations', *International Politics*, 43(3): 342–61.

Paterson, Matthew (2007) *Automobile Politics: Ecology and Cultural Political Economy*, Cambridge: Cambridge University Press.

Paterson, Matthew and Johannes Stripple (2007) 'My space: governing individuals through the carbon market', paper presented at the 4th European Consortium for Political Research General Conference, Pisa, Italy, 6–8 September.

Polanyi, Karl, (1944) *The Great Transformation: The Political and Economic Origins of Our Time*, Boston, MA: Beacon Press.

Ray, Larry and Andrew Sayer (eds) (1999) *Culture and Economy: After the Cultural Turn*, London: Sage.

Robertson, Roland (1992) *Globalization: social theory and global culture*, London: Sage.

Rose, Nicholas (1993) 'Government, authority and expertise in advanced liberalism', *Economy and Society*, 22(3): 283–99.

—— (1996) 'The death of the social? Re-figuring the territory of government', *Economy and Society*, 25(3): 327–56.

Rosow, Stephen, Naeem Inayatullah and Mark Rupert (eds) (1994) *The Global Economy as Political Space*, Boulder, CO: Lynne Rienner.

Neumann, Iver B. and Ole Jacob Sending (2006) 'Governance to governmentality: analyzing NGOs, states and power', *International Studies Quarterly*, 50(3): 651–72.

Shapiro, Michael J. (1993) *Reading 'Adam Smith': Desire, History and Value*, London: Sage.

Thrift, Nigel (2001) '"It's the romance, not the finance, that makes the business worth pursuing": disclosing a new market culture', *Economy and Society*, 30(4): 412–32.

Waever, Ole (1993) *Identity, Migration and the New Security Agenda in Europe*, New York: St. Martin's Press.

Walker, R. B. J. (1993) *Inside/outside: International Relations as Political Theory*, Cambridge: Cambridge University Press.

Walters, William (2002) 'Social capital and political sociology: re-imagining politics?', *Sociology*, 36(2): 377–97.

Weaver, Catherine and Ralf Leiteritz (2005) ' "Our poverty is a world full of dreams": reforming the World Bank', *Global Governance*, 11(3): 369–88.

Weber, Heloise (2002) 'The imposition of a global development architecture: the example of Microcredit', *Review of International Studies*, 28(3): 537–55.

Williams, David (1999) 'Constructing the economic space: the World Bank and the making of homo oeconomicus', *Millennium*, 28(1): 79–100.

World Bank (2004) 'Social capital for development', retrieved 3 February 2007, from *http://www1.worldbank.org/prem/poverty/scapital/index.htm*.

Part 1
Interrogating the classics

1 Undressing the wound of wealth

Political economy as a cultural project

David L. Blaney and Naeem Inayatullah

The 'West' constructs itself, in part, through the discipline of political economy. Political economy, as theory and practice, depends on a utopian self-idealization of the West as wealthy, modern, and civilized that splits it from others, who are poor, backward, and savage. One effect of this split between the West and its others is to hide troubling questions about wealth, modernity, and civilization: is wealth for some bought at the cost of impoverishing others? What benefits of wealth might justify such immiseration? Do savage cultures contain values, critiques, and ways of life that the West still needs?

Economists rarely pose such questions, leaving them, it might be thought, to the cultural critics of economics. The bifurcation of economics and cultural studies shares, however, an understanding of economics as an acultural domain whose logic operates regardless of the particularities of space and time. Economics' purported universalism serves both economics and its cultural critics: economics presents itself as truly scientific while cultural studies can dismiss economics as a mode of inquiry devoid of cultural or ethical meaning. Both ignore the emergence of political economy as a cultural project and, therefore, neither engages the question of wealth.

Despite the dominance of this bifurcation in contemporary disciplines, we find it much less prevalent in the work of major thinkers of the classical tradition of political economy. Figures such as Smith, Hayek, Hegel and Marx help restore our sensitivity to the cultural and ethical content of modern political economic life and allow us to re-imagine political economy as a cultural project. Their work helps us to specify how wealth production inflicts a wound upon the West *and* the world. Festering within this wound are the problems of modern poverty, such as the social deformity of many that is the result of wealth creation, and the subjection of some to others in the name of such values as freedom, equality, and individuality. Turning to these issues permits us to retrieve political economy as a cultural project and, perhaps, to redress the wound of wealth.

Political economy and the utopian/savage slot

The 'West', Michel-Rolph Trouillot (1991: 18, 26–9) explains, constructs itself in comparison to a complex other. 'The savage' marks the earliest state of humankind against which the modern is measured. Superseding this other requires that the 'West' identify and realize certain ideals. Thus, Trouillot (1991: 27) notes that 'the savage is an argument for a particular kind of utopia'. It is against the savage that the 'West' marks itself as a 'utopian projection', a 'universalist' and 'didactic' project. In the disciplinary division of labour, anthropology came to fill 'the Savage Slot' as Trouillot emphasizes. We want to suggest that political economy fills the 'Utopian Slot'.

Political economy serves to articulate the 'West's' greatest ambitions and values – for wealth, social stability, ethical refinement, peace, equality, and freedom, to draw a list from Adam Smith and his Scottish Enlightenment fellows. David Hume (1985: 271, 273) is exemplary: '*industry, knowledge*, and *humanity*, are linked together by an indissoluble chain, and are found, from experience as well as reason, to be peculiar to the more polished, and, what are commonly denominated, the more luxurious age'; 'Law, order, police, discipline: these can never be carried to any degree of perfection, before human reason has refined itself by exercise, and by an application to the more vulgar arts, at least, of commerce and manufacture'. 'Not to mention', Hume (1985: 273) continues, 'that all ignorant ages are infested with superstition, which throws the government off its bias, and disturbs men in the pursuit of interest and happiness'. As Hume's account hints, political economy emerges from a cultural partitioning where others serve as a kind of negative benchmark relative to which modernizing Europe is wealthy, civilized and rational. These others, the developmentally anachronistic are poor, barbaric, and irrational. The savage is precisely what the modern European self is not. We see political economy, then, less as a discipline analysing the commonality and variety of human experience and more a particular cultural project that seeks to split self and other (Benjamin 1988: 25–31, 62–3, 218).

This splitting of the West and the savage is achieved temporally (see Inayatullah and Blaney 2004; Blaney and Inayatullah 2006). While Scottish political economists, for example, ground their political economy in rigorous observation and systematic comparison, they nevertheless locate the West at the apex of temporal development. The savage, while a historical curiosity, is ethically relevant only as a superseded moment of a heroic tale of social progress that culminates in the modern commercial self. Still, the splitting of the savage from the West and the savage slot from the utopian slot are not so easily accomplished. The Scots themselves seemed to sense this difficulty. They deployed a stage-theory of social development to secure this split, erecting a 'temporal wall' between the West and the savage other (Blaney and Inayatullah 2006), but this architectural metaphor simply conceals an overlap of the utopian and savage slots (see Karatani [1995: 6–9], on the power and fragility of architectural metaphors). Though separated and pushed backward, the other finds life within the self. The values and visions of the imagined savage, it seems, are not fully eradicated for the modern. We continue to require savage values both as a mirror for the idealized self and as a corrective for the shortcomings of modernity itself. Further, this uneasy juxtaposition of an idealized image of self and its backward other provides an opportunity for the West to domesticate its most serious anxieties and doubts. Where better to bury doubts than in the richest source of dreams and fantasies – a domain that seems to vindicate the West and represents its greatest historical achievements. Perhaps the separation of self and other is most faithfully defended in political economy because that is where their overlap appears most dangerous.

An investigation of political economy as a cultural project involves, then, not only understanding an identity formation that splits self and other but also the necessary overlap of self and other – an overlap that offers a transgressing vision. Political economy reveals the modern West's most enduring and sacred social and political ideals, its greatest fears and anxieties, and potentially powerful alternative visions of social and political life. Exploring this terrain also means recognizing that political economy sits in the domain of the cultural.

The bifurcation of culture and economy

Political economy and culture are usually set in opposition. Phillip Crang notes that it is often difficult to fix on the relationship of economics and culture because 'the economic and the cultural have long been cast as "self" and "other", each defined by what the other is not' (1997: 4). Cultural critics usually place the blame on economists. Pierre Bourdieu suggests that economic concepts are inappropriately applied 'outside of any reference to the work of historians or social anthropologists' (2005: 3). Stephen Gudeman pits his argument applying cultural categories to economic life against the 'widely accepted view' that 'an economy comprises a separate sphere of instrumental or practical action' (1986: xii). William Jackson's reflections on economics indicate that 'mainstream economists never stray beyond core theoretical assumptions which eschew cultural ideas' (Jackson 1993: 453). Indeed, '[i]ndividualistic, rational-choice theorizing obscures the role of culture'; ideas of efficiency and equilibrium are 'supposedly relevant to all times and places' (Jackson, 1996: 221–2). 'Positing a set of individual motives and capacities as universal', the economist, as Daniel Miller likewise argues, renders 'algorithms that model particular relationships within capitalism' as a 'general and ideal system', bearing little resemblance to a 'holistic' view that considers 'behaviors ... within the larger framework of people's lives and cosmologies' (1997: 8, 17). 'Economy', claims Timothy Mitchell, is therefore thought to refer to a 'realm with an existence prior to and separate from its representations, and thus to stand in opposition to the more discursive constructs of social theory' (1998: 84). Craig Murphy and Christina Rojas de Ferro extend these claims to the field of international political economy, which universalizes 'the categories of capitalism and of the application of laissez-faire principles' in defiance of history and 'cultural, racial or gender differences' (1995: 67). The complaint is that economics sets itself in opposition to culture in order to establish its superior scientific status (its claim to a singular and universal truth).

Most economists would turn the argument on its head and then embrace the complaint. Standard neoclassical economists proudly insist that economic laws operate regardless of the particulars of cultural landscapes. Classical political economy and most Marxist economics are likewise read as working to uncover regularities and laws that operate despite the culturally attuned understandings of actors – though we see our task as partly undoing this reading. As Rob Walker suggests in the conclusion to this volume, to juxtapose culture and political economy is to invoke a tension. The modifier 'culture' threatens to undermine the nomothetic elegance of general laws; it seems to make an aesthetic and logical mess of efforts to get beyond intentions and towards unintended consequences that appear as natural laws or structural regularities. Culture seems to align itself in our imagination as one with the ideographic – culture stands in for cultures and cultures suggest multiple systems of meaning and meaningful interaction. As Phillip Crang has noted, the language of culture does point us to a ' "generic" fact of human life, bound up with the human competencies to make the world meaningful and significant' (1997: 5). But it also points us towards a '"differential" quality, marking out and helping to constitute distinctive social systems' (see Davies, Chapter 2, in this volume). Following the lead of the editors' introduction, to give in to the cultural is to be newly sensitive to cultural variation, seemingly downgrading economics from its status as natural law, to confront alternative meanings and purposes than those central to the modern economy, and to transform economics into an ethnological science.

Though we share the critics' concerns about the discipline of economics – and we take for granted that economy is deeply culturally constituted – our purpose here is somewhat different. Understanding political economy as a cultural project may require that we take seriously the economist's universalist and scientific aims by investigating the social meanings and ethical purposes created by a seemingly acultural and universalistic economics. If political economy is established as the utopian slot in contrast to a cultural savage slot, why is this necessary? What work is enabled by this bifurcation? To ask these questions is not necessarily to absolve economics of its imperial pretensions. Rather, we probe how and why the bifurcation enables both economists and cultural critics to stabilize, naturalize, and overlook the mutually constituting utopian and savage slots. To destabilize and denaturalize the utopian/savage slot requires us to see political economy as a cultural project – as a domain of meaning and ethical purpose. Thus, we do not simply reject modern economics or modern capitalism, though our agenda does require that we construct, as Linda McDowell suggests, 'an understanding of the conflicts and contradictions, the doubts and uncertainties in the multiplicity of practices that constitute "the economic"' (2000: 22). We recognize that economics, despite some protest, necessarily engages, even surreptitiously constructs, a 'moral economy' – a domain of 'moral sentiments and norms' (Sayer 2003: 341; also see Sen 1999: ch. 5).

Thus, we are wary of arguments that drive culture and economy apart. If, as we have noted, the economic stakes a claim to the natural and the universal and the cultural finds its *modus vivendi* in the particular and in difference, then to embrace the cultural may simply pit oneself in opposition to the economic without disturbing their overlap. As Nigel Thrift warns, an emphasis on culture has led many thinkers to take 'remarkably little … note of economics' (2000: 692, 698–9). And, suggesting that this opposition is constitutive of elements of the cultural turn itself, he notes that 'Culture was culture because it had been purified of the taint of the economic' (see also Jackson 2002: 4). To turn to culture may simply reproduce this bifurcation, re-inscribing the boundary so to speak, even as the commentator hopes to recover the cultural for social inquiry.

A cautionary tale may help us to see how secure the bifurcation between economics and culture remains. Richard Ashley is acclaimed for his work challenging conventional international relations theory. His ideas on 'economism' are less well known even if, in our view, they are amongst his most stimulating work. In his 'Three modes of economism' (Ashley 1983), Ashley astutely de-reifies economic logic (Inayatullah and Blaney, 1997). However, he also constructs economy as an 'other', over and against a 'lifeworld' of social meaning and ethical purpose, creative contestation, and thematic ambiguity. Though Ashley does not use the language of culture, preferring to talk about restoring the role of the 'political', his embrace of the 'lifeworld' as a domain of alternative views and social/political action parallels the role that 'culture' plays for some contemporary critics of the economy.

For Ashley the economy presupposes a distinction between 'social system' (society) and 'environment' (nature) (1983: 474–5). Processes *within* the social system are concerned with politics – the contestation of key social purposes. Ashley defines the economy as *relations between* the social system and the environment, but he treats these relations as distinctly asocial. The environment serves society only as a source of objects subject to 'manipulation and control' for social reproduction; the relationship is purely technical or instrumental, a system of inputs and outputs in which the system transforms the environment so 'that it can obtain what it values, requires, or needs in order to maintain or reproduce its given structures' (1983: 474). The definition of (the) economy is thus imbued with familiar neoclassical propositions of scarcity and efficiency that complete the economy's insulation from a world of cultural meanings and purposes.

Ashley fears that the logic of economy is 'an abstract theoretical contrivance' that has led – with the rise of the modern capitalist economy – to the 'conscious contemplation' of all choices in instrumental terms: 'Economic behavior' has become 'self-consciously understood by women and men in just these transparent terms, i.e., in terms of a logic of economy' (1983: 475). Where the logic of economy has a hold on the mind, people are led to accept the social world as 'given' or 'politically neutral' (Ashley 1983: 473). We might add 'culturally neutral', and note that Bourdieu (2005: 5–6) speaks of the supposedly natural laws of economy as involving the inculcation of individuals to the habit of calculation, as a 'conversion' experience. In Ashley's modern economy, technical rationality serves as 'the premier justificatory framework for human action'. This framework presupposes the essential givenness and internal consistency of the decision maker and his values or goals, by regarding as given the definition of a problem (the gap between desirable and actual system conditions) to be solved, and by treating as unproblematic a distinction between values to be served and options to be taken[;] the algorithm exactly reproduces the logic of economy's presupposition of given boundaries between (a) fixed and apolitically defined system structures to be reproduced … and (b) a manipulable environment to be objectified and controlled in the interest of reproducing those structures. Like the logic of economy, technical rationality reflects not at all on the truth content of values or ends, and never on the structures or boundaries of the agent, but only on the efficiency of means. In short technical rationality is the unreflective logic of economy *par excellence* (Ashley 1983: 475–76).

Technical rationality appears to displace all (other?) social and political content from the economy. Thus, the logic of economy embedded in existing capitalist societies is especially debilitating to human political and ethical purposes and as a consequence 'the period of historical economism we are now experiencing is a very dangerous time' (Ashley 1983: 490).

Although we share Ashley's concern that technical rationality often overrides substantial political/ethical concerns, we find it puzzling that he unproblematically characterizes existing capitalist societies as completely dominated by 'technical rational logic'. At one point he admits that 'even within bourgeois culture, conformity to the model [of the logic of economy] has its definite limits', but this admission does not deter the weight of his argument: the internalization of the logic of economy is the 'social pathology of advanced capitalist society', the escape from which is 'the political task of our time' (Ashley 1983: 476, 492). In the end, Ashley depicts the economy as a (social?) practice that is reducible to the logic of technical rationality. We see his *economising of the economy* as an additional mode of economism; he continues to split the economy from social/cultural/political domains.

We are not surprised, then, that Ashley treats the economy as a special source of anxiety against which the 'lifeworld' provides hope for 'salvation' (Youngs 1994: 15). The political logic of 'lifeworld' is 'intrinsically dialectical', capable of 'calling into question the dominant social order on which it depends'. It possesses 'generative power' that can override the merely technical and apolitical logic that governs our participation in the economy (Ashley 1983: 478–80). Thus, a crucial part of this bifurcation of danger/salvation turns on the opposition between an *asocial* economy versus a *social* lifeworld rich with the ethical ambiguity, reflexive questioning, the creative energies of cultural life, and the restorative possibilities of political action.

Ashley's view of the logic of economy and capitalist society thereby stunts our theorizing of political economic possibilities. First, by taking for granted a particular, technical characterization of economy, we are led away from richer, more nuanced accounts of economic life. Ashley's economy is not granted full status as social practice, since he reduces economic practice to technical rationality. But this reduction does not begin to capture the ambitions of political economy as a cultural project. For classical political economy, inquiry is located in the utopian slot; it does not entail a merely technical account of a distinctly economic logic, but envisions an entire way of life, reflecting key ethical meanings and purposes: wealth, order, freedom, equality, etc. At its best, the classical tradition of political economy recognizes that this utopian vision is materialized in limited, complicated, and contradictory ways: the creation simultaneously of wealth and poverty; a market order that is also a source of disorderly booms and busts; a limited understanding of freedom that seems to produce freedoms for some at the expense of others; a formal equality realized but substantively denied; and an expansion of human capacities alongside a vitiation of civic possibilities. Ashley's depiction of economy misses that the instrumental elements of economic logic – a kind of asociality at the heart of the social practice of economy – are a consequence of a rich structuring of social meaning and purpose in which this 'asocial sociality' is pivotal to wealth production. The imperial imposition of technical rationality is motivated and vivified by larger goals, namely an expansion of wealth that serves as a precondition for human freedom and individuality.

Second, Ashley's bifurcation of the logic of economy and lifeworld produces an equally stunted notion of the possibilities of cultural/political life. Though political economy envisions the separation of the economy as a distinct domain, it does not imagine a world in which the other domains of the social whole somehow are insulated or separated from the social meanings and purposes that sustain the economy. It is only by purifying society of the logic of economy that Ashley finds in lifeworld the wholesome motivations, creative energies, and recursive questioning required for our salvation from the logic of economy. However, our modern cultural energies, critical reflexivity, and political and social action do not spring from some place completely free of the operation of technical rationality or insulated from capitalist notions of freedom, equality, and individuality. There is no generative power or creative questioning that *simply* stands outside of and opposed to political economy.

Third, Ashley overlooks that his anxiety about the economy is less a challenge to the political economy tradition than a symptom of fears deeply rooted within that tradition itself; political economy shares the very anxiety that Ashley sets in opposition to a complacent economic logic. Classical political economy comes to us laced with uncertainty about our selves as social beings. That the individual's role in the economy is narrowly self-regarding may be thought to produce certain social goods, but there is also recognition that our civic and familial roles may demand something other than self-interest narrowly conceived. Our contemporary anxieties about the meaning of equality, the purposes of wealth, the possibilities of social order, the character and preconditions of freedom all also lie deeply within the concerns of classical political economy.

Finally, we find it curious that both contemporary economists and Ashley share a common view of the distinctiveness of the logic of economy. Even more curious is that each deploys this claim to justify the purity of their scholarly activity. For the economist, the economy is purified of a cultural/political content that would vitiate claims about the universality and naturalness of this distinct economic logic and immerse them in political/ethical debate. For Ashley, the enclosure of this economic logic allows him to purify the modern lifeworld as a privileged site of critical activity relative to a politically/ethically empty economics. Each needs a certain and fixed boundary to champion their domain and to avoid the ambiguous resources within the overlap. Despite this entrenched bifurcation, the skills we need to recover the resources within this overlap are not scarce. We draw on the rich and often under-appreciated legacy of Hayek, Smith, Hegel and Marx. We can find in these representatives of a more 'classical' tradition a cultural analysis that acknowledges that modern wealth creation is a kind of social wound and that refuses to treat that wound as somehow 'transcended', either historically or dialectically (see Gibson-Graham 2006: xi, and Watson 2005: 18–19).

Reclaiming the classical tradition for cultural political economy

Hayek and Smith: probing the wound (and recoiling)

Friedrich Hayek defends a capitalist political economy for several reasons, not the least of which is that a 'market order' embraces a particular kind of difference. Through the staging of competitions, market society reveals and expresses 'the boundless variety of human nature' and 'the wide range of differences in individual capacities and potentialities'. Market competition uncovers these nature-given differences and energizes them for society, leading humans to produce the things needed by others (Hayek 1979: 67–8). More precisely, the market exposes and punishes less productive efforts, while valorizing productive ones, thereby revealing successful competitive strategies that generate greater wealth at a lower cost (Hayek 1976: ch. 10; 1960: ch. 5). However, for Hayek the market is not simply a technical matter – the means to wealth creation – but is intrinsic to his vision of a good society. Hayek embraces competition because it also promotes and expresses the values of individual equality and liberty. Unlike Ashley, the market, as a discovery procedure, embodies and expresses valued social meanings and statuses. Thus, Hayek sees the market as an expression of, and yet also the unintended consequence of, the particular, independent, and voluntary actions of free and equal individuals (Hayek 1976: 107).

Hayek's spirited defence of a market society is often seen as a fulfilment of the project launched by Adam Smith. Less known is that Hayek's defence of capitalism contains key insights about its failings. While this culture of competition increases everyone's desires, it only can fulfil the desires of some. Despite their best efforts and most skilled contributions, some will be rewarded highly and others will receive few benefits. This outcome is an inevitable and necessary accompaniment of 'a progressive society':

> [W]hile it relies on [a] process of learning and imitation, [it] recognizes the desire it creates only as a spur to further effort. It does not guarantee the results to everyone. It disregards the pain of unfulfilled desire aroused by the example of others. It appears cruel because it increases the desire of all in proportion as it increases its gifts to some. Yet so long as it remains a progressive society, some must lead and some must follow.
>
> (Hayek 1960: 44–5)

Hayek admits that 'pain' is a consequence of differential rewards and that to ignore this difference appears 'cruel'. Yet, such pain and cruelty do not outweigh the fact that the culture of competition generates a wealthy society that endorses, supports, and produces selves that are independent, formally equal, and free. Given these goods, Hayek regards the 'pain' that such an order produces as minor.

Similarly, though more damaging, Hayek admits that there is no necessary connection between individual effort and reward and therefore a cruel deception lies at the heart of capitalist society:

> It certainly is important in the market order (or free enterprise society, misleadingly called 'capitalism') that individuals believe that their well being depends primarily on their own efforts and decision. Indeed, few circumstances will do more to make a person energetic and efficient than the belief that it depends chiefly on him whether he will reach the goals he has set for himself. ... but it leads no doubt also to an exaggerated confidence in the truth of this generalization which to those who regard themselves (and perhaps are) equally able but have failed must appear as a bitter and severe provocation ...
>
> (Hayek 1976: 74)

This tension leads Hayek to a pedagogical problem: 'It is ... a real dilemma to what extent we ought to encourage in the young the belief that when they try they will really succeed, or should rather emphasize that inevitably some unworthy will succeed and some worthy will fail ... ' (Hayek 1976: 4). Hayek quickly sets the dilemma aside; it may prick our conscience now and then, but a progressive society seems to require this noble lie. Nevertheless, Hayek's ultimate conclusions about the benefits of capitalism do not erase his assessments of its deep flaws.

For Adam Smith the deception at the heart of capitalist culture is still more poignant. The pre-eminent theorist of the virtues of a wealthy *society* remains less certain about the benefits of wealth for *individuals*. In *The Theory of Moral Sentiments*, Smith avers that the power and wealth created by the division of labour is quite 'contemptible and trifling':

> Power and riches appear then to be, what they are, enormous and operose machines contrived to produce a few trifling conveniences ... [that] keep off the summer shower, not the winter storm, but leave him always as much, and sometimes more exposed than before, to anxiety, to fear, and to sorrow; to diseases, to danger, and to death.
>
> (Smith 1979: 182–3)

Few perceive that the pursuit of wealth distracts individuals from the search for meaning. Such vision requires, says Smith, a facility with philosophy.

Surprisingly, he regards this failure of popular vision with some relief, for without it 'civilization' could neither be created nor advanced:

> It is this deception which rouses and keeps in continual motion the industry of mankind. It is this which first prompted them to cultivate the ground, to build houses, to found cities and commonwealths, and to invent and improve all the science and arts, which ennoble and embellish human life; which have entirely changed the whole face of the globe, have turned rude forests of nature into agreeable and fertile plains and made the track less and barren ocean a new fund of subsistence, and the great high road of communication to the different nations of the earth.
>
> (Smith 1979: 183–4)

Smith and Hayek thus converge in the belief that progress and civilization rest on deception. Generating wealth and progress requires that individuals regard the market as a producing machine – as a simple relation of inputs and outputs, in which their inputs will be duly recognized; and as ethically justified, not by broader social purposes, but by the individualized and separate ends that it produces. The social purpose of the market is recognized only by theorists, like Hayek and Smith, who provide the ethical justification for the kind of economism that Ashley exposes. Yet these classical political economists regard this economism as pivotal to the ethical purposes of a good society, instead of as an empty instrumentalism.

Despite their convergence on the social purposes of economism, Smith goes further than Hayek in opening a market society to substantive ethical debate, focusing intently on the central feature of his political economy – the division of labour. Smith shows how the wealth-creating division of labour also generates human social deformity and systematic poverty. It is within these arguments that the savage returns, not simply as a foil for progress, but as a commentary on the failings of a commercial society.

In *Lectures on Jurisprudence*, Smith reveals the 'inconveniences' of the division of labour (Smith 1982: 539–41). His replicates his concerns in a famous passage in book V of *Wealth of Nations*:

> In the progress of the division of labour, the employment of the far greater part of those who live by labour, that is, of the great body of the people, comes to be confined to a few very simple operations, frequently to one or two. But the understandings of the greater part of men are necessarily formed by their ordinary employments. The man whose whole life is spent in performing a few simple operations, the effects of which too are, always the same, or very nearly the same, has no occasion to exert his understanding, or to exercise his invention in finding out expedients for removing difficulties which never occur. He naturally loses, therefore, the habit of such exertion, and generally becomes as stupid and ignorant as it is possible for a human creature to become. The torpor of his mind renders him, not only incapable of relishing or bearing a part of any rational conversation, but of conceiving any generous,

noble, or tender sentiment, and consequently of forming any just judgment concerning many even of the ordinary duties of private life. Of the great and extensive interests of his country, he is altogether incapable of judging; and unless very particular pains have been taken to render him otherwise, he is equally incapable of defending his country in war. The uniformity of his stationary life naturally corrupts the courage of his mind, and makes him regard with abhorrence the irregular, uncertain, and adventurous life of a soldier. It corrupts even the activity of his body, and renders him incapable of exerting his strength with vigour and perseverance, in any other employment than that to which he has been bred.

(Smith 1976: 302–3)

Turning the common labourer into a specialist has a number of negative consequences: it makes him 'stupid'; incapable of 'rational conversation'; unable to 'conceive any generous, noble, or tender sentiment' and therefore inept at forming judgments concerning the 'duties of private life' and unqualified to ascertain the 'interests of his country'; and, finally, powerless in 'defending his country in war'. In direct contrast, the absence of a division of labour in savage and barbarous societies means that there exist 'varied occupations' so that inventiveness is 'kept alive'; 'every man is a warrior' and capable of taking his place as a 'statesman'; and each is able to 'form a tolerable judgment concerning the interest of society'. While specialization provides a material plenty unavailable to savage and barbarous societies, this advantage is 'acquired at the expense of [the labourer's] intellectual, social, and martial virtues'. The sober consequence is that 'in every improved and civilized society this is the state into which the labouring poor, that is, the great body of the people, must necessarily fall' (Smith 1976: 303–4).

From these passages we are hard pressed to believe Smith's usual assertions that European working classes are better off than savages. Indeed, so worried is Smith about the fate of workers that he invokes the visible hand of the state. If the state does not provide counter-measures, warns Smith, 'all the nobler parts of the human character may be, in a great measure, obliterated and extinguished in the great body of the people' (Smith 1976: 304).

Smith's treatment of poverty suggests a yet more radical direction. He asserts again and again that a commercial society produces greater material well-being for common people than previous forms of society. Indeed, Smith sets this increased wealth of the lowest ranks as a key criterion by which to assess contemporary society:

No society can surely be flourishing and happy, of which the far greater part of the members are poor and miserable. It is but equity, besides, that they who feed, cloath and lodge the whole body of the people, should have such a share of the produce of their own labour as to be themselves tolerably well fed, cloathed and lodged.

(Smith 1976: 88)

Earlier in the text he promises that, in a 'well-governed society', the 'universal opulence extends itself to the lowest ranks of the people' (Smith 1976: 15). Additionally, Smith is famous for his claim that even the poorest in commercial society are wealthier than savage kings. On his own account, however, such relative comparisons are not entirely favourable to commercial society. He admits to 'indigence' in commercial society: 'Wherever there is great property, there is great inequality. For one very rich man, there must be at least five hundred poor, and the affluence of the few supposes the indigence of the many' (Smith 1976: 232). Systematic production of wealth also generates systematic poverty; this is the unfortunate but necessary side effect of social advance.

We can read a still deeper tension in Smith by highlighting some rather puzzling comments about savage society. Smith suggests that 'extremities of hunger' impose on the savage a kind of 'Spartan discipline' (Smith 1976: 205). It is precisely this condition of scarcity that Smith believes a commercial society brings to an end. However, Smith also presents savages as possessed of the leisure to pursue music and dancing:

> It seems even to be amongst the most barbarous nations that the use and practice of them is both most frequent and most universal, as among the negroes of Africa and the savage tribes of America. In civilized nations, the inferior ranks of people have very little leisure. … Among savage nations, the great body of the people have frequently great intervals of leisure, and they have scarce any other amusement; they naturally, therefore, spend a great part of their time in almost the only one they have.
>
> (Smith 1980: 187)

This abundance of leisure for savages damages Smith's claims: they cannot 'spend a great part of their time' in music and dancing unless they can readily meet their minimum requirements as biological beings, a requirement that would seem to belie claims about their poverty (Levine 1977: ch. 2; Inayatullah 1997).

Smith cannot then sustain the claim that poverty is a condition distinct to savage societies, that it is an original condition for which commercial society is the antidote. Nor can poverty simply be relegated to the past and we cannot therefore so readily ignore the ethical resources offered by 'superseded' forms of society. This point is evocatively made by Eric Cheyfitz:

> Indian kinship economics, which, I want to make clear, I understand not as precapitalist but as anticapitalist, constitute a powerful *and continuing* critique of the waste of an expansive, acquisitive capitalism that … [Europe] could not *afford* to entertain. The loss in social vision was, and is, incalculable.
>
> (Cheyfitz 1993: 118)

While Smith hints at the resources of the savage way of life, his dominant mode of thinking either re-locates savagery to the past or dilutes its potency by pointing to its disadvantages relative to commercial society. Smith's complicated stance indicates that poverty and moral corruption signal a wound within a wealthy society. Smith may not consistently attend to this wound, but he does not ignore it; some part of Smith engages the wound of wealth. His engagement with the cultural other of commercial society – what Cheyfitz above calls the *kinship economics* of the Indians, or what Smith himself alludes to as the *singing and dancing economy of savages* – serves as a potential learning experience for those of us who remain immersed in modern capitalism.

Hegel and Marx: pressing the wound of wealth

Hegel and Marx believe the economy has an ethical purpose. For Hegel, the capitalist economy promotes individuality, equality, and freedom. While Marx sees this promise as largely unfulfilled, he agrees that capitalism promotes pluralized interests and fosters individual initiative and action. For both, modernity necessarily and bloodily destroys past forms of life, thereby freeing the individual from various kinds of pre-modern subordination. Hegel's more positive assessment of modern society is nonetheless qualified. Placing the market at the centre of civil society produces paradox: it generates progress but also alienates many from society; it meets people's expanding needs but also produces poverty. Hegel believes that modern states can resolve these tensions via colonization where the socially disadvantaged may achieve a life of freedom in a colony. However, this 'solution' comes at the expense of backward' peoples and therefore seems little more than a deferral of the problem. Hegel's solution to the wound of wealth inflicts that wound onto others.

In terms similar to Hayek's, Hegel sees 'civil society' as a stage of 'difference' that constitutes people as 'private persons', freeing them from the social and intellectual bondage predominant in particularly African and native American societies. In a modern society each individual is a 'particular' – each with her or his own set of needs and interests and for whom these needs and interests are her/his primary end (Hegel 1991: sections 182–83, 187). The market, as a central institution of civil society, promotes individual self-expression and self-seeking and Hegel recognizes this individuation as a real achievement of modern civil society. The arrival of modern society thus signals the emergence of a historical consciousness, a new era that displaces backward forms. Not all are called to play a role in this rising modern order: '*history*' serves 'as the *world court of judgment*' – a verdict delivered via conquest and the destruction of various savage peoples (Hegel 1991: section 340).

Whatever the limits of past societies, Hegel recognizes that modern society is not without its costs. Civil society lets loose 'boundless extravagance'; the desires are multiplied endlessly and individuals are tempted to define others as a mere means to their escalating ends (Hegel 1991: sections 182, 185). Freed from the political, ethical, and religious strictures of earlier eras, individuals can rend the fabric of society by acting in atomized, narrowly self-interested ways. In contrast with Ashley, however, Hegel recognizes that the logic of economy does not stand alone as a technical, asocial set of practices. Rather, the market is embedded within a wider set of social institutions comprising a specific ethical order (see Dickey 1987: 195, 214–19; Polanyi 1957). Self-seeking can only be 'actualized', says Hegel, within a 'system of all-round interdependence, so that the subsistence and welfare of the individual and his rightful existence are interwoven with, and grounded on, the subsistence, welfare, and rights of all, and have actuality and security only in this context' (Hegel 1991: section 183). The individual appears as a distinctly *social* being, embedded in a system of individual/social needs, and as a bearer of individual rights enforced by the state. This institutional embedding is not merely an external material fact imposing itself on the individual. Rather, by participating in this private sphere, individuals come to recognize that the pursuit of self-interest is possible only in relations of mutual dependence, entailing the recognition of the rights and needs of others (Hegel 1991: section 187; see also Stillman 1987). Though each person is particularized as a self-seeker, civil society is far from being Ashley's asocial or acultural domain: the individual pursuit of goals is richly laden with ethical meaning and value: subjectivity, self-expression, and social recognition.

Hegel's claim does not entail that civil society fully lives up to its ethical promise. A modern society, with an expanded division of labour, may generate prosperity and realize the individuality of many but, like Smith, Hegel is acutely aware that many remain in a state of at least relative privation and social deformity. While the capacity to meet multiplying human needs is expanded '[w]hen the activity of civil society is unrestricted', the *specialization* and *limitation* of particular work also increase, as do likewise the *dependence* and *want* of the class which is tied to such work; this in turn leads to an inability to feel and enjoy the wider freedoms, and particularly the spiritual advantages of civil society (Hegel 1991: section 243).

When a mass of individuals sink 'below the level of a certain standard of living' (by which Hegel means a socially respectable minimum), 'that feeling of right, integrity, and honour which comes from supporting oneself by one's own activity and work is lost' (Hegel 1991: section 244). Though Hegel recommends state action in response to this alienation, he recognizes that providing livelihood *for* people undermines their social respect: state support cannot substitute for the integrity that comes from individual initiative. Unable to resolve this dilemma, Hegel notes that the 'important question of how poverty can be remedied is one which agitates and torments modern societies especially' (Hegel 1991: section 244 [addition]; see also Fatton 1986; Fraser 1996). Here Hegel precisely locates the wound of wealth intrinsic to modern culture.

Nevertheless, Hegel proposes a remedy to poverty; he wants to export civil society via colonization (see Avineri 1972: ch. 7; Serequeberhan 1989; Paquette 2003). Instead of allowing the impoverished to become a rabble that threatens the stability of society, Hegel (1991: sections 247–8) suggests that industry will expand overseas and colonies will be established where a European surplus population might establish for themselves the freedoms of civil society.

Unleashing civil society upon the world appears to resolve the internal problems of civil society, while also advancing backward cultures, but this export carries the wound with it: the inner dialectic of civil society remains unchanged when transposed to the world stage (Siemens 1997).

Marx, as opposed to Hayek, Smith, and Hegel, is usually read as the pre-eminent critic of the logic of capitalist society, yet his insightful analysis of the relative achievements of a capitalist society avoids overly simple readings, like Ashley's, that pit the empty logic of economy against a rich logic of culture. For Marx, the arrival of capitalist society is momentous. It creates a stock of wealth that fuels general social advance and, as he always adds, an eventual transcendence of capitalism (Marx 1973: 325, 540–2). Partly following Smith and Hegel, Marx sees modern freedom and equality as realized first and foremost in the domain of exchange: 'Equality and freedom are thus not only respected in exchange based on exchange values, but, also, the exchange of exchange values is the productive, real basis of all equality and freedom' (Marx 1973: 325). Marx repeatedly suggests that freedom and equality are at the heart of economic and social life in a capitalist society – that 'free individuality' is a central aspiration of this form of society (Marx 1973: 158, 245, 472–4; see also Gould 1978; Keat 1979).

Appearances, Marx warns us, can be deceiving and a deeper analysis of capitalism reveals a darker reality. Capitalism abnegates the promise of equality and freedom: the personal independence of individuals depends on the 'objective dependence' of the worker on a capitalist (Marx 1973: 507–8). In an evocative passage, Marx (1977: 280) suggests that the 'exclusive sphere of Freedom, Equality, Property, and Bentham' offers different experiences for the capitalist and the worker: 'The one smirks self-importantly and is intent on business; the other is timid and holds back, like someone who has brought his own hide to the market and now has nothing else to expect but a tanning'. Like Hegel, Marx sees that capitalism expands human possibilities and 'the development of a rich individuality', but only at a tragic cost: poverty, alienation, and domination. In the modern era, the expansion and enhancement of human needs and capabilities 'appears' also 'as a complete emptying out, this universal objectification as total alienation, and the tearing down of all limited one-sided aims as sacrifice of the human end-in-itself to an entirely external end' (Marx 1973: 325, 488). These strong words may remind us of Ashley's characterization of a politically and ethically empty economy.

Despite the vehemence of his remarks about capitalism, Marx generally regards its capitalism as essential to the eventual emancipation of humanity. Capitalism works in two directions. It fosters a massive process of social destruction that sweeps away the regressive social practices of 'semi-barbarian, semi-civilized communities' that have kept people in bondage far into the misty past. And, by imposing capitalist relations of production, it inadvertently launches the 'social revolution' that moves history beyond capitalism and its brutality to humankind's true 'destiny' (Marx 2001: 65–6). Capitalism's historical role is to give universal shape to human culture as a precondition for the full realization of human capabilities in communism. Marx thus strikes a delicate balance.

Bourgeois society brings progress but also produces history's cruellest and most complete exploitation and alienation. Marx's analysis both supports and inverts the narrative of progress generated by theorists such as Smith and Hegel (Marx 1973: 84; 1977: 169–71) – a 'dialectical' understanding of capitalism that involves 'the *simultaneous* recognition of the "positive" and the "negative"' (Berki 1983: 89). Through this nuanced understanding, Marx avoids a romantic rejection of capitalism and the shameless apologetics he mostly correctly attributes to the economists of his day (McLellan 1979: 180–92; Lichtheim 1969: chs 9 and 10).

His political/ethical stance is also distinguishable from Ashley's. Marx shares Ashley's concern that capitalism, aided and abetted by economists, has constructed a social and a political project that offers only alienation for the vast majority of citizens. Though he rejects Hegel's claims that civil society is a space for realizing freedom and equality, he follows Hegel in recognizing that capitalism serves the historical purpose of connecting wealth with individuality and freedom – if only for the few. For the many, wealth, individuality, and freedom remain aspirations, at least until they act politically to collectively make wealth their own. For *pre*capitalist others, however, the modern era destroys their cultural forms. A destructive and alienating economy must be understood through its historical purposes – purposes that are obscured if we think of the economy as a simple embodiment of an inhuman technical rationality. In Marx's hands, political economic inquiry immerses us in complex system of ethical meanings and purposes. His analysis of successive forms of human self-consciousness suggests that 'objective laws are intertwined with subjective processes' (Ryan 1982: 92) and that our categories must be 'simultaneously philosophic *and* economic' (Blumenberg 2000: 151).

Conclusion

Political economy considered as a cultural project reveals what both economists and cultural critics hide; that wealth creation creates an obstinate wound. With a cultural political economy we can face the ethical claim that cultural critics such as Ashley obscure and economists treat as given by nature: that the institutionalization of technical rationality is central to the creation of wealth and thereby a vital means of promoting freedom, equality, and individuality; that the apparently asocial practice of instrumental reason is not separable from a wider system of social meaning and purpose. Economists and cultural critics share an interest in hiding this ambiguity, but they do so for different reasons. The economists resist because of their almost unquestioned commitment to the net benefits of capitalist practices; the critics because of their refusal to acknowledge or debate the possible virtues of capitalism. An explicit absence of this debate as well as its implicit and unacknowledged persistence is part of the wound of wealth. The pain of this debate is the *real* of cultural political economy (see Zizek 1993: 31; Fink 1995: 24–5) – both what we cannot avoid and cannot seem to face.

Bibliography

Ashley, Richard K. (1983) 'Three modes of economism', *International Studies Quarterly*, 27(3): 463–96.

Avineri, Schlomo (1972) *Hegel's Theory of the Modern State*, Cambridge: Cambridge University Press.

Benjamin, Jessica (1988) *The Bonds of Love: Psychoanalysis, Feminism, and the Problem of Domination*, New York: Pantheon.

Berki, R. N. (1983) *Insight and Vision: The Problem of Communism in Marx's Thought*, London: J. M. Dent.

Blaney, David L. and Naeem Inayatullah (2006) 'The savage Smith and the temporal walls of capitalism', in Beate Jahn (ed.) *Classical Theory in International Relations*, Cambridge: Cambridge University Press, pp. 123–55.

Blumenberg, Werner (2000) *Karl Marx: an Illustrated History*, Douglas Scott (trans.), London: Verso.

Bourdieu, Pierre (2005) *The Social Structures of the Economy*, Cambridge: Polity Press.

Cheyfitz, Eric (1993) 'Savage law', in Amy Kaplan and Donald E. Pease (eds) *Cultures of United States Imperialism*, Durham, NC: Duke University, pp. 109–28.

Crang, Phillip (1997) 'Cultural turns and the (re)constitution of economic geography: introduction to section one', in Roger Lee and James Willis (eds) *Geographies of Economies*, London: Arnold, pp. 3–15.

Dickey, Laurence (1987) *Hegel: Religion, Economics and the Politics of Spirit, 1770–1807*, Cambridge: Cambridge University.

Fatton, Robert (1986) 'Hegel and the riddle of poverty: the limits of bourgeois political economy', *History of Political Economy*, 18(4): 579–600.

Fraser, Ian (1996) 'Speculations on poverty in Hegel's Philosophy of Right', *The European Legacy*, 1(7): 2055–68.

Fink, Bruce (1995) *The Lacanian Subject: Between Language and Jouissance*, Princeton, NJ: Princeton University.

Gibson-Graham, J. K. (2006) *The End of Capitalism (As We Knew It): a Feminist Critique of Political Economy*, Minneapolis, MN: University of Minnesota.

Gould, Carol (1978) *Marx's Social Ontology: Individuality and Community in Marx's Theory of Social Reality*, Cambridge, MA: MIT Press.

Gudeman, Stephen (1986) *Economics as Culture: Modes and Metaphors of Livelihood*, New York: Routledge.

Hayek, Friedrich (1960) *The Constitution of Liberty*, Chicago, IL: University of Chicago.

——— (1976) *Law, Legislation and Liberty, Volume 2: The Mirage of Social Justice*, Chicago, IL: University of Chicago Press.

——— (1979) *Law, Legislation and Liberty, Volume 3: Political Order of a Free People*, Chicago, IL: University of Chicago Press.

Hegel, G. W. F (1991) *Elements of the Philosophy of Right*, Allen W. Wood (ed.), Cambridge: Cambridge University Press.

Hume, David (1985) 'Of refinement in the arts', in Eugene Miller (ed.) *Essays: Moral, Political, Literary*, Indianapolis, IN: Liberty Fund, pp. 268–80.

Inayatullah, Naeem (1997) 'Theories of spontaneous order', *Review of International Political Economy*, 4(2): 319–48

Inayatullah, Naeem and David L. Blaney (1997) 'Economic anxiety: reification, de-reification, and the politics of IPE', in Kurt Burch and Robert Denemark (eds) *Constituting International Political Economy*. Boulder, CO: Lynne Rienner, pp. 59–71.

—— (2004) *International Relations and the Problem of Difference*, New York: Routledge.

Jackson, Peter (2002) 'Commercial cultures: transcending the cultural and the economic', *Progress in Human Geography*, 26(1): 3–18.

Jackson, William A. (1993) 'Culture, society, and economic theory', *Review of Political Economy*, 5(4): 453–69.

—— (1996) 'Cultural materialism and institutional economics', *Review of Social Economy*, LIV(2): 221–44.

Karatani, Kojin (1995) *Architecture as Metaphor: Language, Numbers, Money*, Sabu Kohso (trans.), Cambridge, MA: MIT Press.

Keat, Russell (1979) 'Individuality and community in socialist thought', in John Mepham and David Hillel-Reuben (eds) *Issues in Marxist Philosophy, Volume IV: Social and Political Philosophy*, Brighton: Harvester Press, pp. 127–52.

Levine, David P. (1977) *Economic Studies: Contributions to the Critique of Economic Theory*, London: Routledge and Kegan Paul.

Lichtheim, George (1969) *The Origins of Socialism*, New York: Praeger.

McDowell, Linda (2000) 'Acts of memory and millennial hopes and anxieties: the awkward relationship between the economic and the cultural,' *Social and Cultural Geography*, 1(1): 15–24.

McLellan, David (1979) *Marx Before Marxism*, New York: Harper.

Marx, Karl (1973) *Grundrisse*, Martin Nicholas (trans.), New York: Vintage.

—— (1977) *Capital. Volume I*, B. Fowkes (trans.), New York: Vintage.

—— (2001) 'The British rule in India', in Aijaz Ahmed (ed.) *On the National and Colonial Questions: Selected Writings*, New Delhi: LeftWord Book, pp. 61–66.

Miller, Daniel (1997) *Capitalism: An Ethnographic Approach*, New York: Berg.

Mitchell, Timothy (1998) 'Fixing the economy', *Cultural Studies*, 12(1): 82–101.

Murphy, Craig N. and Cristina Rojas de Ferro (1995) 'Introduction: the power of representation in international political economy', *Review of International Political Economy*, 2(1): 63–9.

Paquette, Gabriel (2003) 'Hegel's analysis of colonialism and its roots in Scottish political economy', *CLIO*, 32(4): 415–32.

Polanyi, Karl (1957) *The Great Transformation: The Political and Economic Origins of Our Time*, Boston, MA: Beacon Press.

Ryan, Michael (1982) *Marxism and Deconstruction: A Critical Articulation*, Baltimore, MD: Johns Hopkins University Press.

Sayer, Andrew (2003) '(De)commodification, consumer culture, and moral economy', *Environment and Planning D: Society and Space*, 21(3): 341–57.

Sen, Amartya (1999) *Development as Freedom*, New York: Anchor.

Serequeberhan, Tsenay (1989) 'The idea of colonialism in Hegel's philosophy of right', *International Philosophical Quarterly*, XXIX(3): 301–18.

Siemens, Robert (1997) 'The problem of modern poverty: significant congruences between Hegel's and George's theoretical conceptions', *American Journal of Economics and Sociology*, 56(4): 617–37.

Smith, Adam (1976) *The Wealth of Nations*, Chicago, IL: University of Chicago Press.

—— (1979) *The Theory of Moral Sentiments*, D. D. Raphael and A. L. Macfie (eds), Indianapolis, IN: Liberty Fund.

—— (1980) 'Of the nature of that imitation which takes place in what are called the imitative arts', *Essays on Philosophical Subjects*, W. P. D. Wightman and J. C. Bryce (eds), Indianapolis, IN: Liberty Fund, pp. 176–213.

—— (1982) *Lectures on Jurisprudence*, R. L. Meek, D. D. Raphel and P. G. Stein (eds), Indianapolis, IN: Liberty Fund.

Stillman, Peter (1987) 'Partiality and wholeness: economic freedom, individual development, and ethical institutions in Hegel's political thought', in William Maker (ed.) *Hegel on Economics and Freedom*, Macon, GA: Mercer University Press, pp. 65–93.

Thrift, Nigel (2000) 'Pandora's box? Cultural geographies or economies', in Gordon L. Clark, Maryann P. Feldman and Meric S. Gertler (eds) *The Oxford Handbook of Economic Geography*, New York: Oxford, pp. 659–703.

Trouillot, Michel-Rolph (1991) 'Anthropology and the Savage Slot', in Richard G. Fox (ed.) *Recapturing Anthropology: Working in the Present*, Santa Fe, NM: School of American Research Press, pp. 17–44.

Watson, Matthew (2005) *Foundations of International Political Economy*, Houndsmill: Palgrave.

Youngs, Gillian (1994) 'The knowledge problematic: Richard Ashley and political economy', Nottingham Trent: manuscript.

Zizek, Slavoj (1993) *Tarrying with the Negative: Kant, Hegel, and the Critique of Ideology*, Durham, NC: Duke University.

2 Works, products, and the division of labour

Notes for a cultural and political economic critique

Matt Davies

As the editors of this volume note in their introduction, something about international political economy (IPE) feels incomplete. This feeling is both evident and subtle: the anomalies and antinomies of current restructurings of the global economy appear most clearly when presented or experienced through the daily social practices of meaning, of consumption, of habit. One of the promises that the cultural turn makes to students of IPE is to 'bring back (?) in' these areas of social life in order to produce better accounts of global restructuring. However, what value does culture add to our analyses; why turn to *culture*? Certainly, to add this 'dimension' to our studies will give more complete descriptions of the global political economy as constituted through social practice. But how does *culture* deepen or strengthen our analyses?

One problematic area for the field of IPE has been the difficulty of and obstacles to making our analyses political. The problem of depoliticization in international relations, in political economy, and in IPE, appears in the way that for the various research programmes, the key processes and forces of the global political economy come to appear as natural or as given, and therefore as subject to 'technical' resolution or management: that is, subject to a correct application of policy, to getting market signals right, to technocracy. There is a parallel political problem for the field of international relations (IR) in general: the discipline has long been structured by a powerful assumption that the domestic is the realm of the polity; thus the international, as a realm of anarchy, appears as a place where conflict and not politics – except in the most restricted sense, as an elite game – orders relations. Arguably, IPE as a sub-discipline of IR emerged as a response to this worldview in a moment where the international came to appear as a realm of cooperation, interdependence, and regimes. However, if for IPE the international was no longer seen as a realm necessarily ordered by conflict, it nevertheless remained a depoliticized realm: a realm for management and regulation.

Thus in the light of neoliberal IPE, grafting 'political' onto international 'economy' did not help bring political questions into focus; rather it continued to obscure them. More successful in this effort to find the politics of international relations were the efforts from the 1980s onward to elaborate critical theories of IR. In historical materialist, poststructuralist, postcolonial, and feminist theories, these efforts began to show how the *separation* of politics from economics was artificial and was contrived to obscure the political moments in analysis and critique. They showed that the 'economy' was always already political.

'Bringing culture into political economy' could be as tricky as bringing politics into international economics proved to be. This chapter takes this lesson from the last 25 years of critical IR theory to heart: before culture can be 'brought back in' to IPE, the nature and conditions of its prior separation must be clarified. This separation – its genesis and its maintenance – is crucial for the dominance of technocratic approaches to political economy. These preliminary reflections on separation and the fragmentation of collective life stem from Henri Lefebvre's definition of everyday life as the 'residue' remaining after specialized occupations or 'higher' activities, such as reflection or philosophy, have been separated from daily life. Lefebvre's understanding of this 'residue' is very complex – a point to which we will return below – and has been the object of some trenchant (if misguided, see Gardiner [2004] for a good discussion) criticisms of Lefebvre. But the separation is what prompts this chapter, because the process of separation suggests both that everyday life is itself an historical creation, that is, a particular way of organizing daily life, and that this separation is linked to broader processes of historical development, in particular, the division of mental labour from manual labour. Thus the general question this essay will address is how a turn to culture can help to politicize IPE.

The cultural turn is relevant to these concerns not only because culture – understood as a 'whole way of life' – could provide important concepts and methods for investigating everyday life, but also because the cultural turn has provided some important innovations in recent studies of political economy (see especially Ray and Sayer 1999; and du Gay and Pryke 2002). This important body of work in cultural economy has helped to bring into question the conceptual and methodological dualism of culture versus economy. This questioning has taken several forms. An original and now sadly neglected approach came out of the work on cultural imperialism from the 1960s and 1970s, such as in the investigations of Herbert Schiller (1971) or Armand Mattelart (e.g. Dorfman and Mattelart 1984). Taken as a whole, this approach combined investigations into the political economy of the culture industries and their role in establishing and maintaining American dominance or hegemony in the post-Second World War era with semiotic readings of the cultural products of the American cultural industries in the receiving contexts of the developing world (Davies 1999).

A more contemporary and influential approach is the culturalization thesis that suggests that crucial political economic processes have taken on increasingly cultural characteristics. This thesis of an epochal shift in the global political economy is primarily identified with Lash and Urry (1994) but it also informs the arguments of Manuel Castells (2000) on network societies, Robert Reich (1991) and others on knowledge or information economies, Nigel Thrift (Chapter 9, this volume) on the increasing importance of the cultivation of 'talent' for contemporary economies, or Hardt and Negri (2000) on 'empire' and 'immaterial labour' (see also Lazzarato 1996; Wittel 2004). Another contemporary approach, one that questions this notion of culturalization, sees cultural meanings as embedded in or even determining economic life. This type of approach relies frequently on a discursive analysis and examines the discursive construction of economic activity (see the various contributions in du Gay and Pryke 2002; see also Castree 2004). A third contemporary approach, less influential but even more compelling than the previous two, is the call for an 'ethnographic international political economy' of Naeem Inayatullah and David Blaney (2004). They combine the approach in economic history and economic anthropology of Karl Polanyi with insights taken from Tzvetan Todorov and from Ashis Nandy to call for an approach to international relations that can address the 'problem of difference'.

Unlike the cultural imperialism thesis, which did not set out to critique the dualism of culture and economy, these latter three approaches do critique this dualism by questioning the analytical and/or practical separations of culture and economy. For this reason, the cultural turn opens a space where everyday life might find a place in political economic thinking. However, there are problems in these approaches that are either intrinsic to them or that would prevent them from giving an adequate account of culture and of everyday life.

The culturalization thesis, in the first place, preserves the dualism between culture and economy even as it asserts the increasing importance of culture for political economy (see Ray and Sayer 1999). This happens in a number of ways but particularly problematic, and most clearly evident in the 'immaterial labour' thesis, is the way that those political economic activities that take on a cultural dimension tend to be the *dominant* activities, i.e. characteristic of more developed countries or of more highly remunerated or skilled occupations. The assertion that domination in the economy rests with cultural processes or products implies that subordinate actors, activities, regions, or processes are somehow *not* cultural. When Wittel (2004: 18) writes: 'It seems fairly obvious that in the middle of the nineteenth century, most types of labour (e.g. coal mining) were less interwoven with cultural knowledge and communication skills than most types of labour today ... cultural and communicational expertise were not intrinsic to work and performance in the same way as they are today', he ignores the centrality of culture and cultural change for the emergence of industrial labour: for example, the development of 'Pitmatic' as a dialect specific to mines and mining in Northeast England (Griffiths 2007). The implication that culture can be confined to specific, dominant economic activities can only be sustained if culture is somehow distinguished from economy – that is, if the dualism between culture and economy is preserved.

This assumption can be questioned from a variety of theoretical perspectives. By positing an epochal shift towards more culturalized, aestheticized, or information driven economies, this thesis misses the way that *all* economic activity rests on culturally driven or constructed meanings. A strong version of this critique can be derived not only from the classic works of economic anthropology (e.g. Polanyi 1968; Mauss 2000) but also from sociological analyses of the role of trust in economies in Durkheim (1964), or of religion in economic development in Weber (1958), or of conspicuous consumption in sustaining social hierarchies in Veblen (1965).

Similarly, discursively oriented critiques insist on the necessary inscription of economic activities into systems of power and knowledge that can define a particular process or act as 'economic'. However, contemporary discourse-oriented approaches, such as those in du Gay and Pryke, tend to invert the dualism between culture and economy rather than undermine it. That is, instead of seeing culture as a 'superstructure' reflecting an analytically prior economic 'base', discourse-oriented approaches run the risk of reducing the economy into something epiphenomenal or derivative of apparently pre-economic cultural forces. Treating the economy as a discursive effect itself depends on a prior, 'intransitive' separation of mental from manual labour. Thus both the culturalization thesis and discourse oriented approaches to cultural political economy uncritically reproduce or assume, to greater or lesser degrees, the dominance of mental labour over manual labour and the dominance of 'higher' or specialized activities over everyday life – precisely the kinds of problems that the critique of everyday life examines. The risk of reductionism can be mitigated by situating discourse – central to shaping crucial contingent social practices and strategies – in relation to extra-discursive or 'intransitive aspects, which include the tendential impacts of the law of value, the abstract formal separation of the market and the state in capitalism as well as intransitive dimensions of technology' (Ryner 2006: 149), as well as the development of the division of labour. In part, this means analysing discursive practices in terms of the social and other forces that enable them.

I have much more sympathy with Inayatullah and Blaney's ethnographic approach to this problem. For them, political economy is ordered by separations and differences, 'otherings' that culturally constitute both the West and its 'savage' other. However, they tend not to foreground production and the social relations of production (though these concerns are not absent from their investigations, see Blaney and Inayatullah, Chapter 1, this volume), which I will argue are crucial if we are going to critique the mental/manual division of labour. I will explore this question in greater detail below.

What is needed first is a conception of culture that can help to overcome the dualism that persists in the predominant approaches to cultural political economy and that can open a space for the critique of everyday life in international political economy. In an effort to rethink the cultural turn, I will look to Raymond Williams's cultural materialist approach to culture and Henri Lefebvre's conception of everyday life. The two reasons I think that existing concepts of culture used in economics or political economy are too thin are (1) these fields tend to reduce culture to discourse, immaterial practices, semiotics, values, etc., and this depends on (2) not thinking about *how* we can come to experience culture as a separate sphere of life from other practices (e.g. economics).

The second part of the chapter will examine this separation. The argument is that the separation is real but, like everyday life, artificial: the product of a particular development of human society (especially capitalist modernity). The artifice depends on the ways we have of dividing labour: first, the mental/manual division of labour (the way we separate the tasks of thinking about how and what to produce and the tasks of producing), which becomes a hierarchically ordered social division of labour, which also organizes complex productive tasks into a technical division of labour (that under capitalism yields abstract labour with its social consequences).

Then the final part of the paper will go back to the idea of labour and work, and examine – in a kind of utopian way, perhaps – how work can never have its mental and creative aspects completely abstracted from it, and how both the analytical and political projects of re-integrating culture and political economy depend on organizing work in a way that gives workers the chance to (1) re-integrate their own creative capacities and creative practices into the work process and (2) re-integrate work into life itself in a way that does not just subsume living into working life, especially as the latter is organized by the hierarchies rooted in historical forms of the social division of labour.

What is culture?

In 1958, Raymond Williams provided a crucial starting point for understanding culture in his manifesto, 'Culture is Ordinary':

> A culture has two aspects: the known meanings and directions, which its members are trained to; the new observations and meanings, which are offered and tested. These are the ordinary processes of human societies and human minds, and we see through them the nature of a culture: that it is always both traditional and creative; that it is both the most ordinary common meanings and the finest individual meanings. We use the word culture in these two senses: to mean a whole way of life – the common meanings; to mean the arts and learning – the special processes of discovery and creative effort. Some writers reserve the word for one or other of these senses; I insist on both, and on the significance of their conjunction.
>
> (Williams 1989: 4)

Williams is insisting on the conjunction of these two meanings because he is arguing against the then predominant view of culture as an elite property, as in 'high' culture. The view was associated with both left and right critiques of the emergence of 'mass' society and, in effect, ratified the separation of culture from economy by deeming the mass (working classes and middle classes) incapable of appreciating culture, thereby restricting them to merely economic functions.

In his etymological studies in *Keywords*, an extended appendix to *Culture and Society*, Williams shows how the development of the idea of culture enabled this restricted elitist understanding of culture to come about. His analysis illustrates how the development of the concept is linked to the separation and hierarchization of culture and economy. The root word for culture was the Latin term *colere*, which had several meanings: to inhabit, to cultivate, to honour with worship. From the sense of inhabiting we get the modern English term 'colony' and from the sense of worship we get the term 'cult'. Cultivation or husbandry initially gave the term 'culture' a sense of process, so that over time the culture of animals or 'sugar beet culture' could yield a notion of the culture of the mind or of the spirit: education as husbandry. From here, the more familiar modern senses of culture took form. Williams distinguishes three contemporary senses for culture:

(i) the independent and abstract noun which describes a general process of intellectual, spiritual and aesthetic development, from [the Eighteenth Century]; (ii) the independent noun, whether used generally or specifically, which indicates a particular way of life, whether of a people, a period, a group, or humanity in general, from Herder and Klemm. But we have also to recognize (iii) the independent and abstract noun which describes the works and practices of intellectual and especially artistic activity. This seems often now the most widespread use: culture is music, literature, painting and sculpture, theatre and film.

(Williams 1988: 90)

If we reflect on the persistence of the dualism of culture and economy in cultural political economy, we can see that it stems in part from a tendency to understand culture in one of these three more restricted senses. For example, the culturalization thesis tends to understand the changes it perceives in the economy in terms of 'sign-value' and aesthetics: its understanding of culture is located very near to the third and most widespread use of the term. Similarly, the discourse analyses, by focusing on how culture endows economic meaning to particular social activities, can be seen to locate culture in the first sense Williams identifies: a general process of intellectual, spiritual, and aesthetic development. These two understandings of culture are near to the way cultural studies often understands culture, in contrast to the way that material culture predominates for some archaeologists and anthropologists. By insisting on the ordinariness of culture and culture as a whole way of life, Williams's approach is not to privilege one of these senses of the term over the others but to propose a more holistic understanding. The narrower understandings are not in themselves wrong; the point is to understand the ways they emerge from particular historical circumstances and how they interact to shape the cultural possibilities for a particular class, society, or people.

The ordinariness of culture in Raymond Williams recalls Henri Lefebvre's insistence on the importance of everyday life. The reception of Lefebvre in the English speaking context has tended to fragment his prolific contributions into different camps: today, principally, there is the spatial or urban Lefebvre of *The Production of Space* and the cultural or sociological Lefebvre of the several volumes of *The Critique of Everyday Life*. But this fragmentation of his thought is unwarranted. Everyday life was at the core of his research and theory for over 50 years. It informed his philosophical writings as much as his political writings; his programmes for sociological research as much as his theoretical considerations of space and the state; his observations on urbanism as much as his investigations into rural life.

I have already mentioned Lefebvre's description of everyday life as a 'residue' that remains after specialized or 'higher' activities are separated out. But this separated everyday residue is not inert: it is itself productive.

> In terms of these activities, the first definition of everyday life is a negative one. If in our minds (by a sort of abstraction) we remove the highly specialized occupations from man and from the human, what is left? An apparently very scanty residue. In reality the so-called residue contains a 'human raw material' which holds hidden wealth, as our study shows. The higher activities derive from it, they are at one and the same time its ultimate expression, its direct or indirect critique and its alienated form – albeit an alienation embodying a more-or-less conscious and successful attempt to achieve 'disalienation'.
>
> (Lefebvre 1991a: 86)

Thus this 'residue' is also productive. It is what Lefebvre describes as the 'fertile soil' in which the 'flowers' of the higher activities bloom (Lefebvre 1991a: 87).

If, as Raymond Williams suggests, our contemporary understandings of culture emerge as a part of a broader historical process, so also does everyday life emerge from historical change. Lefebvre provided his own terminological clarification, situating everyday life in history:

> Let us simply say about daily life that it has always existed, but permeated with values, with myths. The word everyday designates the entry of this daily life into modernity: the everyday as an object of a programming (*d'une programmation*), whose unfolding is imposed by the market, by the system of equivalences, by marketing and advertisements. As to the concept of 'everydayness', it stresses the homogenous, the repetitive, the fragmentary in everyday life'.
>
> (Lefebvre 1988: 87)

The qualification of 'everyday' for everyday life thus describes a way of living; capitalism and modernity shape the 'values and myths' – or the 'intellectual, spiritual and aesthetic development', as Williams would have us investigate – in order to provide the 'programming' that is 'imposed by the market, by the system of equivalences, by marketing and advertisements'. This also signals the way the liberalism construes freedom as freedom of circulation and exchange and privileges such exchanges over other, therefore marginalized, practices of social and cultural life.

Everyday life is evidently also a class-determined concept, with a hierarchical class structure reflecting the dominance of higher activities over daily life, culture over economy, mental over manual labour. The critique of everyday life counterposed the banality and repetitions of daily life to philosophy and contemplation, to religious transcendence in art, or to heroism and virility in war, for example. Lefebvre suggests that such a critique of daily life betrayed contempt for other people on the part of the critic. The writer, the artist, or the philosopher, freed from the banality of labour, showers labour with contempt:

> These criticisms have a common element: they were the work of particularly gifted, lucid and active *individuals* (the philosopher, the poet, etc.). However, this individual lucidity or activeness concealed an appearance or illusion, and therefore a hidden, deeper reality. In truth their work belonged to a time and a class whose ideas were thus raised above the everyday onto the level of the exceptional and the dominant. Hence the criticism of everyday life was in fact a *criticism of other classes*, and for the most part found its expression in contempt for productive labour; at best it criticized the life of the dominant class in the name of a transcendental philosophy or dogma, which nevertheless still belonged to that class.
>
> (Lefebvre 1991a: 29)

This is the same contempt Raymond Williams finds expressed in the disdain for ordinary lives in the 'culture' of the Cambridge teashop:

> When I now read a book such as Clive Bell's *Civilisation*, I experience not so much disagreement as stupor. What kind of life can it be, I wonder, to produce this extraordinary fussiness, this extraordinary decision to call certain things culture and then separate them, as with a park wall, from ordinary people and ordinary work?
>
> (Williams 1989: 5)

Williams's point here is to insist on the creative capacities of ordinary people. This creativity underscores the dialectical nature of the separation of specialized, higher activities from everyday life in Lefebvre's conception: the separation is at once effective, shaping the forms of class domination, and artificial, incomplete:

> Superior, differentiated and highly specialized activities have never been separate from everyday practice, they have only appeared to be so. Their consciousness of being separate from it was in itself a link; they implied an indirect or implicit criticism of the everyday only inasmuch as they raised themselves above it. Thus French eighteenth-century philosophy, literature, art, ethics, and politics corresponded to *the everyday life* of the bourgeoisie: the new pursuit of happiness, pleasure, luxury, profit, and power. In the same way eighteenth-century rationalism corresponded to the everyday attitude expressed in 'commonplace books'. And every time a scientist comes up with a formula or a law, he is of necessity condensing a long experience in which the lowliest assistant and the simplest tool have had their part to play.
>
> (Lefebvre 1991a: 86–7)

Thus, if we return to the problem of how a cultural political economy can contribute concepts and methods for situating everyday life in the global political economy and for overcoming the neglect of everyday life in international political economy, we can begin by specifying that *culture* for a cultural political economy must be understood in terms of what Raymond Williams signalled as the conjunction between ways of living and the intellectual, spiritual, or aesthetic development of a group, class, people, or humanity in general. Through Lefebvre's critique of everyday life and through Williams's arguments against elitism in culture, we can also specify that conceptions that hypostatize or reify culture by locating the common meanings, habits, and repetitions of everyday life in the world of ordinary people and their work while locating discovery and creative practice in the world of the superior, higher activities can apprehend neither the creative practices of subordinates in social relations nor the irruption of the mundane and prosaic into the practices of planning, programming, and controlling everyday life.

Furthermore, the *political economy* of a cultural political economy cannot apprehend everyday life if it restricts its focus to the economic practices of circulation and exchange. It must focus on the power relations articulated in the social relations of production, and on work and production themselves. That is, the power relations conjoining employers or managers with workers, technocrats, and planners with inhabitants, or more generally dominants with subordinates, are the social relations that constitute the global political economy. The creative practices of the subordinate groups, or rather, the conjunction of the inherited, repetitive, common meanings with the practices of discovery and creation point to the ways in which everyday life – as well as its critique – is both a burden and a resource for subordinate groups. To elaborate this idea, we will now turn to the problem of work.

Production and the division of labour

It may be helpful to recapitulate some of the observations so far: the project of a cultural political economy comes out of a perceived need to overcome an analytical or conceptual dualism between culture and economy. Contributions to this project have been provocative but have largely been unsatisfying, in part because they rely on a thin notion of culture and, furthermore, a conception of political economy that privileges circulation and exchange. In order to come up with a more satisfactory conception of culture, we turned first to Raymond Williams, who shows how culture is *both* the process and product of general intellectual, spiritual, and aesthetic development, *and* the 'whole way of life' of a group of people. This conception helped remedy what had been a wilful neglect of the culture of ordinary people among cultural theorists of the day and to bring together the two distinct understandings of culture.

Williams's conceptual moves were then linked to Henri Lefebvre's theoretical work on everyday life. Like the separations that characterized the understanding of culture as Williams critiqued it, everyday life is also determined by a fundamental separation of 'higher' specialized activities, especially philosophy or reflection, from the mundane and repetitive in daily life. Like Williams, Lefebvre's investigations show how this separation is, first, an artifice, that is, a product of a particular historical development of collective life, and second, a process that is never fulfilled or completed.

These separations – of culture from economy, of intellectual and aesthetic developments from the ordinary lives of people, of specialized activities from mundane, prosaic everyday life – are linked to and directly invoke another fundamental separation that is itself a central concern for political economy: the division of labour, and in particular the division between mental labour and manual labour.

In his study of the social and historical foundations for epistemology, Alfred Sohn-Rethel argues that abstract thinking (philosophy and science) is enabled by the social abstraction of commodity exchange (Sohn-Rethel 1978). In effect, what he calls a 'society of appropriation' under capitalist social relations develops abstract ways of thinking on the basis of the need to separate the knowledge of the production process from the direct producers. An artisan, for example, holds both the knowledge to produce a particular product and the skill to execute the production; but as labour itself becomes a commodity, control over the production process shifts to the capitalist who 'produces' by bringing together the disparate elements of the production process. Following Marx, Sohn-Rethel argues that the separation of intellectual labour from manual labour flows out of the political struggle over the control over the production process. This is a sophisticated version of the familiar 'de-skilling' argument regarding industrial labour; however, it is not necessary to accept de-skilling as an inevitable outcome of this struggle, nor to assume that the terrain of this struggle would remain the same throughout the historical development of capitalist economies. Indeed, the separation of mental from manual labour is linked to and undergirds the separation of culture from economy, the separation of specialized activities from everyday life, and the fragmentation of everyday life.

We can see some of the consequences for work of dividing mental from manual labour through Henri Lefebvre's (Lefebvre 1991b) review of Marx's use of the notion of production. To overturn the received, transcendental notion of space as a pre-existing 'container' for being, Lefebvre had to undertake a counter-intuitive project: to examine how space is *produced*. To make this theoretical move, however, he first had to analyse the notion of *production*, to specify it as a concept. In this analysis, Lefebvre begins with Hegel, for whom production has a 'cardinal role' (Lefebvre 1991b: 68). In Lefebvre's account, Hegel's conception of production was indeterminate and Marx made the move of endowing the concept with a substantive content or positivity by conflating the broad philosophical sense of production with a concrete, political economic content. This move was extremely powerful. It allowed Marx to move between an indeterminate, 'broad' conception of production – 'humans as social beings are said to produce their own life, their own consciousness, their own world' (Lefebvre 1991b: 68) – and a 'narrow', positive conception, where a product is increasingly a thing, a product: '… whereas a *work* has something irreplaceable and unique about it, a *product* can be reproduced exactly, and is in fact the result of repetitive acts and gestures. […] Humanity, which is to say social practice, creates works and produces things' (Lefebvre 1991b: 70–1).

Here, Lefebvre is playing with the double meaning of the French word *oeuvre*, which signals both work as an activity and the notion of a work of art. The more that the idea of production denotes programming, repetition, and abstraction, the closer it lies to its narrow, political economic sense: 'the more restricted the notion becomes the less it connotes creativity, inventiveness, imagination' (Lefebvre 1991b: 69). But just as there are no 'purely economic' activities – that is, economic activities cannot take place outside of the cultural systems that give them meaning, endow value, or provide for a category of 'economic' as distinct from other activities – so also works and products imply each other and exist in conjunction with each other. Lefebvre illustrates this dialectical unity by examining Venice: is the city a work or a product (Lebfebvre 1991b: 73–5)? Greatly simplifying Lefebvre's account, it is both: both an imaginative creation and the practical product of labour; both the mundane practices and festival; both everyday life and theatricality.

The logic underlying these separations of mental from manual labour or of works from products is also historical. In *The Critique of Everyday Life Volume 1*, Lefebvre demonstrates how the separations occasioned changes in work and living spaces and is worth quoting at length:

> In those [past] eras, in those modes of production, productive labour was merged with everyday life: consider the lives of peasants and craftsmen, for example. What distinguishes peasant life so profoundly from the life of industrial workers, even today, is precisely this inherence of productive activity in their life in its entirety. The workplace is all around the house; work is not separate from the everyday life of the family. Formerly the imperatives of the peasant community (the village) regulated not only the way work and domestic life were organized, but festivals as well. Thus up to a point a way of living which strictly speaking did not belong to any one individual, but more the a group of men committed to the ties – and limits – of their community or guild, could be developed.
>
> With bourgeois society these various elements and their relations were overturned: in one sense they became differentiated, separate, in another they came to constitute a unified whole. Bourgeois society reasserted the value of labour, above all during the period of its ascendancy; but at the historical moment when the relation between labour and the concrete development of individuality was emerging, labour took on an increasingly fragmented character. At the same time the individual, more and more involved in complex social relations, became isolated and inward-looking. Individual consciousness split into two (into the private consciousness and the social or public consciousness); it also became atomized (individualism, specialization, separation between differing spheres of activity, etc.) … Family life became separate from productive activity. And so did leisure.
>
> (Lefebvre 1991a: 30–1)

The separation of mental from manual labour thus structures the social division of labour. In the first place, this takes place by creating hierarchies in which the intellectual processes and intellectual development are deployed to control the production process. To do so required controlling manual labour and, as the separation proceeded, it required the control of insubordinate skilled workers (Marx, *Capital Volume 1*, cited in Sohn-Rethel 1978: 120). This process extends from the social division of labour – in which one's social position is at least in part determined by what one does in the world of work – to the technical division of labour – in which the production process is divided into isolated tasks to be reintegrated in the product itself.

To understand these processes, it is necessary to examine the technical and social divisions of labour more carefully. In classical political economy, especially in Adam Smith, the division of labour is central to the functioning of the market. Markets bring together dispersed producers as their products (commodities) circulate. In the classical tradition, the social division of labour is determined by the way that the market links and distributes these independent producers. In this realm, the producers are 'free' to pursue their own ends; moments of creativity and discovery are rewarded by the market and increasingly complex needs can develop and be met spontaneously. The role of the market – or catallaxy, in the term used by the liberal Hayek but also embraced by the radical Andrew Sayer – is celebrated for its capacity to maximize the kinds of social needs that can be met and thus expanding the realm of freedom through circulation and exchange.

The technical division of labour takes place within an enterprise. Adam Smith's example of the manufacture of pins through a detailed division of the tasks involved highlighted not only the gains in efficiency – more pins can be produced at lower costs with extensive technical divisions of the process – but also the de-skilling of the workers, the threat to personality, and their subordination to the control of the capitalist (this point is taken up in Blaney and Inayatullah, Chapter 1, this volume). This argument was often extended to show how the technical division of labour could be a precursor to mechanization, making workers redundant and weakening their position in the market for their labour and thus in society.

Consequently, on the face of things, creativity is squeezed out of the labour process (and the worker) within the enterprise. Taylorism can be understood as an expression of this struggle for control over the bodies of workers and Fordism as an extension of Taylorism, to attempt to control the whole ways of life of workers (Gramsci 1971: 301–10). This effort to extend command over the production process to the economy – and society – as a whole in Fordism is what Lefebvre referred to as the 'bureaucratic society of controlled consumption' (Lefebvre 1984) and, in the first instance, it problematizes the notion that the market and its social division of labour can be a realm of freedom.

However, the logic and functioning of the technical and social divisions of labour are not the same and social formations and the forms of social relations of production are more complex than a notion such as society-as-factory can describe. These three aspects of the division of labour – mental/manual, social, and technical – interact to create complex social formations in which producers circulate between multiple forms of power relations in production, which are themselves articulated and connected to extend power exercised at the point of production throughout the social formation and into the state (Harrod 1987). Thus the processes Lefebvre describes as characteristic of everyday life – hierarchy, homogenization, fragmentation – are realized in the complex and political processes of dividing labour.

This complexity differentiates between different kinds of work and different qualities of working. For some, Taylorism persists in extreme forms. Fast food enterprises are organized and their labour processes are designed to have a high turnover rate in employment. The control over the labour process is encoded into the machines and buildings themselves and workers are literally interchangeable. Workers in call centres are under constant and intense surveillance: the key strokes on their keyboards and the number of calls made are counted, scripts are provided; creative deviation from the scripts is not permitted.

For other workers, the process is quite different. The post-Fordist factory was an attempt to address a specific problem in the struggle to control the labour process. Workers remain creative: the received, inherited common meanings of the moments of the labour process could not be entirely separated from the moments of creativity and discovery. Thus, workers on an assembly line, for example, could still have a superior collective knowledge of the manufacturing process and find ways to create down-time through cooperation. Post-Fordist labour practices, in contrast, encourage creativity on the part of workers but as a way of finding gains in efficiency, for the benefit of the enterprise rather than as a way for the workers to gain control over the labour process. Indeed, as Thrift (Chapter 9, this volume) argues, the cultivation of 'talent' has become instrumental to the redefining of the labour process (at least with regard to dominant processes and firms in contemporary capitalist economies). Rather than squeezing the space for creativity out of work, these techniques seek to appropriate the creativity, the 'form-giving fire' (Marx 1973: 361).

Reintegrating culture and political economy is an analytical *and* political task

One possible objection to the foregoing arguments is that focusing on work and production risks truncating the contribution to international political economy that an engagement with culture and with everyday life could provide. The problem lies in what Lefebvre refers to as a 'metaphysics of labour': 'Put differently, praxis is not restricted to the utilitarian transformation of external nature through repetitive, instrumental action. It also involves love, sensuality, the body – a plethora of creative, emotive and imaginative practices Lefebvre calls *poesis* in his as yet untranslated 1965 work *Métaphilosophie*' (Gardiner 2000: 80).

Such an objection is correct to the extent that the conceptions of culture, everyday life and work for investigations into international political economy are themselves stripped of the moments of discovery and creation, of reflection, and of creative practice. The separations structuring culture, everyday life, and work examined in this chapter must be investigated and analysed as part of the processes that characterize the global political economy.

A cultural turn for international political economy, or a cultural political economy, represents the possibility for beginning such an analysis. However, a 'thin' notion of culture will not provide the perspective needed to effect this analytical reintegration of culture and political economy. The conception of culture must be open to the conjunction between the general processes of intellectual, spiritual, and aesthetic development and ordinary, habitual ways of life. It must be open to the creative practices of ordinary people in everyday life.

The one-sided conception of culture also truncates political economic analysis. To focus on the products themselves, as in the culturalization thesis, or to focus on the circulation of meanings, as in discursive critiques of political economy, tends to invoke the economic relations of exchange in cultural political economy and therefore to ratify an uncritical perspective on the market and the social division of labour. In contrast, to emphasize the cultural and political economic dynamics of work and production helps to clarify the power relations that define the social relations of production. To avoid the traps of a 'metaphysics of labour', the critical analysis of work and production must address the political economic dynamics that drive the ways in which creativity is integrated into work or suppressed or appropriated in production.

To return to the problem of depoliticization, then, a cultural turn for international political economy can – among other necessary theoretical tasks as outlined throughout this volume – signal how change in the political economic ordering of life is a manifestation of the struggle over the creative moment in work. This struggle takes place at various scales, from intimate and bodily political economies, as illustrated through the HSBC advertising images analysed by Best and Paterson in the Introduction to this volume, to the global scale. Crucially, however, a strong notion of culture for cultural political economy directs our attention not only to these varying scales of political economic processes but also across the technical, social, and mental/manual divisions of labour. A cultural political economy will feel as incomplete as IPE has felt if it restricts culture to the cultivation and control of innovation among dominant agents and economies or to the received patterns of habitual, mundane meanings among the dominated. Culture, as Williams insists, requires that we grasp common meanings and whole ways of life, *and* the special processes of creative effort, *and* their conjunction. The processes of dividing labour, into which political economy has provided much insight, provide an important starting point for bringing this conjunction into analytical focus.

Work does not exhaust the concepts of culture and of everyday life – though work often exhausts the energies of the worker. The analytical reintegration of culture and political economy can be thought of as part of a political project for the reintegration of creative practice and work. However, as was seen in the discussion of post-Fordist methods of organizing production, this reintegration is not itself a guarantee that the workers become free of the compulsions of the workplace.

To the extent that work can become creative practice, the fragments of everyday life must be re-socialized such that 'love, sensuality, the body – [the] plethora of creative, emotive and imaginative practices' become the organizing forces in social relations. In this regard, then, the *critique* of everyday life – the criticism of banality from the perspective of creativity and the criticism of hierarchy from the perspective of everyday life – is an essential tool in the critique of the global political economy.

Bibliography

Castells, Manuel (2000) *The Rise of the Network Society, 2nd edition*, Oxford: Blackwell.

Castree, Noel (2004) 'Economy and culture are dead! Long live economy and culture!', *Progress in Human Geography*, 28(2): 204–26.

Davies, Matt (1999) *International Political Economy and Mass Communication in Chile: National Intellectuals and Transnational Hegemony*, International Political Economy Series, New York: St Martin's Press.

Dorfman, Ariel and Armand Mattelart (1984) *How to Read Donald Duck: Imperialist Ideology in the Disney Comic*, New York: International General.

du Gay, Paul, and Michael Pryke (eds) (2002) *Cultural Economy: Cultural Analysis and Commercial Life*, London: Sage Publications.

Durkheim, Emile (1964) *The Division of Labor in Society*, New York: Free Press.

Gardiner, Michael E. (2000) *Critiques of Everyday Life*, London: Routledge.

—— (2004) 'Everyday utopianism: Lefebvre and his critics', *Cultural Studies*, 18(2/3): 228–54.

Gramsci, Antonio (1971) *Selections from the Prison Notebooks*, New York: International Publishers.

Griffiths, Bill (2007) *Pitmatic: The Talk of the North East Coalfields*, Newcastle: Northumbria University Press.

Hardt, Michael and Antonio Negri (2000) *Empire*, Cambridge, MA: Harvard University Press.

Harrod, Jeffrey (1987) *Power, Production, and the Unprotected Worker*, New York: Columbia University Press.

Inayatullah, Naeem and David Blaney (2004) *International Relations and the Problem of Difference*, New York: Routledge.

Lash, Scott and John Urry (1994) *Economies of Signs and Space*, London: Sage Publications.

Lazzarato, Maurizio (1996) 'Immaterial labour', in Paolo Virno and Michael Hardt (eds) *Radical Thought in Italy: A Potential Politics*, Theory Out of Bounds, Vol. 7, Minneapolis, MN: University of Minnesota Press, pp. 133–47.

Lefebvre, Henri (1984) Everyday Life in the Modern World, Sacha Rabinovitch, (trans.), New Brunswick, NJ, and London: Transaction Publishers.

Lefebvre, Henri (1988) 'Toward a leftist cultural politics: remarks occasioned by the centenary of Marx's Death', in Cary Nelson and Lawrence Grossberg (eds) *Marxism and the Interpretation of Culture*, Urbana, IL: University of Illinois Press, pp. 75–88.

—— (1991a) *Critique of Everyday Life Volume 1: Introduction*, John Moore (trans.), London: Verso.

—— (1991b) *The Production of Space*, Donald Nicholson-Smith (trans.), Cambridge, MA: Blackwell.

Mauss, Marcel (2000) *The Gift: The Form and Reason for Exchange in Archaic Societies*, London: Routledge.

Marx, Karl (1973) *Grundrisse*, New York: Vintage Books.

Polanyi, Karl (1968) *Primitive, Archaic, and Modern Economies: Essays of Karl Polanyi*, New York: Anchor Books.

Ray, Larry, and Andrew Sayer (eds) (1999) *Culture and Economy: After the Cultural Turn*, London: Sage Publications.

Reich, Robert B. (1991) *The Work of Nations: Preparing Ourselves for 21st Century Capitalism*, New York: Knopf.

Ryner, J. Magnus (2006) 'International political economy: beyond the poststructuralist/historical materialist dichotomy', in Marieke de Goede (ed.) *International Political Economy and Poststructural Politics*, International Political Economy Series, Basingstoke: Palgrave, pp. 139–56.

Schiller, Herbert I. (1971) *Mass Communications and American Empire*, Boston, MA: Beacon Press.

Sohn-Rethel, Alfred (1978) *Intellectual and Manual Labour: A critique of epistemology*, London: The Macmillan Press.

Veblen, Thorstein (1965) *The Theory of the Leisure Class*, New York: Augustus M. Kelley.

Weber, Max (1958) *The Protestant Ethic and the Spirit of Capitalism*, New York: Charles Scribner's Sons.

Williams, Raymond (1988) *Keywords: A Vocabulary of Culture and Society*, London: Fontana Press.

—— (1989) 'Culture is ordinary', in Robin Gable (ed.) *Resources of Hope: Culture, Democracy, Socialism*, London: Verso, pp. 3–18.

Wittel, Andreas (2004) 'Culture, labour and subjectivity: For a political economy from below', *Capital and Class,* 84: 11–29.

Part 2

The cultural constitution of economic history

3 'To the ends of the earth'

Culture, visuality and the embedded economy

Rob Aitken

In 1940, aboard the *S.S. Mariposa* en route to Australia, John Grierson, a figure key to the early use of film across the Anglo-American world, wrote to his friends in Canada and Britain about the dramatic possibilities of documentary film. Imagining the new world that would emerge after the war, Grierson identified film as the art that would be most central to the new order to come. It was film – what Grierson referred to as 'a medium with its own special art' – which could both deliver a world from war and help construct a post-war order in which cooperation would predominate.

This story raises some intriguing questions about both the post-war order as well as the broader territory of 'culture' and 'economy.' Perhaps the most prominent conceptualization of the post-war order has been the notion of 'embedded liberalism.' Coined by John Ruggie, embedded liberalism has come to occupy important locations in our imagination of both the post-war moment as well as our globalized present. Embedded liberalism is a form of political-economic order which seeks 'to manoeuvre between ... two extremes' of economic nationalism and classical free trade and to achieve a certain reconciliation between domestic stability and openness to global economic exchange (Ruggie 1982: 393). This notion of embeddedness, however, is often figured in international political economy (IPE) in ways which sharpen a contrast between the post-war order and the kinds of neoliberal political-economic arrangements which characterize our contemporary globalized world.

This is particularly characteristic of critical approaches in the field which often tend to sketch out an epochal note of transformation in which embedded and disembedded worlds are placed on either side of a supposed divide. This is a divide, notes Robert Cox, which materialized in the crises of the 1970s; 'a threshold marking a transition from one world order to another' (Cox 1987: 400). Although there have been recent attempts to diagram more subtle and concretely-situated accounts of embedded liberalism (Blyth 2002; Rupert 2000), much of the discussion of the embedded order has entailed significant reification.

This generalized notion of an embedded order leaves intact several striking questions regarding the specific contours of how – and through what specific rationalities and forms of knowledge – the embedded economy was constituted. What, other than a structural necessity, was the embedded economy? What were its conditions of possibility and its surfaces of emergence? What modes of knowledge and expertise – 'economic,' 'cultural,' 'social' – did it occupy and assemble? What lines of disruption *and* persistence does it inhabit in relation to our present?

To begin to answer some of these questions, this chapter mounts a particular argument about the role of cultural knowledge in the formation of the 'embedded economy.' Although the post-war order is often framed in material terms as an object uniquely constituted in relation to tangible forms of practice – mass production, material knowledge, work – I argue in this chapter that the embedded economy was intimately cultural. One of the lines along which the embedded economy was constituted was the newly consolidating cultural sciences of the interwar and post-war moment.

Although much has been made over the past 20 years regarding the question of culture and its relation to economy, I draw in this chapter on a recent conceptualization formulated by Tony Bennett. For Bennett, 'culture' is not an anthropological but a historical reality, given meaning only in a web of historically specific contexts. Of particular concern for Bennett is the relation between the 'cultural' and the 'social.' For Bennett 'cultural' knowledge, itself historically contingent, has often helped shape the 'social.' Interrogating this relation requires a:

> focus on the material processes through which culture has come to be ... differentiated by the social ... It also involves attending to the further work through which culture, in its varied differentiated forms, then acts on the social through the 'working surfaces on the social' that it produces. These are organized by specific cultural knowledges and techniques of intervention which operate ... to format the social for specific kinds of action and intervention.
>
> (Bennett 2007: 32–3)

Drawing on Bennett, the main claim I want to make in this chapter is that culture was key to – a 'working surface' for – the embedded economy. Although culture is, as Bennett notes, deeply implicated in the 'social,' it is also, I will argue in this chapter, key to 'economy' and to the ways in which 'economy' could be (re)shaped and organized. An 'embedded' economy was not, I argue, only constituted in and through 'economic' forms of knowledge and practice (in Keynesian bodies of practice for example) but also in 'cultural' practices and institutions.

To make this kind of argument I draw on a particular empirical case: the work of one specific, but particularly influential, Anglo-American network of cultural workers, social scientists, and bureaucrats who, over the 1920s and 1930s became keenly interested in the ways in which film and other visual practices (poster-art) could be used to constitute a new order. This network, centered around John Grierson, emerged out of the British documentary film movement and became key to the institutional practices of film and public culture throughout the interwar and post-war periods: the Empire Marketing Board, the public film practices of the Canadian and Australian governments, the UK General Post Office Film Unit, the International Labour Organization and some of the early discussions that led to the formation of UNESCO.

This network sought to insert culture and visual practice, in particular, into the formation of a new – embedded – economy in two main ways. First, Grierson's network sought to articulate public culture as part of the state machinery required to construct an international economic order animated by concepts of planning and cooperation. Drawing on a language of Keynesian intervention, Grierson sought to redefine the role of public culture in terms of state intervention and social stability. Second, and more specifically, Grierson marked out a particular role for public culture as a technique of identification. For Grierson visual practices could play a dramatic role in the new embedded order by inserting individuals directly into global space and by cultivating a mode of self and citizen – and a kind of worldly being – in which individuals could confront their own roles as agents in a new world (see Thrift, Chapter 9, this volume, on the process of 'worlding').

This argument is intended not only to address a historical curiosity – to highlight the relation between certain forms of public culture and the broader realm of embedded liberalism. Rather, it is offered as a provocation intended to unsettle the ways in which we use the concept of embedded liberalism as a critical device. By highlighting the intimate relation between self and the world these cultural/visual experiments sought – and the concept of worldly being they pursued – I intend to evoke a more complicated genealogy of embedded liberalism, not only as form defined in stark difference from our own neoliberal present, but as a more multiple, complex and ambiguous category.

To pursue an argument in these terms, this chapter is divided into three broad sections. The first section reviews the concept of 'embedded liberalism' as used in IPE. This section notes the widespread use of 'embedded liberalism' as a somewhat unproblematic or overly generalized concept. This is especially true of the constitutive feature of embedded liberalism; a bounded economy amenable to domestic intervention. A second section turns to the case of Grierson and his network. This section reviews the ways in which Grierson sought to use public culture – and visuality in particular – as practices central to how a new economy could be constituted. A third section turns squarely to the conception of worldly being Grierson sought to promote in and through these visual practices. Drawing in particular on poster campaigns managed at the Empire Marketing Board this section assesses the complex notion of self and citizen promoted in and through Grierson's early experiments in making visible an international integrated economic space. As this section describes, these experiments sought to cultivate forms of active agency among everyday actors but also limited that agency by a conception of difference as a problem to be overcome or contained. The conclusion to this chapter synthesizes the argument as a whole by returning to broad themes of 'culture' and 'economy' and the relations between them. Developing analyses more attuned to cultural governance, I conclude, can help develop more varied and multiple stories of our economic present; a conclusion which implies the need to rethink the ways in which we use embedded liberalism as a critical device.

Embedded economy

The concept of embedded liberalism lies at the core of many conversations in IPE. The global spread of free-market and neoliberal forces over the past generation has often been understood, especially, perhaps, among critical voices, as a violation of a program of 'embedded liberalism' which first emerged in the early post-war period. The notion of an embedded liberalism is inspired by the prescient analysis of Karl Polanyi. For Polanyi no society prior to the nineteenth century attempted a form of economy or a mode of market exchange which was not embedded in 'society' or somehow responsive to social relationships. The 'self-regulating' market that emerged in the wake of industrialization (and empire) in Britain of the nineteenth century was conspicuous precisely as one such attempt to establish a market governed only by 'economic' logic (Polanyi 1944). By commodifying land, labor and money, the self-regulating market removed economic life from its social conditions of existence in ways that triggered disastrous environmental and social consequences. Normally, noted Polanyi, 'the economic order is merely a function of the social in which it is contained. Under neither tribal, nor feudal nor mercantile conditions was there, as we have shown, a separate economic system in society' (Polanyi 1944: 71).

For Ruggie, the post-war order negotiated at Bretton Woods was an attempt to re-embed market relations within society. This sought to 're-embed' the economic order by constructing a 'compromise' which both facilitated an open international economy *and* created conditions for effective domestic macro-economic management. This compromise entailed a delicate maneuver between the kinds of economic nationalisms of the interwar period and classical modes of *laissez-faire* capitalism. Offering a suggestive analysis, Ruggie places domestic intervention at the center of a renewed post-war economic arrangement. 'The task of post-war institutional reconstruction,' notes Ruggie, 'was to manoeuvre between … two extremes and to devise a framework which would safeguard and even aid the quest for domestic stability … This was the essence of the embedded liberal compromise … its multilateralism would be predicated upon domestic interventionism' (Ruggie 1982: 393).[1]

As Jacqueline Best notes, both the concept of embedded liberalism and the kind of economic arrangements it sought to foster rotate around a distinctive social purpose. The reconciliation of international liberalization with domestic stability is not merely a technical objective but, rather, a set of arrangements deeply animated by a normative grid. Embeddedness is a 'social purpose' designed not so much to effect a certain set of economic objectives, but to facilitate a broader form of social stability and compromise (Best 2003: 365). Unlike the classical doctrine of *laissez-faire*, embedded liberalism explicitly framed itself in normative terms. Embedded liberalism, states Best, was 'self-reflexively normative and discursive, setting out to constitute particular practices and expectations in order to stabilise economic relations … a social purpose that recognised itself as such' (Best 2003: 368).

At the heart of this vision is John Maynard Keynes (see Keynes 1936; Kirshner 1999). Keynes, the key British figure at the Bretton Woods negotiations, established the overall discursive coordinates of embedded liberalism. Beginning in his reaction to the peace in Versailles in 1919 (Keynes 2004[1919]) and continuing throughout his complex negotiations with classical liberalism, Keynes articulated what Jonathan Kirshner has referred to as a 'middle way.' This middle way sought to avoid both what he perceived as the problems of classical *laissez-faire* capitalism as well as the difficulties inherent in socialist or collectivist alternatives. As Kirshner notes, 'the "middle way" [pursued] a capitalist economy in which some market forces would be managed and contained' (Kirshner 1999: 314). This entailed, importantly, not only macro-economic planning, but also social policies which would enhance forms of social solidarity and protection. As Steffek has noted, this entailed a kind of opposition in which 'domestic' and 'international' space exist on either side of a divide. In this formulation, international space is characterized by mechanisms of economic regulation designed to facilitate smooth and gradual forms of liberalized exchange. Domestic space, by contrast, is criss-crossed by regimes of intervention committed to social stability and social security. 'Only national politics', notes Steffek, 'is supposed to realize the overarching political goals such as distributive justice and social stability. The task of embedding liberalism is allocated exclusively to the national level' (Steffek 2006: 53).

In many respects, embedded liberalism rightly resides at the core of conversations in IPE. Foregrounding embedded liberalism usefully opens up a consideration of the kinds of critical distance which now exist between the normative grids of neoliberalism and its predecessors. Moreover, placing 'social purpose' at the center of our political-economic analysis facilitates a certain kind of critique which locates norms and political discourse at the core of how political-economic arrangements are constituted. Critical voices, in addition, have also been able to usefully deploy narratives of embedded and disembedded liberalism as critical devices capable of emphasizing the political transformations that have been at the heart of neoliberalism (see Gill 2003; Rupert 2006). Despite these important contributions, discussions of embedded liberalism have tended not to pay particular attention to the object which lies at its core – the 'embedded economy.' Although much attention has been paid to the political conditions which gave rise to embedded liberalism and to some of the specific practices through which it operated (see Best's [2003, 2005] discussion of the purposeful role of ambiguity in the post-war order), there has been less attention given to the specific practices and knowledge with which a new form of economy – an embedded and national economic space – became constituted and reshaped. What, in more specific terms, was the embedded economy? What knowledges and forms of expertise established its basic coherence? Out of what practices and accidents, disruptions and persistences was it assembled?

Perhaps because the shift to (and away from) embedded liberalism has so frequently been read as an effect of broader macro-structural forces, the specific contours of the embedded economy have been left relatively uninterrogated. Before an economy can be governed, however, it must first be constituted and rendered imaginable/apprehendable (du Gay 1996; du Gay and Pryke 2002;

Miller and Rose 1993; Rose 1999). Although embedded liberalism remains a notion central to both mainstream and critical voices in the field, the specific ways in which the object which lies at its core – a systematized economic space amenable to domestic intervention – has been left surprisingly insulated from critical investigation. This was an image of economy, moreover, deeply implicated in 'culture' and in the newly reorganizing cultural knowledges.

Economy, culture, visuality

Over the period between 1920–45 the ways in which 'economy' and 'culture' are organized – the institutional networks through which they become governable, the lines of force between state, citizen, and world they become implicated in – underwent dramatic change. In the case of 'economic' science and practice, the period before and during the Second World War is a moment deeply animated by shifts in the way in which the economy is conceived. Even though it is often treated as an unproblematic category in much of the social sciences, the 'economy' has been constituted and 'performed' in a variety of ways over time (Mitchell 2002; see also Mackenzie *et al.* 2007). The interwar and wartime periods were a moment, as noted by Timothy Mitchell, when a radically new understanding of the economy as a systematized, national, and self-contained space, was invoked. This is not to suggest that the idea of a national economy (associated, for example, with the European empires or with processes of 'late development industrialization') did not exist prior to this moment. Rather, in the interwar period the 'national economy' was *redefined* in ways which began to sketch out a functionally integrated space coincident with the borders of the nation. Even though this notion was key to the emerging post-war order – and central to the conception of 'interventionism' which lies at the heart of embedded liberalism – the actual forms of knowledge and discourse through which this novel reworking of the economy emerged has often been assumed rather than investigated in IPE.

This reworked idea of the national economy emerged by assembling knowledge from diverse locations – early national accounting practices, new quantitative sciences, a Keynesian language of macro-economic planning, and older notions of the economy as a mechanical system borrowed from physics – in ways that sharpened the notion of the 'economy' as a discrete space and system (see Mirowski 1989). 'What was new about the idea of the economy,' argues Mitchell, 'was the notion that these processes form a singular and self-contained totality … The reworking of the mechanical imagery of the 1930s … to imagine the possibility of … a completely closed system marks the birth of the idea of the economy' (Mitchell 1998: 87; see also Foucault 1991; Hindess 2002; Mitchell 2002).[2]

The organization and management of 'culture' also underwent significant shifts over this same period of time. Although not reducible to a single impulse, the period beginning after the First World War initiated a long process through which 'culture,' the way it is organized and the method with which it confronts everyday life, underwent rapid consolidation and change. By the end of the Second World

War, 'culture,' at least in the Anglo-American, world became institutionalized and deeply implicated in a new web of consolidated and professionalized sciences. This consolidation occurred heterogeneously across a range of fields: the field of cultural policy (Druick 2007), the advertising and marketing sciences (Bird 1999; Ewen 1996; Firat and Venkatesh 2003; Griffith 1983; Henthorn 2006; McFall 2004; Stole 2001); the consolidation of private networks of control over key broadcast technologies (Newman 2004); the construction of new national and public media institutions and the concerted effort by private and public authorities to expand the reach of a new consumer culture (see Denning 2004).

These two moments of transformation – of economy and culture – are not separable from each other. Although they occupy heterogeneous territories, the reorganization of 'culture' and 'economy' – and something of our contemporary usage of each of those terms – occupied a shared moment of experience in the period from 1920–45. Put a bit differently, the reorganization of culture and economy, although distinct and heterogeneous processes are, at least in some important ways, also *interior* to each other. One of the main arguments I want to advance in this chapter is the claim that the *economic* changes that occurred in this period – changes that were key to the formation of an 'embedded' economy – were deeply implicated in forms of knowledge and practice often labeled as *cultural*. Although some important work has mapped genealogies of the practices through which the national economy emerged in this period (see Callon 1998; Hindess 2002; Mitchell 2005), these genealogies have been preoccupied with the work of *economic* knowledge and practice. Although important, this neglects the ways in which a broader range of knowledge and practice beyond formally economic science, including cultural knowledge, has been implicated in the making and performing of economic space.

Visuality and the embedded economy

One particular element of *cultural* knowledge which became deeply implicated in the rise of the embedded economy is a concern with visuality. Visuality, more or less rationalized attempts to govern visual display and projection, became increasingly central to the political, social, and commercial cultures of the interwar and war periods. Although it is not the only cultural technique given prominence in this period (there is, of course, a great deal of interest in the aural possibilities of radio broadcasting), the period just before and during the Second World War witnessed a relatively systematic set of experiments in the use of visuality as a technique capable of intervening into the everyday lives of citizens. What I want to argue in this section of the chapter is that these experiments in visuality were directly implicated in attempts to constitute a new form of economic practice consistent with an embedded economy.

To focus this argument I want to review the cultural-visual rationality developed by one network organized around the figure of John Grierson.[3] Much of this network was hired beginning in 1926 by the new Empire Marketing Board (EMB). The EMB, a British-funded offshoot of the Imperial Economic Committee, was concerned to develop statistical analysis, films, posters, and other publicity related to the British Empire and the imperial economy. After a productive and intensive period at the EMB (which involved groundbreaking work on the use of film and poster-art) Grierson continued to influence the emerging cultural sciences as a high-level film advisor to the Australian and Canadian governments, as a Director of the General Post Office Film Unit (UK), as the founder of the National Film Board of Canada and the inaugural National Film Commissioner, as a private film producer, and as a key figure in New York and Paris during the formation of UNESCO.

In the promotion of poster-art and, most importantly, film, Grierson described visuality as a particularly effective technique of intervention. This was, in its most ambitious form, an argument about the unique ways in which visuality, unlike more rational forms of cultural expression could be harnessed for socially purposive ends. For Grierson, the new visual practices are intimately bound up with the problem of 'economic integration' and planning. It is imperative, notes Grierson, that film helps dramatize and address the 'problems of economic integration, either nationally or internationally' (Grierson 1943). At one level, this involved articulating the project of filmic visuality in a language consistent with 'domestic interventionism.' The archival record is riddled with the lexicon of macro-economic planning and state intervention.[4] Public culture is depicted in a language consistent with the Keynesian 'middle way'; as a state enterprise committed to the possibilities of a planned capitalist economy.

Echoing the themes of embedded liberalism, those who became preoccupied with visuality – a network which itself was international in scope – began to promote its own form of 'middle way' in which virtues of economic planning and individual initiative would exist together. Echoing in important ways the Keynesian position that was installed at the core of Bretton Woods, Grierson situated the Film Board and other visual initiatives in a space in which a process of planning would regulate, but not suffocate, economic practice. This process of planning, Grierson notes, is one that exists across international space:

> ... we are entering upon a new and interim society which is neither capitalist nor socialist, but in which we can achieve central planning without loss of individual initiative, by the mere process of absorbing initiative in the function of planning ... As one watches the implications of the New Deal and of what is happening today in the development of centralized planning ... one sees that hope not only on a national scale but on an international one too.
>
> (Grierson 1943)

In these terms, the cultural practices of visuality are deeply implicated in the new embedded economy. These kinds of cultural practices are fully, explicitly, designed to constitute a kind of embedded economy; a form of cultural governance in which, in Tony Bennett's terms, culture becomes implicated in, becomes one of the 'working surfaces' upon which other categories or objects – such as economy – are constituted (Bennett 2007). An embedded economy amenable to domestic interventionism is an object assembled at a diverse set of sites. These are locations dominated not only by economic science but also by explicitly cultural practice and knowledge. This assembling of the embedded economy is, moreover, not only a question of 'making up' an economy figured in Keynesian terms (systematically integrated, functionally interrelated) but also a question of specifying grids of a particular kind of identification.

'Seeing our neighbors as ourselves': identification and an 'international self'

As his assessment of the need for a new post-war order became urgent, Grierson began to make a case for a new 'international self.' In contrast to the old national information services (the propaganda machines of the First World War, the old Government Motion Picture Bureau) which orbited around more traditional forms of propaganda, or around the need to project national culture abroad, the new cultural institutions had a much different and more dynamic mandate. The primary role of the new cultural institutions was to mobilize citizens in relation to the requirements of the new international order. This was a task of training the information services more squarely onto the new issues of international cooperation. As Grierson envisioned it, this required the old information services to abandon the goals of projecting a kind of national story, instead replacing it with the projection of a kind of 'international self':

> … the national information services should think less of presenting their own nations to the world and more of presenting the new cooperative world to which their nations are pledged … international relationships and dependencies … In the concern for social progress … the national interest is often, and deeply, the interest of others. I see in this fact a new phase for the information services: larger in prospect than ever before … through the offices of … UNRRA, ILO. … the best service that we can do for our country will be in the articulation and projection of its larger international self.
>
> (Grierson 1945)

But what did it mean to say visual culture – and film in particular – could be centered around the goals of an international self? What kind of ambition was this? What, beyond mere rhetoric, did this signify? I want to argue in this section of the chapter that this dream of a kind of 'international self' resides at the core of Grierson's ambition for film, and how film might help constitute an embedded order. The most significant ambition associated with film was its possibility as a *technique of identification*. For Grierson, film could, in Paul du Gay's terms, be key to the 'making up' of new forms of identity – new modes of self and citizen – 'required' of the new order (du Gay 1997; 2007). As du Gay notes, a focus on identity in these terms involves 'an understanding of the specific forms of "personhood" that individuals acquire as a result of their immersion in, or subjection to, particular normative and technical regimes of conduct' (du Gay 2007: 11).

This attempt to constitute visual practice as a technique of identification entails a particular argument about visual form as a non-rational and even 'intimate' medium. Because visual display and projection operated at a level beyond (or above) rational process, visual forms had an immediacy not easily forged in other types of cultural expression. In order for art to address the problems of the world, noted Grierson, it 'must bring it alive, so that people will live intimately ... You can only do it in those dramatic terms which present the life of the thing and the purpose of the thing and make intimacy possible. The radio, the picture, the poster and the story are the more obvious instruments in your hand' (Grierson 1944a).

Visuality, in more significant ways than other forms of rational language or culture, was a deeply resonant and intimate form of communication and experience. 'We shall,' Grierson simply put it, 'have to learn and speak a new language ... the way of rational explanation will not serve ... The new language ... must in fact be something more in the nature of a dramatic language than a rational one' (Grierson 1926). This focus on visuality, however, was not so much the domain of the spectacle – the exceptional visual experience – but a more mundane and personal form of visual display aimed directly at everyday life. 'Speaking intimately and quietly about real things,' argued Grierson, 'will be more spectacular in the end than the spectacle itself' (Grierson 1944a). At its core this preoccupation with visuality and with film in particular is a kind of claim about citizenship and the dramatic but mundane ways in which visual forms are capable of intervening directly into everyday spaces. Filmic visuality can, in these terms, quite literally nurture and nourish an identification with the wider world:

> In film ... we have an instrument much more suited ... than any other of the arts. It really can bring the outside world alive to the growing citizen. It really can extend his experience ... it can, if it is mastered and organised, provide this necessary umbilical to the community outside.
>
> (Grierson 1926)

This conception of visual form as an intimate and yet broadening device draws upon a much older, and dubious, set of assumptions about the need to confront and govern 'everyday' and 'working class' populations with technologies which are sensual and not rational. Assuming that everyday populations are incapable of digesting or mediating rational forms of cultural expression, this argument foregrounds visuality as a practice particularly suited to/suitable for the 'uncivilized' spaces of everyday life. For Lewis, for example, an early proponent of visual practices in financial advertising, visuality was useful as a 'primitive art' uniquely capable of intervening within the degraded spaces of everyday life. 'This is called primitive art,' notes Lewis:

> which fascinates primitive peoples. The ignorant like bright colors and a lot of them, and all in violent contrast ... The unrefined man is attracted by 'loud'

things ... He discounts all claims to culture, hence you must paint the picture gaudily in order to impress him.

(Lewis 1908: 98)

An intimate form of worldly being

As promoted by Grierson and his network, visual practices were particularly suited to the creation of an intimate world. This intimacy was twofold. On one hand this was an intimacy of form in which film, as a direct and immediate experience, struck a particularly intimate relation with individual viewers. On the other hand this was an intimacy of being-in-the-world. Visual practice was forceful enough, according to Grierson and his colleagues, to bring individuals into direct relation with – perhaps even confrontation with – the *world* beyond local horizons. By helping to dramatize the world, by bringing individuals into dramatic relation with distant 'others,' film created the space in which individuals could confront the world. In this sense film made the world more intimately knowable; a possibility which allowed everyday individuals to create a world for themselves and to situate themselves directly, unavoidably, within that world.

This attempt to articulate film and visual practice as a technique of worldly identification was formulated in complicated terms. Perhaps most directly these experiments sought to mark out a certain territory deeply linked to a 'social' form of citizenship. Social citizenship enmeshes individuals within and across the social body (Rose 1999). Social governance articulates problems not as individual pathologies but as concerns (and hence risks) which can be located across the social whole. Influenced both by this emergent form of social governance and by his own Chicago training in social science, Grierson attempted to install this notion of the social at the heart of filmic visuality. Film, noted Grierson, 'must first be socialized. By that I mean that it must at every turn take hold of its role as a social instrument' (Grierson 1944a). In order to achieve this kind of social goal, experts began to champion the role of film in delineating the ways in which citizens could occupy a kind of functional role in 'society.' 'The people as we know them,' asserted Grierson, 'want film materials which will help them in their actual and present citizenship: films ... about a world which is organically related to their own interests and their own functions within the nation' (Grierson 1940).

This form of 'social' self, however, was not singular or unidimensional. For Grierson, citizens were to be imagined not only as passive recipients of 'information' but as agents who could use cultural material in ways that would allow them to engage with the world. Although we often conceive of the post-war moment of social citizenship/governance and the active citizenship of our own neoliberal present as occupying distinct and quite separate worlds, the experiments with visuality in the interwar and war periods sought a certain kind of reconciliation between the two.[5] Citizens were envisioned as an active and instrumentalized component in cultural practice. In Grierson's terms, the new visual forms are 'imaginative media' which no longer rely on passive audiences. Citizens, Grierson puts it, are 'in part, at least, thinking beings. They have been encouraged in individual judgement by a liberal era. They have their own sentiments, loyalties, ideas and ideals ... They cannot be considered automata' (Grierson 1941; see also Druick 2000).

This attempt to use visual practice to address an audience in active terms – a theme that would be pursued consistently by the 1930s and 1940s – was innovated during the 1920s at the EMB.[6] The EMB was established by the British government and the Imperial Economic Committee to cultivate 'publicity' which would promote images of the imperial economy among consumers (Constantine 1986; Druick 2007). Although it presented a particular, if short-lived, notion of imperial economy, it is at the EMB that Grierson developed the conceptual underpinnings for the kind of visuality he wanted to pursue as part of a larger project committed to a planned and integrated international economy.

Beginning in 1927, for example, the EMB formalized its call for a 'voluntary preference' as the cornerstone of its publicity campaigns. 'Voluntary preference' referred not to any state-imposed trade preference but to a certain voluntary consumer practice in favor of domestic and imperial goods. The EMB launched an advertising and postering campaign designed to encourage consumers to voluntarily adopt preferential consumption behavior. According to the Committee, the voluntary preference sought to mobilize a kind of 'latent preference' for empire and to 'translate' it 'into a practical scheme under state guidance and on a scale commensurate with the productive facilities of the Empire. The scheme rests on the free will of the individual citizen as consumer' (Imperial Economic Committee 1927: 4). In this formulation, the preference is an attempt to sketch out an intimate connection between the space of voluntary consumption and the larger space of imperial practice.

Most fully, however, this keen interest in visuality was an ambition to cultivate a kind of practice of worldly being.[7] To pursue the dream of film at the center of a kind of international self, Grierson and his colleagues placed particular emphasis on the possibilities of civic engagement across and through filmic space. At the core of these arguments about visuality is a contention about the possibilities of using visual practice to create a space in which distant 'others,' others separated by spaces of immense geographic and social distance, could engage directly in each others' lives. The visual territory created by and through films is a space in which everyday citizens can meet and, in some measure, can confront the requirements of the new era. An embedded economy – an economic space which requires mutual cooperation and planning – is, for Grierson, an object that needs to be forged in the first instance in the spaces of filmic visuality. 'We know more about our international duty,' argues Grierson, 'because we have all, at least imaginatively, flown in airplanes, crossed frontiers and seen our neighbours as ourselves' (Grierson 1942). The unique space of filmic visuality is actually the territory on and through which cooperative practice between citizens who are geographically distinct can be forged and mobilized. 'Miraculously,' notes Grierson, '… men spatially distant and unknown to each other combine each day in great and co-operative dramas'

(Grierson 1942). It is in these terms that visuality was conceived as a technique of worldly being; as a mechanism which could place individuals directly into the world.

This attempt to mobilize a kind of citizenship and form of cooperative practice among 'distant' populations became key to much of the visual practice of the EMB throughout the 1920s and 1930s. Although the centerpiece of all EMB publicity was a diagram which linked 'British' consumers with the wider world of British imperial possessions, this was a diagram which took many forms.[8] In one series of early advertisements, for example, a 'progressive' notion of empire is mobilized in which active agents are inserted in empire as a self-consciously humane force. In this formulation, the imperial economy, and the subjects at the heart of that space, are components of a system capable of generating socially useful outcomes. Invoking a proto-Keynesian language of a systematically integrated economic space, the advertisements in this series link the active work of the British consumer-citizen with a stable and 'socially secure' system.[9] 'When you are buying,' the text implores its audience, 'remember the unemployed.' The advertisement emphasizes the ways in which 'imperial consumption' can 'attack unemployment' and, at the same time, can also help maintain 'British standards of civilisation.' 'Whenever you have an opportunity of giving a voluntary preference to British Empire products,' the advertisement asserts, 'do it in the interests of British standards of civilization, British trade and industry and the employment of your fellow British citizens' (EMB 1929).

In these kinds of initiatives the EMB sought to visualize, and make real, not only a 'progressive' (and systematically integrated) imperial economy, but also a form of active citizenship at the core of that system. In this vein, a connection is attempted between the intimate and active space of consumption and the broadest possible spaces related to an empire global in scope. This is a rationality which seeks out a space made systematic by and through the active work of choosing subjects. It is also a method with which individuals can be located directly into the world. This 'action on the self by the self' (see Dean 1999) constitutes the empire as a systematically integrated space and locates individuals in direct relation to 'distant' places and others. Although the EMB marks out an imperial diagram, it does so in a manner that experiments with a formulation – everyday actors as agents in global space – that would become key to the ways in which Grierson and others attempted to paint an embedded order. As Figure 3.1 notes, this is a connection, such as it is, that is forged out of and within the active work of consumers themselves. 'Such simple words as yours,' notes the text in reference to the mundane work of consumption, 'find their way to the ends of the earth' (EMB 1930).

These poster advertisements, among the earliest experiments of the new visuality, begin to mark out a kind of active citizen stretched across global space. The appeals to a form of global citizen, to a kind of worldly being, prefigure, at least in some ways, a kind of global relationality which has become common in today's mode of globalization (see the HSBC advertisements in the Introduction). The global subject of our present, active in his/her citizenship, is embedded in a

Figure 3.1 'How you can help the empire.'
Source: EMB (1930).

much longer and more complicated history than is often acknowledged. This is a mode of identification, however, that is as much concerned with maintaining global difference as it is in overcoming it.

Envisioning a field of danger/difference

Although excited about the possibilities of using visual practice to overcome distance, Grierson also expressed deep concerns about the 'dangers' inherent in the new sciences of visual culture. Placing citizens in direct confrontation with each other in the visual spaces created by films is, notes Grierson himself, a risky task. As Grierson suggests, 'the paradox of a shrinking world is that what is less distant may be felt to be all the more dangerous' (Grierson 1944b). Establishing the kind of intimate connections among citizens was an entirely new 'pattern of dramatic statement.' Although optimistic about the possibilities of locating culture and visuality in particular at the core of this new dramatic statement, Grierson frequently acknowledged the difficulty of establishing a kind of cultural practice based not on rational technique but on the less cognitive processes of visual communication.

Of particular concern is an anxiety about the question of difference. Like most modes of liberal government, cultural experiments associated with visuality not only specify modes of active citizenship, but sketch out the lines which separate active citizens from those that are governed in more coercive modes. 'Liberal political reason,' notes Hindess, 'has been as much concerned with paternalistic rule ... as with the government of autonomous individuals, as much concerned with the subject peoples of imperial possessions as with the free inhabitants of Western states' (Hindess 2002: 93).

Although visuality is a practice capable of reformulating distance, it cannot overcome the problem or fear of difference. Without exception the active agents addressed in the posters and films of the EMB are British 'home' populations. The visual practices of the EMB invoke a fundamental ambiguity about the 'you' addressed. On the one hand, the images diagram a cooperative space in which all members of the empire are stitched into a single body. On the other hand, however, there are often ambiguities (and anxieties) about who is addressed at the core of this body and which races form its center. In one 1927 example (*Your Great Inheritance*), the text is clearly addressed to a partial 'you' and to an inheritance based on its own expansive racial prerogatives:

> As a citizen of the British Empire, you are one of the trustees of an inheritance more vast and splendid than the world has ever known before. You have your personal share of responsibility for the future of an Empire comprising more than one quarter of the whole earth ... immense areas still awaiting settlement by men and women of our own race.
>
> (EMB 1927a)

This is a striking, if ambiguous, formulation. On one hand the narrative addresses a particular 'you' and summons that body in an active tone invoking his/her 'responsibility' as a personal agency central to empire and its ongoing integrity. On the other hand, it marks a notion of governance drawn in an image of 'our race.' This implies a particular, deeply racialized, relationship to difference. Difference is not so much accepted as it is integrated into a singular form defined in relation to the superior culture and practice of Anglo-European races. The 'fear of difference,' note Inayatullah and Blaney, 'remains strong ... Differences remain the problem to which creating a uniform world order is the solution' (Inayatullah and Blaney 2004: 89).

At another level, however, the visual practices key to the EMB not only sought to overcome but also to mark out lines of difference. EMB posters, for example, draw idealized images of colonies as 'strange' and 'romantic' spaces. The colonies are imagined as occupying a kind of timelessness distinctly foreign from the logic of the 'home economy.' Because they are targeted to a unique audience, the spaces of what Anne McClintock has referred to as 'commodity spectacle,' these images are a productive attempt to assemble imperial languages of difference

Figure 3.2 'East of Suez.'

Source: EMB (1927b).

and 'orientalism' in a unique manner (McClintock 1995). Figure 3.2 (*East of Suez*), for example, foregrounds an imperious difference in the 'Eastern' empire. Although a source of commodities (tea for tired British citizens) it is also a source of wondrous and romanticized difference. 'Has it ever occurred to you,' asks the text, 'to connect the homely, household things you eat and drink and handle daily with the strange, romantic places of the East whence they came?' (EMB 1927b). This image seeks to forge a connection between the daily consumption act at 'home' with the strange and mysterious spaces of the 'other.' In doing so, however, and in seeking to adopt a certain link between those spaces, it also productively paints and reaffirms a particular conception of difference and otherness.

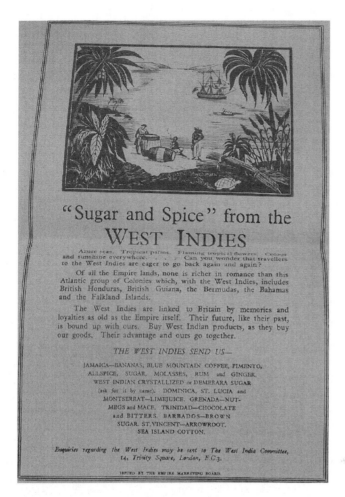

Figure 3.3 'Sugar and Spice' from the West Indies.
Source: EMB (1927c).

Figure 3.3, in addition, mobilizes a common metaphor by painting colonial possessions in terms of the naturalized and immutable ground of memory. In this rationality the colonial 'other' is depicted as a timeless space connected to the world at large not in rational terms but through the unspeaking vectors of memory. A source of simplicity and pleasure, colonial space is imagined as occupying a beautifully distant location, as well as a strangely resonant link to the heart of empire itself. 'Travelers to the West Indies,' the text notes, 'are eager to go back again and again ... The West Indies are linked to Britain by memories and loyalties as old as the Empire itself. Their future, like their past, is bound up with ours' (EMB 1927c). Firmly connected to empire through myth and memory, colonial spaces remain sharply distinct from the 'home' of empire by lines of difference and strangeness.[10]

These visual practices are also designed, however, to emphasize the instrumental role of empire as a source of 'civilization' and 'improvement'; a mode of transition which, if not overcoming difference, can at least contain it in some fashion. One of the earliest waves of advertisements from the EMB, for example, not only encourage 'our' participation in imperial space as consumers, but mobilize this active capacity by diagramming the 'progressive' role of imperial practice in dislocating modes of 'savagery.' One proof from this campaign, *News For You from West Africa*, notes that 'Britain has given West Africa great gifts – the end of slavery and tribal war – a new era of peace, happiness and prosperity ... There you see how Empire trade benefits both the producer Overseas and your own people at home' (EMB 1927d). It is in these terms, and marked out in contentious rationalities of difference and civilization, that the visual experiments of the interwar period invoke notions of a 'reciprocal' economy – an embedded economy – and a particular kind of subject capable of actively engaging in global space. These images are early, and often experimental, attempts to craft ways of imagining 'our' relation to 'them' in an economy that is both distant and strangely intimate.

In these attempts, it is possible to construct an 'other' story of embedded liberalism. These experiments explicitly attempt to invoke a notion of 'economy' deeply consistent with – often explicitly drawing upon – the concepts key to what would become known as embedded liberalism: planning, cooperation, an economy amenable to domestic intervention and international exchange. At the same time, they reveal an ambition for a certain kind of intimate form of worldly being. Constituting an embedded economy was not merely, for Grierson, a question of assembling a cooperative and planned economic space, but also, crucially, of cultivating a certain mode of identification. It sought to insert citizens directly in the world and to mobilize a kind of intimacy which might bring distant populations into direct contact with each other.

At the same time, however, this intimate form of worldly being was marked not only by the possibilities but also by the dangers of intimacy. The visual practices Grierson's network sought to cultivate sketched a world criss-crossed by intractable lines of difference and imperious distance. In these terms, these experiments in visuality pursued a delicate balance keen to overcome distance but committed, at the same time, to a conception of difference as a 'problem' to be managed and contained. It is in these terms – in a language of the possibilities and limits of worldly being – that these early experiments in visuality drew a particular image of global citizenship. Although clearly expressed in a language and practice resonant of its moment of emergence, this formulation nonetheless has lines of affinity, however uneven, with the neoliberal conceptions of global being which circulate in our political present. Often understood in ways which emphasize its contrast to the globalized world of neoliberalism, this story of embedded liberalism and worldly being helps establish some of the lines and partialities with which we might actually place the two in a shared line of force. This type of story, in turn, allows us to recover something of the plurality and ambiguities of embedded liberalism, not as a singular 'order' but as a diverse field constituted in relation to a heterogeneous range of knowledges and practices. This is a sense of ambiguity, moreover, made visible not in conventional political economies of embedded liberalism, but only in a form of analysis attuned to the importance of culture.

Conclusion: 'cultural' and 'economic' governance in embedded liberalism

From the mid 1920s until the late 1940s John Grierson existed at the center of a network particularly committed to visual practices. For Grierson these visual practices were to be central to the new world that was in construction and to the kinds of everyday citizenship practices that this world required. Although this was a project dedicated, in some important ways, to what John Ruggie has called 'embedded liberalism,' it foregrounds a different story about that moment than is normally told. For Grierson and his network the formation of an embedded order – one which sought a world governed by national planning *and* international openness – was not merely or even primarily a question of marking out Keynesian lines of economic governance or structures of international economic management. Rather it was a question of using film and other visual techniques to mobilize everyday populations in a particular kind of way. Most fully it was an attempt to use cultural and visual practices to intervene directly into everyday life, to use visual space as one of the 'working surfaces' upon which a new economy could be developed. This was an attempt to directly confront everyday actors with a world in which they were to be active agents, to cultivate a practice of worldly being in which they were intimately connected to a world with which they could engage. The central argument I have put forward in this chapter is that embedded liberalism was an intimately *cultural* project in which cultural practices were cast as central to the ways in which citizens might be asked to confront the world in a new and direct manner. This was also styled, self-consciously, as a 'dangerous' ambition; one that needed to manage and contain difference in a particular way.

Retelling this story about public culture and embedded liberalism reveals more than a historical curiosity. It foregrounds, also, something of the ambiguity of embedded liberalism and the ways in which we use it as a critical device. One of the contributions that cultural analysis can make is an ability to unsettle concepts that remain given or unproblematized. In IPE the concept of embedded liberalism is often treated in a singular manner as a form of world order distinctively separate from the world of contemporary neoliberalism and globalization. As this chapter suggests it may be useful to rethink this overly general approach.

As I have argued, the cultural experiments associated with embedded liberalism attempted to use filmic and visual practices as techniques of identification that could cultivate the kind of worldly being among everyday citizens required of a global economy which orbits around international planning and cooperation. What is striking about these experiments is the complicated way in which they situate embedded liberalism in a longer genealogy of global or worldly being; a genealogy which is stitched, unavoidably, into the fabric of our own neoliberal present. This is not to suggest that anything like a direct line could be traced between the kind of 'international self' promoted by Grierson and the more fully globalized 'enterprising self' of our neoliberal moment (see Rose 1999). This is to suggest, however, that any genealogy of worldly being, of attempts to locate citizens in the world, would need to encompass both embedded and neoliberal moments. Put a bit differently, the cultural story I have told about embedded liberalism suggests the need to locate these experiments as a moment – perhaps even a formative moment of some kind – in a long and complex genealogy of global/international citizenship. Neither is this to suggest that something of our contemporary notion of global personhood (see the HSBC advertisements discussed in the Introduction) was 'born' in the various lines of force sketched out in the experiments associated with embedded liberalism. What I have put forth, however, is a complex genealogy, and a complex set of persistences and disruptions, which cannot be diagnosed with any simple story which places embedded liberalism and neoliberalism on either sides of an opposition or as part of a story of epochal disruption. As a critical device, embedded liberalism needs to be rethought not as a singular story of change, but as a set of moments that are assembled in diverse, multiple, and even surprising, sometimes counter-intuitive, ways.

In turn, this story of Grierson and the network he assembled raises significant questions regarding 'cultural' and 'economic' governance and the lines of force between them. At a more general level, this story reaffirms the contention that 'economic' space and practice is culturally constituted. As the narrative I have retold indicates, economic spaces and practices are not given, nor do they exist in some manner prior to their representations, but are, rather, historically shifting practices brought into being by the representations which are said only to be their effects (see Aitken 2007). The story retold in this chapter also implies a second, and more specific, methodological contention regarding the relation between 'economy' and 'culture.' Following Bennett, I conclude by re-emphasizing the importance of developing cultural analyses capable of making visible the historically shifting ways in which 'cultural' and 'economic' practices are deeply implicated in each other. This is not to collapse the distinction between 'culture' and 'economy' but to highlight, precisely, the historically shifting ways in which 'culture' has been defined and the diverse methods with which 'cultural' knowledge can shape new forms of 'economy.' This is, to use Bennett's language, an attempt to foreground the ways in which 'cultural' practices, themselves a historical and not 'anthropological' reality, constitute a kind of 'working surface' upon which 'economic' change can be shaped or directed. This implies the importance of adopting nothing like a general definition of 'culture' but, precisely, a set of analyses sensitive to the shifting ways in which 'culture' has been mobilized for particular purposes in diverse ways. 'What one should, perhaps, avoid trying to do,' affirm du Gay and Pryke (2002: 12), 'is to impose a general analytic distinction between "economy" and "culture" on one's material prior to examining … its practical constitution.' This implies the importance of cultural-economies capable of inspiring not generalized types of analyses, but analyses of the mundane and heterogeneous conditions which lie at the heart of international political economy and of how that 'economy' might be reformulated.

Notes

1 It should be noted that this cooperative world order was conceived not as a zero-sum game but, rather, as a form of economic order in which all countries could devise mutually beneficial economic arrangements. As American official Henry Morgenthau noted at the Bretton Woods conference: 'What we have done here in Bretton Woods is to devise machinery by which men and women everywhere can exchange freely, on a fair and stable basis, the goods which they produce through fair labor. And we have taken the initial step through which the nations of the world will be able to help one another ...' (Morgenthau 1944).

2 Central to the conditions of existence for the national economy are Keynesian lines of force. See Keynes (1933: 760); see also Radice [1982] for a more detailed analysis of the relationship of Keynes' view to nationalism, see Esty (2000).

3 Although it is a bit beyond the scope of this chapter to develop a detailed treatment of Grierson, it should be noted that I conceive of Grierson as a figure indicative of a broader network of actors – both private and public – keen to explore film and other visual forms throughout the period.

4 See Grierson (1943): ' ... we shall find new concepts coming more powerfully into our lives; and we shall find ourselves dramatising them so that they become loyaliteis and take leadership of the Will ... We shall talk less about free enterprise and competition and more about the State and Control. There will be less about Liberty and more about Duties ... there will be less about words and more about action and less about the past and more about the future. Already you hear the new words in the air: Discipline, Unity, Co-ordination, total effort, Planning.'

5 It is beyond the scope of this chapter to fully delineate the literature around 'active citizenship' and the ways in which 'active' and 'social' citizen might relate. Although much of the critical literature around neoliberalism has rightly stressed the ways in which neoliberalism has invoked an active form of self and citizen, this literature has not as often stressed the ways in which social governance or social citizenship has also invoked notions of active citizenship in a different manner (see Walters 2004).

6 Although it invoked an imperial imaginary, the argument I want to make is that the cultural rationality developed at the EMB actually prefigures the kind of uses film and poster-art were put to when Grierson began working at the NFB and began thinking more systematically about culture and the embedded order. The themes that would dominate his work in the 1930s and 1940s – how to use film and visual practice to constitute an active and international mode of citizenship – was a theme clearly innovated while working at the EMB. As an early experiment, furthermore, the work at the EMB is actually revealing as a moment when this rationality was being worked out and articulated with a certain clarity and openness.

7 For Grierson film constitutes a kind of 'international exchange': 'we have potential machinery for the international exchange of the living materials of social consideration and achievement ...' (Grierson 1944b).

8 One series of advertisements, for example, sought to mark out this intimate consumer-imperial relation in terms of a broader geopolitics of liberal peace. 'Peace,' one of the advertisements announces, is the 'strongest Bulwark in the British Empire ... You want Peace too. There you have another reason for "shopping within the Empire"' (EMB 1928).

9 See EMB 1927e: 'Why is this worth doing? Most people feel instinctively that they would rather buy from their own people ... by adopting the policy of the EMB in your daily shopping, you will not merely be satisfying that instinct, you will be taking a real part in a planned and concerted effort to make the British Empire lead the world in organized production and the preservation of waste ... That way lies the advancement of the standard of life in every empire country and the defeat of unemployment in your own.'
10 Although there is not enough space in this chapter to develop it, this argument has affinities to a distinction Wendy Brown has recently noted between those 'who have culture' and those (other) populations 'who culture has' (see Brown 2006).

Bibliography

Aitken, Rob (2007) *Performing Capital: Toward a Cultural Economy of Popular and Global Finance*, New York: Palgrave.

Bennett, Tony (2007) 'The work of culture', *Cultural Sociology*, 1(1): 31–47.

Best, Jacqueline (2003) 'From the top down: the new international financial architecture and the re-embedding of global finance', *New Political Economy*, 8(3): 363–84.

—— (2005) *The Limits of Transparency: Ambiguity and the History of International Finance*, Ithaca, NY: Cornell University Press.

Bird, William L. Jr (1999) *'Better Living': Advertising, Media and the New Vocabulary of Business Leadership*, Evanston, IL: Northwestern University Press.

Blyth, Mark (2002) *Great Transformations: Economic Ideas and Institutional Change in the Twentieth Century*, Cambridge: Cambridge University Press.

Brown, W. (2006) *Regulating Aversion: Tolerance in the Age of Identity and Empire.* Princeton: Princeton University Press.

Callon, Michel (1998) *The Laws of the Market*, Oxford: Blackwell.

Constantine, Stephen (1986) 'Bringing the empire alive: the Empire Marketing Board and imperial propaganda, 1926–33' in John M. Mackenzie (ed.) *Imperialism and Popular Culture*, Manchester: Manchester University Press.

Cox, Robert W. (1987) *Production, Power and World Order*, New York: Columbia University Press pp. 192–231.

Dean, Mitchell (1999) *Governmentality: Power and Rule in Modern Society*, Thousand Oaks, CA: Sage.

Denning, Michael (2004) *Culture in the Age of Three Worlds*, London: Verso.

Druick, Zoe (2000) 'Documenting government: re-examining the 1950s National Film Board films about citizenship', *Canadian Journal of Film Studies*, 9: 55–79.

—— (2007) *Projecting Canada: Government Policy and Documentary Film at the National Film Board*, Montreal: McGill-Queen's University Press.

du Gay, Paul (1996) *Consumption and Identity at Work*, London: Sage.

—— (1997) *Production of Culture/Cultures of Production*, London: Sage.

—— (2007) *Organizing Identity: Persons and Organizations After Theory*, London: Sage.

du Gay, Paul and Michael Pryke (eds) (2002) *Cultural Economy*, London: Sage.

Empire Marketing Board (1927a) *Your Great Inheritance*, Ottawa: Archives Canada, RG 17 Vol. 3310, Folder 848–1(3).

—— (1927) *Why is This Worth Doing?* Ottawa: Archives Canada, RG 17 Vol. 3310, Folder 848–1(3).

—— (1927b) *East of Suez*, Ottawa: Archives Canada, RG 17 Vol. 3310, Folder 848–1(3).

—— (1927c) *Sugar and Spice from the West Indies*, Ottawa: Archives Canada, RG 17 Vol. 3310, Folder 848–1(3).

—— (1927d) *News for You From West Africa*, Ottawa: Archives Canada, RG 17 Vol. 3310, Folder 848–1(3).

—— (1928) *Peace: Its Strongest Bulwark is the British Empire*, Ottawa: Archives Canada, RG 17 Vol. 3310, Folder 848–1(3).

—— (1929) *When You are Buying, Remember the Unemployed*, Ottawa: Archives Canada, RG 17 Vol. 3310, Folder 848–1(3).

—— (1930) *How You Can Help the Empire*, Ottawa: Archives Canada, RG 17 Vol. 3310, Folder 848–1(3).

Esty, Joshua (1999) 'National objects: Keynesian economics and modernist culture in England', *Modernism/Modernity*, 7(1): 1–24.

Ewen, Stuart (1996) *PR! A Social History of Spin*, New York: Basic Books.

Foucault, Michel (1991) 'Governmentality', in Graham Burchill, Colin Gordon and Peter Miller (eds) *The Foucault Effect: Studies in Governmentality*, Chicago, IL: University of Chicago Press.

Firat, Fuat A. and Alladi Venkatesh (2003) 'An interview with Sidney J. Levy', *Consumption, Markets and Culture*, 6(2): 111–113.

Gill, Stephen (2003) *Power and Resistance in the New World Order*, New York: Palgrave-Macmillan.

Grierson, John (1936) *Broadcasting and the Cinema as Instruments of Education*, London: National Union of Teachers.

Grierson, J. (1942) "The Documentary Idea:," *Documentary News Letter*.

—— (1940) *Correspondence to M. Kelly, Honolulu 6 February 1940*, Ottawa: Archives Canada, MG 30 D77, Vol. 22.

—— (1941) *The Nature of Propaganda: Part I, Propaganda on the Offensive*, Ottawa: Archives Canada, MG 30 D77, Vol. 22.

—— (1943) *Propaganda and Education*, Montreal: National Film Board Archives, Speeches File.

Grierson, John (1944a) *Films and the International Labor Organization*, Montreal: National Film Board Archives, Speeches File.

Grierson, John (1944b) 'Film in international affairs, part 1', *The Nation*, 31 November.

—— (1945) 'Film in international affairs, part 2', *The Nation*, 13 January.

Griffith, Robert (1983) 'The selling of America: the Advertising Council and American politics, 1942–60', *Business History Review*, LVII(3): 388–412.

Henthorn, Cynthia Lee (2006) *From Submarines to Suburbs: Selling a Better America, 1939–1959*, Athens, OH: University of Ohio Press.

Hindess, Barry (1998) 'Neo-liberalism and the national economy', in Mitchell Dean and Barry Hindess (eds) *Governing Australia: Studies in Contemporary Rationalities of Government*, Cambridge: Cambridge University Press, pp. 210–226.

—— (2002) 'The liberal government of unfreedom', *Alternatives*, 26(1): 93–111.

Imperial Economic Committee (1927) *Report on the Functions and Work of the Imperial Economic Committee*, London: Imperial Economic Committee.

Inayatullah, N. and David Blaney (2004) *International Relations and the Problem of Difference*, London: Routledge.

Keynes, J. M. (1933) 'National self-sufficiency', *The Yale Review* XXII: 755–69.

—— (1936) *The General Theory of Employment, Interest and Money*, London: Macmillan.

—— (2004[1919]) *The Economic Consequences of the Peace*, New York: Prometheus Books.

Kirshner, Jonathan (1999) 'Keynes, capital mobility and the crisis of embedded liberalism', *Review of International Political Economy*, 6(3): 313–37.

Lewis, E. St Elmo (1908[1985]) *Financial Advertising*, New York: Garland Publishing Inc.

Mackenzie, Donald, Farbien Muniesa and Lucia Siu (eds) (2007) *Do Economists Make Markets? On the Performativity of Economics*, Princeton, NJ: Princeton University Press.

McClintock, Anne (1995) *Imperial Leather: Race, Gender and Sexuality in the Colonial Contest*, New York: Routledge.

McFall, Liz (2004) *Advertising: A Cultural Economy*, London: Sage Publications.

Miller, Peter and Nikolas Rose (1993) 'Governing Economic Life', in Mike Gane and Terry Johnson (eds) *Foucault's New Domains*, London: Routledge.

Mirowski, P. (1989) *More Heat Than Light*, Cambridge: Cambridge University Press.

Mitchell, Timothy (1998) 'Fixing the economy', *Cultural Studies*, 12(1): 82–101.

—— (2002) *Rule of Experts: Egypt, Techno-Politics, Modernity*, Berkeley, CA: University of California Press.

—— (2005) 'The work of economics: how a discipline makes its world', *European Journal of Sociology*, 46: 297–320.

Morgenthau, H. (1944) "Closing address by Secretary of the Treasury Henry Morgenthau. July 22, 1944." *Pillars of Peace Pamphlet # 4*. Washington: United States Army Information School.

Newman, Kathy (2004) *Radio Active: Advertising and Consumer Activism*, Berkeley, CA: University of California Press.

Polanyi, Karl (1944) *Great Transformations: The Political and Economic Origins of Our Times*, Boston, MA: Beacon Press.

Radice, Hugo (1982) 'The national economy: a Keynesian myth?', *Capital and Class*, 22: 111–40.

Rose, Nikolas (1999) *Powers of Freedom: Reframing Political Thought*, Cambridge: Cambridge University Press.

Ruggie, John Gerard (1982) 'International regimes, transactions and change: embedded liberalism in the post-war economic order', *International Organization*, 36(2): 379–415.

Rupert, Mark (2000) *Ideologies of Globalization: Contending Visions of a New World Order*, London: RIPE/Routledge.

—— (2006) *Globalization and International Political Economy: The Politics of Alternative Futures*, Oxford: Rowman and Littlefield.

Steffek, Jens (2006) *Embedded Liberalism and Its Critics: Justifying Global Governance in the American Century*, London: Palgrave Macmillan.

Stole, Inger L. (2001) 'The advertising industry goes to war with America: critics and the fight over the excess profits tax during the Second World War', in Charles R. Taylor (ed.) *Proceedings of the 2001 Conference of the American Academy of Advertising*, New York: American Academy of Advertising, pp. 90–97.

Walters, William (2004) 'Some critical notes on "governance" ', *Studies in Political Economy*, 73: 25–42.

4   The culture of money doctoring

American financial advising in Latin America during the 1940s[1]

Eric Helleiner

How has culture constituted political economic practices historically? This chapter addresses this question with reference to one of the more enduring aspects of North–South economic relations over the past century: the extension of international financial advisory missions to poorer countries. Most scholarly literature on these missions has examined the activities of foreign 'money doctors' with conventional political economy questions in mind, e.g. what were their economic and political goals, and whose interests were served (e.g. Drake 1989, 1994; Flandreau 2003; Woods 2006)? A recent exception, however, can be found in Emily Rosenberg's (2003) important study of US financial advisors in Latin America in the 1900–30 period: *Financial Missionaries to the World*. One of the central themes in her work is that the activities of US money doctors in this era cannot be fully understood without examining how they were culturally constituted. One influence was that of the 'mass culture' of American society as a whole at the time. Equally if not more important, however, was the significance of the more specific culture of experts involved in financial advising; a culture that embodied the kinds of socially acquired dispositions that is perhaps closer to Bourdieu's (1977) concept of 'habitus.'[2]

In this chapter, I reinforce Rosenberg's thesis by carrying the argument forward historically. I examine a much-neglected episode in US international financial advising history that took place during the 1940s vis-à-vis Latin America. The episode is particularly significant because US financial advisors in this period developed an entirely new approach to money doctoring that contrasted with the better known US financial advisory missions from the pre-1930s period in personnel, content and style. There is no doubt that this new approach served changing US strategic and economic goals at the time. But echoing Rosenberg, I will try to show that cultural shifts – both among both expert groups and broader American society – also constituted this change in important ways.

In so doing, I aim not just to highlight how traditional political economy scholarship can be enriched by devoting greater attention to the role of culture in shaping political economic practices. My goal is also to encourage the field of 'cultural political economy' to recognize how distinct cultural influences can exist simultaneously, and reinforce each other, at different levels. In more specific historical terms, the chapter is also designed to reinforce the argument made by

Rob Aitken in Chapter 3 that IPE scholars need to recognize the importance of the cultural content of the post-war era of 'embedded liberalism.' Aitken focuses on culture as a 'technology' – the form of an emerging professional visual arts sector – which helped to constitute the new 'embedded' conceptions of the economy. In this chapter, I highlight the cultural influences on political economic practices of embedded liberalism emerging from both mass society and expert economist circles.

The era of dollar diplomacy: two cultural influences

Rosenberg's book examines how the first generation of US international money doctors emerged in the context of the country's 'dollar diplomacy' in the 1900–30 period. In her words, 'dollar diplomacy' describes 'the process of arranging loans in exchange for some kind of financial supervision' (Rosenberg 2003: 2). In some places, beginning with the Philippines, this kind of financial supervision took place in the context of US colonial rule. In other locations, independent governments in Latin America and elsewhere invited well-known US economists to advise them on various financial and monetary reforms. The advice of these US money doctors – including Charles Conant, Jeremiah Jenks and most famously Edwin Kemmerer – was very similar in each context. In the fiscal realm, they pushed for the adoption of strict accounting practices and administrative rationalization. In the monetary spheres, they recommended that currencies be tied to the gold standard and managed automatically by an independent central bank or currency board.

US financial advisory missions in this period certainly served some broader US economic and strategic goals. Encouraging fiscal reforms and the spread of the gold standard abroad helped US businesses that were expanding internationally at a rapid pace by creating a more stable financial and monetary environment. When countries held gold reserves in New York, US financial interests also benefited and the city's standing as an international financial center was bolstered. Dollar diplomacy was also linked more generally to the expansion of US political influence abroad, particularly in Latin America.

In Rosenberg's view, US money doctoring in this era was also linked to two broad cultural influences. The first was the emergence of a 'professional-managerial discourse' among financial experts, many of whom were professional economists. The discourse drew on neoclassical liberal economic ideas that emphasized the national and international benefits of self-regulating markets and the spread of free trade and international investment. But it was more than an economic ideology. The discourse was part of a broader cultural framework involving 'faith in professionalism' (Rosenberg 2003: 187) and 'emphasizing masculine duty, objectivity, and civilization' (2003: 260).

Rosenberg argues that, for these experts, the liberal economic advice offered in financial advisory work was a scientific truth and part of a civilizing mission bringing modern progress to 'backward' regions of the world. Most of the money doctors began their careers in the US colonial service (especially in the

Philippines), and they 'considered US imperialism to be a benevolent carrier of science and civilization that would uplift backward economies and people' (Rosenberg 2003: 24). They believed, in Rosenberg's words, that 'financial expertise was a universal and scientific product' (2003: 194). The advice offered was thus almost identical in each context they encountered. As Paul Drake notes, 'hardly a word in his [Kemmerer's] reports varied from Poland to Bolivia. In purely technical terms, he could have delivered most of his laws by mail' (1989: 25).

In their view, the spread of markets would bring not just prosperity but also individual freedom and moral progress in the form of greater individual discipline, regularity and responsibility. Rosenberg argues that these latter values were closely linked to Victorian middle class conceptions of masculinity wherein the strength of individual character was defined in terms of self-control and self-mastery. Indeed, one of the key attributes Kemmerer looked for when hiring people for his missions was whether they were 'manly.' As Rosenberg puts it, 'his science of economics and his commitment to bringing orderly financial systems to what he viewed as disorganized, profligate territories inscribed his convictions about moral behavior and its gendered assumptions' (2003: 35). More generally, she argues:

> Gender distinctions had symbolic links to the emerging political economy that was to be organized by dollar diplomacy. Just as manhood implied restrained self-mastery, and supervision over dependents, uncivilized peoples were marked by feminine attributes, especially lack of planning and weak self-discipline. Against the moral and financial effeminacy of unbacked, inflating paper money could be set the manly, civilizing force of a gold standard, careful regulation of a national banking system, and supervised revenue collection and expenditure.
>
> (2003: 33–4)

This culture of neoclassical liberal economics intersected with a 'fascination with primitivism' (Rosenberg 2003: 219) in broader US society in this period. In the general popular culture, peoples in Latin America and other poorer regions were often portrayed as exotically primitive. These images were frequently heavily racialized and gendered. For example, some of the leading US university textbooks on Latin America in this period stressed the importance of the racial mix of each country in explaining their relative political stability and economic situation. More broadly, Rosenberg argues:

> mass culture provided images of feminized and subordinated primitives. Primitivism – with its tropes of race, gender, and nature – reinforced the naturalness of hierarchical financial arrangements and, like the standardized programs of financial advising itself, helped project the image of peripheral areas of the world as undifferentiated others.
>
> (2003: 260)

By the 1920s, there was a growing support for the idea that culture was malleable rather than biologically determined. But the same distinction between primitive culture and civilization remained, and Rosenberg argues that it continued to provide justification for financial supervisory missions. In her words, 'the proof that culture was malleable; that race was not destiny; and that the modern mind could be successfully introduced to backward people were all themes that pervaded the rhetoric of dollar diplomacy' (2003: 207). Summing up, Rosenberg concludes:

> As US investments and expertise spread to the world, financial advisory relationships both shaped and were shaped by two highly representational systems. The first, finance, emphasized masculinized duty, control and objectivity; the second, mass culture, provided images of primitive, subordinated, and feminized settings in which nature met the forces of civilization.
>
> (2003: 217)

Is Rosenberg's cultural political economy approach useful in understanding and explaining other episodes of international money doctoring? It is tempting to apply it to the recent period since a number of scholars have drawn parallels between pre-1930s US money doctoring missions and those of the IMF and World Bank during the past two decades. It is certainly true that financial advisory missions from these international institutions have often promoted free market advice that is similar in some respect to that in the earlier period. Have changing cultural contexts reinforced the revival of this kind of money doctoring activity in the recent context?

Instead of trying to answer this question, I attempt to demonstrate the potential usefulness of Rosenberg's approach in a different manner. Rather than looking for parallels to the pre-1930s period, I examine an important, but much-neglected, *discontinuity* in the practice of international money doctoring. During the 1940s, the US government launched a series of financial advisory missions to Latin America that differed dramatically from those of the pre-1930s period. After describing these missions briefly, I argue they cannot be fully explained without reference to some broader cultural shifts in both expert and mass culture.

A new kind of money doctoring: US financial advising in the 1940s

The first US financial advisory mission to Latin America during the 1940s was sent to Cuba in 1941–2. It was, in fact, the first such mission since Kemmerer's missions of the 1920s, and it was immediately apparent that its content and style would be very different. To begin with, the mission was staffed not by private economists, but rather by government officials. It was led by Harry Dexter White from the US Treasury and included other Treasury officials as well as some staff from Federal Reserve Board.

The mission's recommendations were also very different. In its final report, the mission advocated a complete overhaul of the Cuban monetary system. At the time, Cuba had no central bank and its monetary system was dominated by the use of US dollars. The Cuban government was now advised to de-dollarize and create a new government-controlled central bank. The latter was to be empowered not just to act as a lender of last resort, but also to lend to the government and to conduct a more activist monetary policy aimed more at domestic needs rather than solely at maintaining the external balance. The US advisors also recommended the creation of a stabilization fund to help protect the stability of the Cuban currency, and even allowed for the use of exchange rate adjustments and foreign exchange controls to correct payments imbalances (American Technical Mission to Cuba 1942).

Most of these recommendations would have been seen as rather heretical by Kemmerer and his associates in the pre-1930s period. They had recommended independent central banks with limited powers and whose primary purpose was that of maintaining the convertibility of the currency into gold at a fixed rate. The advice given to the Cuban mission provoked strong opposition from New York bankers and the banking community – composed of both Americans and Cubans – within Cuba (a group whose membership on the US technical mission had been explicitly rejected by the State Department). The mission's advice was also questioned by the newly appointed and conservative US Ambassador, Spruille Braden, whose views were subsequently overruled (US Government 1963: 296–315; 1962: 128–33, 191–5, 302–11; Braden 1971: 305–6).[3]

It soon became clear that White's Cuban mission was no exception. Around the time of the Cuban mission, another request for US financial advice came from Paraguay, a country that also lacked a central bank and had a monetary system dominated by foreign (primarily Argentine) currency. Paraguay at this time was headed by a government strongly committed to a statist economic program aimed at pursuing nationalist objectives. US officials once again accommodated these sentiments by recommending similar, if not even more ambitious, reforms as had the White mission – reforms that were then implemented between 1943 and 1945. They argued that Paraguay needed to create a new national currency and a government-controlled central bank that could lend to the government and manage the currency in an activist manner to serve domestic goals. External imbalances were to be corrected primarily with the help of exchange controls, and exchange rate adjustments would also be permitted in exceptional circumstances.

This mission was led by Robert Triffin, the new chief of the Latin American section of the staff of the Federal Reserve's Board of Governors, who explicitly rejected – using much stronger language than White – the monetary ideas of past US money doctors to Latin America, such as Edwin Kemmerer, as outdated. In his Paraguayan recommendations and other publications at this time, Triffin (1944, 1946), argued forcefully that the interwar experience had clearly demonstrated the need for Latin American countries to move beyond liberal monetary orthodoxy. Kemmerer's central banks had pursued a passive monetary policy that responded automatically to changes in the balance of payments. In Triffin's view, this monetary automatism was too costly and disruptive to the domestic economy given the vulnerability of Latin American countries to sudden changes in their balance of payments due to such developments as crop failures, changes in export markets, or volatile capital movements.

What was needed, in Triffin's view, was a new form of monetary management that insulated the national economy from international disruptions and focused on domestic goals, particularly those of promoting national economic development and industrialization. These objectives required not just the use of exchange controls, adjustable exchange rate pegs, and the abolition of the rigid link between the national monetary supply and the country's gold and foreign exchange reserves. They also required the establishment of central banks equipped with strong powers to promote national economic development in an activist manner. Kemmerer had assumed Latin American central banks would influence the national monetary supply via open market operations and discount rate changes. But Triffin noted that these tools were ineffective in Latin America because domestic financial markets were underdeveloped and the banking system was dominated by foreign banks that responded primarily to monetary developments in their home country. In this context, central banks needed to be empowered to impose reserve requirements on private banks and to control private lending, and perhaps even lend directly to the public. Central bank lending to the public might also be useful, Triffin argued, in the promotion of specific development projects that foreign banks refused to finance. And of course the introduction of a new domestic and activist focus for monetary policy required the creation of a national currency in countries where foreign currency had previously dominated the monetary supply, such as Paraguay and Cuba.

The Paraguayan reforms attracted attention across the region and quickly came to be seen as a model for reforms elsewhere. Invitations soon streamed into the Federal Reserve Board for Triffin's advisory services. He took up many of the invitations, including those which involved major monetary and central bank reforms such as Guatemala (1945–6) and the Dominican Republic (1945–7). In these later cases, the local governments specifically requested that Triffin 'do the somewhat the same sort of job for them as he did for Paraguay.'[4] The significance of the Paraguayan reform also attracted attention outside of Latin America and Federal Reserve advisors soon found themselves overseeing monetary reforms based on the new model in countries such as Ceylon (1950), South Korea (1950) and the Philippines (1949). Triffin himself did not participate in these later missions; he left the Federal Reserve Board in July 1946 to work at the IMF. But his ideas continued to be influential on these and other missions to Latin American countries in the late 1940s and early 1950s. In Korea, for example, US officials noted that their advice was 'adhering rather closely to the so-called Triffin pattern.'[5] In the Latin American context, the leadership of the Federal Reserve activities passed to David Grove after Triffin's departure, and he adhered closely to Triffin's line of thinking until his departure in the early 1950s.[6]

The Triffin missions in the 1940s differed from those of the pre-1930s period not just in terms of their personnel and content but also in their style. The advice of Kemmerer and his colleagues rarely differed from country to country, and their recommendations were usually presented as a *fait accompli* to the local governments. By contrast, Triffin went out of his way to highlight how his advice was differentiated and tailored specifically to each unique situation. For example, in explaining why his proposals for the Dominican Republic differed from those for Guatemala, he told a Dominican official: 'They are due to the very different circumstances of the two countries. You know that I do not believe that the same legislation can serve as a passkey for every country in Latin America.'[7]

Triffin also went out of his way to consult not just with local officials but also with leading monetary thinkers across Latin America. He was keen to contrast his willingness to learn from Latin American experience with Kemmerer's approach in the 1920s when, as he put it, 'orthodox, but thoroughly alien, central banking reform attempted to transplant bodily in La Paz or Quito the monetary and banking mechanisms of older financial centers.' Triffin insisted that his proposals would 'no longer be mere copies of foreign legislation. Every effort will be made to adapt them to regional needs and conditions and to profit from the experience accumulated by central banks in the 'twenties, 'thirties and early 'forties.'[8] To this end, Triffin devoted considerable time to the study of the experience of Latin American central banks that had experimented with unorthodox policies during the 1930s such as exchange controls, activist monetary policies, and central bank involvement in agricultural and industrial project financing. He quickly gained a detailed understanding of these policy innovations and was keen to acknowledge their influence on his thinking.

Particularly important and interesting was his willingness to learn from and consult with Raúl Prebisch who was one of the best known monetary thinkers in Latin America at the time. Prebisch was already a strong advocate at this time of state-supported industrialization that might help Latin American countries escaping the declining terms of trade associated with agricultural exports.[9] In the monetary sphere, he argued in an unpublished 1943 book proposal for an activist monetary policy that was devoted to three main tasks: (1) preventing volatile business cycles that were provoked by the impact of foreign trade and fluctuating agricultural prices; (2) promoting development and full employment; and (3) fostering rapid economic growth and industrialization. At the core of Prebisch's monetary thought was a commitment to national policy autonomy: 'To resist subordination of the national economy to foreign movements and contingencies, we must develop inward, strengthen our internal structure, and achieve autonomous functioning of our economy' (quoted in Dosman 2001: 90).

After meeting in Mexico, Prebisch and Triffin quickly struck up a close personal friendship characterized by mutual intellectual respect.[10] Triffin frequently cited his debt to Prebisch's 'pioneering work' in his publications (e.g. Triffin 1966: 141fn2). Triffin went further than just drawing on Prebisch's ideas in his own work. He also invited Prebisch to assist him on various Federal Reserve Board financial missions, including the all-important Paraguayan mission. Prebisch spent three months in Paraguay in early 1945 during which he helped draft legislation for the new central bank and reforms of exchange control regulations. Prebisch was also very supportive of Triffin's final Paraguayan report, and suggested that it heralded the start of a new era in US–Latin American relations.[11]

The Federal Reserve Board's archives contain many other examples of Triffin's efforts to consult with and learn from other Latin American policymakers and thinkers. In contrast to Kemmerer and his associates, Triffin was constantly asking for advice and comments on his ideas from local experts and authorities. He often discussed the ideas of Hermann Max, a Chilean economist who endorsed domestically oriented monetary policy, exchange rate adjustments and direct lending to the public by central banks. Max had advised Costa Rica (1936), Venezuela (1939) and Nicaragua (1940) on monetary reforms, and Triffin felt his proposals were 'better adapted to the basic economy and financial characteristics of the countries involved' than Kemmerer's initiatives in the 1920s which had been 'characterized by their extreme conventionality and rigidity.'[12] He also corresponded frequently with Victor Urquidi, an official at the Bank of Mexico who was emerging as a leader thinker in this area. In addition, Triffin pushed successfully for the Federal Research Board to hire Latin Americans into its Latin American research division, including Prebisch's Harvard-trained first cousin Julio Gonzales Del Solar.[13]

Further evidence of a new attitude among US financial advisers was the fact that they sought to encourage more intra-Latin American exchanges of financial expertise of the kind that Prebisch had offered to the Paraguayan government.[14] Their rationale was that Latin American policymakers often could learn much more from each other than they could from US officials. This goal was present from the start in the Paraguayan mission when Triffin invited not just Prebisch but also a Bank of Colombia official Enrique Davila to assist the US mission. Arrangements were then made to send Paraguayan officials on a training mission to Costa Rica to study the administration of that country's central bank.

Explaining the new approach to money doctoring

The US financial advisory missions of the 1940s thus represented a dramatic departure from those of the pre-1930s period in personnel, content and style. How do we explain this departure? A more conventional political economy focus on changing US interests is clearly important. Since the late 1930s, US officials had become increasingly concerned about growing Nazi economic and military influence in the region. They also increasingly sought to offset the growing influence of Latin American 'revolutionary nationalism' (Green 1971).[15] In the wake of the Great Depression, liberal regimes across Latin America were increasingly challenged by domestic political groups – on the right and left of the political spectrum – who rejected the *laissez-faire*, export-oriented economic policies of the pre-1930s era in favor of more statist economic policies that promoted industrialization, the growth of an internal market, national ownership, and better social conditions (e.g. Rock 1994). Some aspects of this trend of Latin American economic policy clearly threatened US economic interests in the region, as dramatic developments such as Bolivian and Mexican confiscation of US oil property in 1937 and 1938 highlighted well.

From the perspective of US government and business elites, it became increasingly important for the US government to endorse a new model of economic cooperation with Latin America to offset both the Nazi influence and the appeal of radical economic ideologies. This included a new commitment to provide financial and technical assistance to Latin American governments that could help diminish German influence, promote political and economic stability, secure investments, and cultivate markets. This program was also explicitly designed to support many of the new 'developmentalist' goals of Latin American governments. While rejecting radical economic policies, US officials were willing to back moderate economic nationalist objectives of using targeted state intervention to support industrialization and other domestic economic and social goals.

The financial advisory missions were clearly part of this policy shift. Their advocates and participants were very clear that the missions served broader US strategic and economic objectives in the region. Federal Reserve officials had called attention to the role that financial missions to Latin America could play in bolstering US influence in Latin American as far back as mid-1939 and they reiterated it frequently thereafter.[16] Triffin's all-important Paraguayan mission was also strongly backed by the State Department on the grounds that it would help counter German influence in the country. The Paraguayan government at the time was strongly devoted to a nationalist economic program, and Triffin's recommendations fit perfectly with the government's broader economic objectives. Accommodating and supporting Paraguayan economic nationalism helped to cultivate a Paraguayan–US political alliance.[17]

As the German threat diminished by the end of the war, Federal Reserve officials continued to see their Latin American research and financial advisory missions as a way to increase US influence and prestige in the region. They also felt that the missions served many US economic interests. Although they might have been unpopular with some US financial interests, they benefited other US groups economically by promoting monetary and financial stability abroad, and by creating more diversified economies in Latin America which could boost US exports, particularly in capital equipment.

Although changing interests help to explain the new US financial missions, my reading of the evidence has led to me to the conclusion that they do not offer a complete explanation. In particular, I would like to suggest that the missions cannot be fully understood without reference to two cultural shifts paralleling those described by Rosenberg: one at the level of expert culture and the other in mass culture.

The culture of Keynesianism

The first key change was the Keynesian revolution in the professional economics community. This revolution is usually portrayed primarily as a shift in economic ideology. To be sure, this aspect of the Keynesian revolution was enormously significant. It undermined the neoclassical liberal faith in free markets and gave birth to a whole new branch of economic inquiry: macroeconomics. At the international level, it also encouraged the emergence of what Ruggie (1982) has called an embedded liberal ideology which sought to reconcile the nineteenth-century liberal belief in an open multilateral economic order with a new commitment to domestic interventionist economics.

But the Keynesian revolution also involved a broader cultural shift in the economics profession. Keynes made clear that his thought was rooted in the broader philosophical culture of the Bloomsbury group with which he was closely associated. The Bloomsbury group forcefully rejected many of the values of the Victorian age that Kemmerer and his associates held in such high regard. In addition to Victorian conceptions of appropriate masculinity, this included what Keynes called its 'Benthamite' economism.

Keynes's willingness to challenge orthodox thinking also stemmed from what Kirshner calls his 'extraordinary pragmatism.' In contrast to the pre-1930s US money doctors, Keynes was deeply skeptical of claims of universal truths. In Kirshner's (2007) words, he would 'consider each problem with fresh eyes' and he seemed to delight in the challenge of orthodox beliefs if they did not make sense in a new empirical reality. His willingness to experiment intellectually, and to see theory and practice as reciprocally inter-related, infused Keynesianism with a spirit of pragmatism.

Finally, by his example, Keynes encouraged economists to see themselves as engaged professionals serving the common good through public service. As Parker (2005: 96) puts it, 'Keynes presented a model of the economist as an engaged and political purposive intellectual.' In the context of the economic chaos of the 1930s, this model was important. Many neoclassical economists advocated inaction during the Great Depression, arguing that markets would eventually clear. But Keynes, particularly after the publication of the *General Theory*, gave economists a sense that something could be done through public action (Parker 2005: 86). In this way, as Hirschman (1995: 151) contends, Keynes 'raised public-spiritness' and his followers infused into government 'a spirit of energetic dedication to public service and accomplishment.'[18]

These aspects of Keynesianism encouraged a cultural shift in the economics profession, particularly among younger economists who were beginning their careers during and after the Great Depression. It is from this generation that the US financial advisors to Latin America were drawn. Scholars who have examined the spread of the Keynesian revolution to the US in the late 1930s and 1940s have identified the US Treasury and the US Federal Reserve as the government agencies that were the earliest and deepest affected (Hirschman 1995; Salant 1989). Many of the Keynesians in these government agencies were also linked to Harvard University's economics department which had emerged, in Galbraith's words, as 'the principal avenue by which Keynes's ideas passed to the United States' (1972: 49).[19] The key figures associated with Latin American financial advising emerged from these Harvard–Treasury–Federal Reserve circles.

We have seen how the Treasury, initially under White's leadership and then the Federal Reserve under Triffin, took the lead role in the money doctoring movement. Both White and Triffin also did their PhDs at Harvard, and were associated with many of those at the university who were seeking to challenge liberal orthodoxy. So too did many other economists involved in Latin American financial advising, including even many of the key Latin American economists such as Prebisch. Triffin also made special efforts to recruit other Harvard economists to the Latin American research division throughout his tenure.[20]

The impact of Keynesianism on the Latin American money doctors can be seen at both the level of economic ideas and at the level of deeper culture. With respect to the former, the content of the economic advice offered to Latin American governments was very much in keeping with embedded liberal thought. As we have seen, US money doctors placed a high priority on the defense of national policy autonomy in order to enable Latin American governments to pursue domestic interventionist policies. Indeed, they explicitly saw the reforms they promoted as helping to boost the overall embedded liberal economic values of the Bretton Woods system being constructed at this time. Ruggie suggests that the embedded liberal ideology of Bretton Woods was designed to protect the welfare state and Keynesian macroeconomic planning, both of which had emerged prominent in rich countries in the wake of the Great Depression. In the Latin American context, however, the domestic interventionist practices that had emerged from the 1930s consisted of state-led developmentalist policies.

The distinction was brought out well by Prebisch who was one of the first Latin American economists to recognize the Keynesian revolution, and published the first Spanish language introduction in Latin America to Keynes' *General Theory* in 1947 (Ferrer 1990; FitzGerald 1994: 96). At the core of his Prebisch's monetary thought was a commitment to national policy autonomy, as noted above. This commitment to policy autonomy echoed that of Keynes, but the two men's respective rationales for policy autonomy were somewhat different. Prebisch was in fact quite critical of the fact that Keynes had ignored the distinct circumstances and difficulties facing poorer agricultural exporting countries. In Prebisch's view, 'policy autonomy' was needed in these countries not to protect a kind of Keynesian welfare state but rather to enable state-supported industrialization and economic development to take place without tight external constraints.

The US officials involved in financial advisory work were initially hardly experts on state-led developmentalist economics. But we have seen how Triffin and others showed a strong willingness to learn from Latin American experience and knowledge to develop some innovative ideas in this field. Their willingness to do so, I believe, was linked to the deeper Keynesian culture.

Triffin provides the most prominent example of a figure who brought this Keynesian culture to the Latin American work. In advising Latin American governments, he rejected what Keynes had called Benthamite economism, embracing the idea that economic policy might serve broader nation-building goals rather than simply economic gain. He was also deeply committed to the role of the economist as a public activist. As he later put it, 'Economists are citizens and cannot elude their responsibility to participate in the democratic process' (Triffin 1981). He also displayed a remarkable pragmatism, citing Keynes as a model in this respect:

> policy-oriented economic analysis should obviously be based on a correct appraisal of the assumptions most relevant to the problem at hand, rather than on assumptions far remote from the facts of the case and whose only merit is to lend themselves more easily to abstract mathematical, so called econometric, reasoning. This made the greatness of Keynes.
>
> (Triffin 1981: 248–9)

Triffin's pragmatism manifested itself not just in his humility and willingness to learn from Latin American experience and knowledge vis-à-vis state-led development policies. It was also apparent in the manner in which he went out of his way, Keynes-like, to trumpet the unorthodox nature of the new monetary and central banking laws, describing them as 'revolutionary' (Triffin 1946: 25) and 'a fundamental departure from the central banking structures previously established in Latin America' (US Federal Reserve 1945: 528).

The culture of the new deal and the good neighbor policy

The second important cultural shift involved a shift in mass American culture in the context of the New Deal. Several aspects of the New Deal were significant in this respect. The first was what Rosenberg calls its 'anti-banker discourse.' This discourse had long historical roots in US society on both the left and right of the political spectrum. It associated money and banking with greed, corruption and exploitation instead of with progress, efficiency and civilization, as had been the case in the 'professional-managerial' discourse of the dollar diplomacy era. During the 1920s, Rosenberg describes how critics of dollar diplomacy increasingly drew on this anti-banker discourse to argue that the policy was driven by greedy financiers and associated with imperialism, militarism and exploitation. The growing influence of these views encouraged the US government increasingly to distance itself from direct involvement in money doctoring missions in the 1920s.

It was with the arrival of the New Deal, however, that this discourse achieved its greatest influence and prominence. Rosenberg (2003: 150) notes how 'suspicion of bankers ... became a dominant political and cultural motif in some of the rhetoric and programs of the early New Deal.' Many New Dealers saw the New York financial elite as having contributed to the Great Depression. They also felt a sense of solidarity with Latin America because they saw it as having been the victim of the same US financial elite that they blamed for the US's economic troubles. This latter connection had been highlighted particularly by the 1933 Pecora hearings which had mandated by the Senate to investigate the nefarious lending practices of New York financiers during the 1920s. The hearings attracted widespread and sympathetic attention within the US, and they devoted considerable attention to the Latin American loans of that era. Pecora's final report portrayed the bankers as greedy and corrupt, and concluded that 'foreign securities is one of the most scandalous chapters in the history of American investment banking' (quoted in Rosenberg 2003: 252).

During the era of dollar diplomacy, Americans had generally attributed Latin America's economic problems to Latin Americans themselves. Their poverty was a function of their 'primitivism.' In the wake of the Depression, however, many Americans identified more with the Latin American economic plight. As mass poverty became a domestic US reality, there was what Frederick Pike (1995: 19) calls a kind of 'Latin Americanization' of the US that encouraged Americans to see Latin America's poverty in a whole new light. Latin America was no longer to be looked down upon but rather now seen as an equal victim of financial and corporate elites. In this context, many Americans welcomed an opportunity to correct past wrongs in US economic relations with the region. In this way, the 'anti-banker' discourse increasingly mixed with an anti-imperialist one.

Reinforcing these shifts was the broad concern for social justice that was the hallmark of the New Deal. The project of extending economic assistance to Latin America provided an opportunity to translate this concern for social justice onto the international stage. As Roosevelt famously noted in early 1940, the new approach to US–Latin American relations was designed to 'give them [Latin America] a share' (quoted in Gardner 1964: 109).

Finally, the broader enthusiasm of the New Deal for political reform that challenged the power of established elites encouraged New Dealers to look sympathetically at many of the political changes in Latin America in the 1930s. The challenges to oligarchic elites and their free market values seemed to parallel many of the reform efforts of the New Deal. As Pike (1995: 53) holds, 'Democratic leaders especially among northern intellectuals could sympathize with and even enthuse over Latin American predilections toward the interventionist state.'

These shifts in mass American culture encouraged a changed approach to US–Latin American relations. In place of dollar diplomacy, enthusiasm grew for what came to be called a 'Good Neighbor' policy. Initially, this phrase symbolized a commitment by the US not to intervene politically and militarily in Latin America. By the late 1930s and early 1940s, however, the Good Neighbor policy came to be associated with the more active idea of a close economic partnership on more equal terms with Latin America, designed to promote economic development in the region. The partnership was driven partly by some economic and strategic goals, as we have seen, but it also reflected this mass cultural shift within US society. Frederick Pike (1995: 33) is the scholar who has highlighted the latter most effectively: 'the Depression produced a virtual revolution in American attitudes [towards Latin America], and that out of this revolution issued the public attitudes that enabled FDR to forge a Good Neighbor policy.'

Although Pike does not analyse the financial advisory missions of the 1940s, they reinforce his thesis about the significance of this shift in American mass culture. Many of the key figures involved were strong exponents of the New Deal.

This was certainly the case with Harry Dexter White who played a central role in reorienting US financial policy towards Latin America in the late 1930s more generally. The clash between the old culture of the dollar diplomacy and that of the New Deal was well evidenced in White's interactions with American conservatives and bankers during the Cuban mission. The latter objected to White's proposals not just on economic grounds but also on the grounds that the Cuban people were not sufficiently ready in a cultural and moral sense to run a central bank properly. White and other New Dealers responded by challenging this perspective as outdated and as representing an attempt to 'to deny to Cuba the sovereignty over these [monetary] matters which is enjoyed by all independent countries' (US Government 1963: 303).

Triffin and many of the other Federal Reserve officials involved in Latin American financial missions also embraced the culture of the New Deal. Triffin himself had little sympathy for the kinds of imperialist attitudes that had encouraged the top-down advisory model of the pre-1930s. As we have seen, he treated Latin American officials more as equals and went out of his way to highlight how much there was to learn from their ideas and experience. He also clearly saw his initiatives as in the spirit of these progressive ideals of the activist Good Neighbor economic policy.[21] In true New Deal fashion, we have seen how he enjoyed challenging the old liberal orthodoxy in international monetary thought. He also rejected Kemmerer's gendered conceptions of who would make an appropriate money doctor and had no hesitation including female economists in his Latin American research division.[22] When in Paraguay, Triffin's colleague Bray Hammond aptly expressed the New Deal perspective on why the US should be helping Latin America at this time. The rationale was 'humanitarian': 'They are not so well off as we, they are victims of a lot of hard luck, their situation is disadvantageous, and it won't hurt us to give them some help.'[23]

More generally, Triffin's political sympathies were with those in Latin America who sought to challenge the old oligarchies and promote democratic social, political and economic reform. He was, for example, particularly enthusiastic about his work for the newly elected reformist government of Juan José Arévalo in Guatemala in 1945 which came to power after the ousting of a dictator.[24] By contrast, he disliked his stay in Bolivia, where he noted: 'I have never met anywhere such an extreme contrast between wealth and destitution. ... The government seems to be in the hands of the foreign mining companies and graft is open and insolent.'[25] His Federal Reserve colleague Bray Hammond similarly lamented how the Bolivians 'to us appeared dominated by a harsh and brutal spirit of anti-social exploitation.' Hammond continued: 'The central bank is run to make money, and there seems to be no sense of public responsibility.'[26]

Triffin and other Federal Reserve Board officials also saw the financial advisory missions as yet one more part of their struggle against the power of the traditional New York financial elite. One of the key reforms of the New Deal had been to assert greater centralized political control over both private financial firms and the privately owned Reserve Banks of the Federal Reserve System, especially the powerful FRBNY. With the Banking Act 1935, the locus of power within the Federal Reserve System had shifted decisively to the Washington-based Federal Reserve Board whose members were all appointed by the US president. Federal Reserve Board officials saw the Latin American missions as a way to 'strengthen its [the Board's] own position in international affairs and in this country'[27] and they actively resisted efforts by the FRBNY to take the lead on these missions.

Like White, Triffin sometimes encountered resistance from individuals who retained the 'old' mass cultural attitudes towards Latin America. In objecting to Triffin's ideas, people such as the head of the FRBNY, Allan Sproul, expressed concern about the kind of advice offered by Triffin, arguing that it would be unfortunate 'to recommend and devise monetary and banking legislation which, though fitted to a country's economic situation, is beyond the administrative competence and integrity of its people.'[28] The US ambassador to Paraguay during the early 1940s also expressed a negative view of the capabilities of Paraguayans. In one 10-page memo, he outlined a very negative view of the character of the people, advising all US policymakers to be aware of their 'peculiar psychology,' including traits such as 'indomitability,' 'refractariness' and 'belligerency,' which he attributed partly to their race.[29] Back in Washington, officials skeptical of this kind of analysis and its 'rather gloomy view of the people there' wondered whether some of these traits simply reflected 'their [the Paraguayans'] resentment at our assumption that we do know just how and for what purposes the money we are willing to lend them should be spent.' They called for an overhaul of 'our whole conception of economic cooperation,' an approach that Triffin's much more open-minded and generous view of the capabilities of Paraguayans subsequently provided.[30]

Conclusion

To sum up, my analysis of US financial advising missions to Latin America during the 1940s has led me to a very similar conclusion as that reached by Emily Rosenberg: that the study of financial advisory missions is enriched by a 'cultural political economy' approach. The dramatic change that took place during the 1940s in the nature of US money doctoring, I have suggested, was linked not just to changing US strategic and economic interests. Also important were cultural shifts among both expert groups and broader American society. Regarding the former, the Keynesian revolution ushered in an expert culture that embraced public activism, non-economic values, pragmatism and intellectual innovation in ways that were quite distinct from the expert culture that Rosenberg shows influenced the earlier generation of US money doctors. At the broader societal level, the mass culture of the New Deal substituted the concept of the US as a 'good neighbor' for the 'primitivist' discourse that Rosenberg suggests had informed US attitudes towards Latin America in the pre-1930s era.

If culture shaped political economic practices in this episode, it is important to recognize the two distinct realms of culture involved. The first – that of mass culture – is the more familiar. But equally if not more important was the culture of experts. Within traditional political economy literature, Keynesianism is usually portrayed primarily as a new set of economic ideas. However, I am suggesting that it also involved an important shift in the culture of professional economic discourse and practice. This shift, I believe, influenced not just domestic policy but also US foreign economic policy towards Latin America during the 1940s. It fostered a kind of money doctoring that was quite distinct not just from that of Kemmerer but also from that of the more recent neoliberal 'Chicago boys' in the 1970s and 1980s. The culture of Keynesianism encouraged Triffin and other 'Harvard boys' during the 1940s to pioneer a model for international financial advising that was much less rigid in both its style and content. In this way, the culture of Keynesianism reinforced the impact of mass cultural shifts in US society associated with the New Deal.

The combination of these cultural influences played an important role in fostering a new kind of US foreign economic policy, a policy that is characterized well by Ruggie's phrase 'embedded liberalism.' In his chapter for this volume, Rob Aitken (Chapter 3) highlights how Ruggie's analysis neglects the cultural content of embedded liberalism. My analysis certainly reinforces this point. At the same time, I have also shown how Ruggie's analysis has wider significance than he initially acknowledged. In his pioneering work, Ruggie portrayed the new embedded liberal approach as significant primarily in US postwar economic relations with other advanced industrial countries. This chapter has shown how it had relevance to US–Latin American relations as well.

Notes

1 I am very grateful to the Social Sciences and Humanities Research Council of Canada for helping to support the research on which this chapter draws. I also thank Jacquie Best, Mat Paterson, and all the participants in this workshop for their very helpful comments.
2 Rosenberg herself does not invoke Bourdieu's concept.
3 In the end, domestic opposition from the banking community within Cuba prevented the recommendations from being implemented until 1948.
4 These are Gardner's words describing the views of a Dominican government representative in: Gardner to Governor Szymczak, May 12, 1945, p. 1, US National Archives Record Group (RG) 82, ISF, Box 221, File: 'Foreign Missions, Dominican Republic (1945).'
5 'Meeting of Staff Group on Foreign Interests' May 1, 1950, p. 11, RG82, ISF, Box 215, File: 'Foreign and International Problems, Minutes and Agenda, March–June 1950.'
6 See for example David Grove 'The Potentialities of Monetary Policy in the Economic Development of Latin America,' June 18, 1951, RG82, ISF, Box 156, File: 'Latin America, General (June 1946–54)'; and David Grove, 'Objectives and Potentialities of Monetary Policy in Underdeveloped Countries' Feb 18, 1952, RG82 ISF, Box 20 'File: Banking Central Bank Conference, Havana, Cuba – 1952.'
7 Triffin to Alfonso Rochac, Jan. 7, 1946, p. 1, RG82, ISF, Box 221, File: 'Foreign Missions, Dominican Republic (1946–54).'
8 Robert Triffin, 'Address to the Pan American Society on Recent Monetary and Exchange Developments in Latin America' April 11, 1945, p. 2, 14, RG82, ISF, Box 156, File: 'Latin America, General (1943–May 1946).'

9   This aspect of Prebisch's thinking is often associated with his later career as head of ECLA after 1949, but Dosman (2001) shows that he had already developed this core idea in the early 1940s.

10 I am grateful to Ed Dosman for this point. For example, Triffin reported that his wife 'wishes me to express again our gratitude and friendship to you and Adelita. We feel that we have few friends that we like and appreciate as much as the two of you and we hope fervently that circumstances will again unite us in the near future,' Triffin to Prebisch, July 23, 1945, p. 4, RG82, ISF, File: 'Paraguay, Monetary and Banking reform.'

11 Prebisch to Triffin, June 17, 1945, p. 2, RG82, ISF, Box 162, File: 'Paraguay, Monetary and Banking Reform.' Triffin was very appreciative, thanking Prebisch 'for the nicest letter I have received in a very long time'; Triffin to Prebisch, July 23, 1945, p. 1, RG82 ISF, File: 'Paraguay, Monetary and Banking Reform.'

12 Triffin to Gardner, April 9, 1943, p. 1, RG82 ISF, Box 162, File: 'Paraguay, Monetary and Banking Reform.'

13 Triffin to Manuel Noriega Morales, Jan 29, 1946, RG82, ISF, Box 138, File: 'Guatemala, Monetary and Banking Reform (1945–June 15, 1946)'; Triffin to Szymczak, 'Work of the Latin American Group and Personnel Needs,' Feb 6, 1945, RG82 ISF, Box 264, File: 'International Training Program General 1938–Aug 1945.'

14 Treasury officials had also supported this idea in 1939 in discussing the virtues of the Inter-American Bank: 'It is likely that in this way Latin American countries will receive more technicians from other Latin American countries rather than from the United States, a step which would be highly desirable in view of the poor record of American advisers in Latin America and especially in view of the ever-present danger that the suggestions of American advisers may become political footballs that rebound to the disadvantage of the United States.' Hanson to White, Dec. 7, 1939, p. 1, RG56, 450/81/02/03, Box 66, File: 'Monetary Inter-American Bank Memoranda. etc. Vol. 1.'

15 For the ideas in this and the next paragraph, see also Gardner (1964), Gellman (1979, 1995), Gilderhus (2000), Grow (1981), Guerrant (1950) and Pike (1995).

16 Gardner to Eccles, May 29, 1939, RG82, ISF, Box 236, File: 'Foreign Missions, General (1922–Feb 1945).' See also Gardner, 'Latin American Field,' May 25, 1943, RG82, ISF, Box 231, File: 'Foreign Missions, Paraguay (1942–Oct. 1943)'; Gardner to Goldenweiser, July 24, 1943, p. 3, RG82, ISF, Box 148, File: 'Latin America 1923–54, Banking, General.'

17 For the State department's recognition of the importance of Triffin's work, see also Hammond to Triffin, June 20, 1944, RG82, ISF, Box 231, File: 'Foreign Missions, Paraguay (June–July 1944).'

18 See also Best and Widmaier (2006).

19 This is not to suggest that the department was uniformly supportive. Indeed, many of the faculty were quite hostile to Keynesianism and the New Deal, leading to a number of deep splits within the department during the 1930s. See Parker (2005: ch. 2).

20 Gardner to Szymczsk 'Tentative Program'; Triffin to Govr Szymczak, 'Work of the Latin American Group and Personnel Needs', Feb 6, 1945, RG82 Intl Subject Files, Box 264 File: International Training Program General 1938–Aug 1945.

21 See especially Triffin to Arthur Schlesinger, May 13, 1946, RG82, ISF, Box 156, File: 'Latin America, General (1943–May 1946).' He had also been sympathetic to center-left reformist movements in Belgium in the 1930s (Triffin 1990).

22 He had hoped to include them in his trips to Paraguay and Brazil, although he encountered resistance to this idea from the Federal Reserve Board; Triffin to Gardner, June 8, 1944, RG82, Intl Subject Files, Box 231, File: Foreign Missions, Paraguay (June–July 1944)-Triffin to Gardner, June 23, 1944, in RG82, Intl Subject Files, Box 231, File: Foreign Missions, Paraguay (June–July 1944). I have not yet been able to determine from the archives the reasons for the Board's resistance. One official did,

however, hint about a concern that their gender might 'constitute a barrier in those [Latin American] countries.' Gardner, 'Latin American Field,' p. 1, May 25, 1943 in RG82 Intl Subject Files, Box 231, File: Foreign Missions, Paraguay (1942–Oct. 1943).
23 Hammond to Govrnor, p. 2 Oct. 18, 1943, in RG82 Intl Subject Files, Box 231, File: Foreign Missions, Paraguay (1942–Oct. 1943).
24 Triffin to Board of Governors, Oct. 2, 1945, RG82, ISF, Box 221, File: 'Foreign Missions, Dominican Republic (1945).' See also Triffin (1990: 28). Gilderhus (2000: 145) notes that the programs of this government were 'reminscent of the New Deal in the United States.'
25 Triffin to Captain Marion Allen Leonard (US Army, Miami Beach), p. 3, Nov. 18, 1943 in RG82, Intl Subject Files, Box 231, File: Foreign Missions, Paraguay (Nov 1943–Feb 1944).
26 Hammond to Governor Szymczak, p. 3, Sept. 9, 1943, in RG82 Intl Subject Files, Box 231, File: Foreign Missions, Paraguay (1942–Oct. 1943).
27 Gardner to Szymcak, Nov. 11, 1943, p. 2, RG82, ISF, Box 231, File: 'Foreign Missions, Paraguay (Nov 1943–Feb 1944).'
28 Sproule to Szymcak, July 13, 1945, RG82, ISF, Box 221, File: 'Foreign Missions, Dominican Republic (1945).' See also O. E. Moore to Sproul, 'Dr. Herman Max', Oct. 29, 1940, RG82 ISF, Box 180, File: 'Venezuela General (1923–54).'
29 Frost to Hull, 'Paraguay's Peculiar Pyschology' Aug. 10, 1942 in Oberlin, Frost Papers, Dept. of State: Messages Sent by Wesley Frost, 1941–42.
30 Philip Bonsal to Mr. Duggan, Aug. 28, 1942 in RG59 250/44/7/7, Box 58, File: Paraguay Jan. 1 through August 1946.

Bibliography

American Technical Mission to Cuba (1942) 'Report to the Cuban government of the American technical mission to Cuba', *Federal Reserve Bulletin*, August: 774–801.
Best, Jacqueline and Wesley Widmaier (2006) 'Micro- or macro-moralities? Economic discourses and policy possibilities', *Review of IPE*, 13(4): 609–31.
Bourdieu, Pierre (1977) *Outline of a Theory of Practice*, Richard Nice (trans.), Cambridge: Cambridge University Press.
Braden, Spruille (1971) *Diplomats and Demagogues*, New Rochelle, NY: Arlington House.
Dosman, Edgar (2001) 'Markets and the state in the evolution of the "Prebisch Manifesto"', *CEPAL Review*, 75: 87–102.
Drake, Paul (1989) *The Money Doctor in the Andes: The Kemmerer Missions 1923–1933*, Durham, NC: Duke University Press.
Drake, Paul (ed.) (1994) *Money Doctors, Foreign Debts and Economic Reforms in Latin America from the 1890s to the Present*, Wilmington, DE: Scholarly Resources.
Ferrer, Aldo (1990) 'The early teaching of Raul Prebisch', *CEPAL Review*, 42: 27–33.
FitzGerald, E. V. K. (1994) 'ECLA and the formation of Latin American economic doctrine', in D. Rock (ed.) *Latin America in the 1940s: War and Postwar Transitions*, Berkeley, CA: University of California Press, pp. 89–108.
Flandreau, Marc (ed.) (2003) *Money Doctors: The Experience of International Financial Advising, 1850–2000*, London: Routledge.
Galbraith, John Kenneth (1972) 'How Keynes came to America', in J. K. Galbraith (ed.) *Economics, Peace and Laughter*, Boston, MA: Houghton Mifflin, pp. 44–56.
Gardner, Lloyd (1964) *Economic Aspects of New Deal Diplomacy*, Madison, WI: University of Wisconsin Press.
Gellman, Irwin (1979) *Good Neighbor Diplomacy: United States Policies in Latin America 1933–1945*, Baltimore, MD: Johns Hopkins University Press.

—— (1995) *Secret Affairs: Franklin Roosevelt, Cordell Hull, and Sumner Welles*, Baltimore, MD: Johns Hopkins University Press.

Gilderhus, Mark (2000) *The Second Century: U.S.–Latin American Relations Since 1889*, Wilmington, DE: Scholarly Resources Inc.

Green, David (1971) *The Containment of Latin America: A History of the Myths and Realities of the Good Neighbor Policy*, Chicago, IL: Quadrangle Books.

Grow, Michael (1981) *The Good Neighbor Policy and Authoritarianism in Paraguay: United States Economic Expansion and Great-Power Rivalry in Latin America During World War II*, Lawrence, KS: Regents Press of Kansas.

Guerrant, Edward (1950) *Roosevelt's Good Neighbor Policy*, Albuquerque, NM: University of New Mexico Press, 1950.

Hirschman, Albert (1995) 'How the Keynesian revolution was exported from the United States', in Albert Hirshman (ed.) *A Propensity to Self-Subversion*, Cambridge, MA: Harvard University Press, pp. 139–153.

Kirshner, Jonathan (2007) 'Keynes, legacies and inquiry', Mimeo.

Parker, Richard (2005) *John Kenneth Galbraith*, Chicago, IL: University of Chicago Press.

Pike, Frederick (1995) *FDR's Good Neighbor Policy*, Austin, TX: University of Texas Press.

Rock, David (1994) 'War and postwar intersections' in D. Rock (ed.) *Latin America in the 1940s: War and Postwar Transitions*, Berkeley, CA: Univeristy of California Press, pp. 15–40.

Rosenberg, Emily (2003) *Financial Missionaries to the World: The Politics and Culture of Dollar Diplomacy 1900–30*, Harvard, MA: Harvard University Press.

Ruggie, John (1982) 'International regimes, transactions and change', *International Organization*, 32: 379–405.

Salant, Walter (1989) 'The spread of Keynesian doctrines and practices in the United States', in P. Hall (ed.) *The Political Power of Economic Ideas: Keynesianism Across Nations*, Princeton, NJ: Princeton University Press, pp. 27–52.

Triffin, Robert (1944) 'Central banking and monetary management in Latin America', in Syemour Harris (ed.) *Economic Problems of Latin America*, New York: McGraw-Hill, pp. 94–108.

—— (1946) *Monetary and Banking Reform in Paraguay*, Washington, DC: Board of Governors of the Federal Reserve System.

—— (1966) 'National central banking and the international economy', (ed.) *The World Money Maze*, New Haven, CT: Yale University Press.

—— (1981) 'An economist's career: what? why? how?' *Banca Nazionale Del Lavoro Quarterly Review*, 138: 239–60.

—— (1990) 'Conversation avec Catherine Ferrant et Jean Sloover', in Catherine Ferrant and Jean Sloover (eds) *Robert Triffin: Conseiller Des Princes*, Brussels: Editions Ciaco, pp. 9–69.

US Federal Reserve (1945) 'Monetary developments in Latin America', *Federal Reserve Bulletin*, 31(6) (June).

US Government (1963) *Foreign Relations of the United States, 1942: Diplomatic Papers: Volume 6 – The American Republics*, Washington, DC: Government Printing Office.

—— (1962) *Foreign Relations of the United States 1941: Diplomatic Papers: Volume 7 – The American Republics*, Washington, DC: US Government Printing Office.

Woods, Ngaire (2006) *The Globalizers*, Ithaca, NY: Cornell University Press.

Part 3

Culture as concealing political economic practices

5   Anti-political economy

Cartographies of 'illegal immigration' and the displacement of the economy[1]

William Walters

> What distinguishes the map from the tracing is that it is entirely oriented toward an experimentation in contact with the real. ... The map is open and connectable in all of its dimensions; it is detachable, reversible, susceptible to constant modification. It can be torn, reversed, adapted to any kind of mounting, reworked by an individual, group, or social formation. It can be drawn on a wall, conceived of as a work of art, constructed as a political action or as a meditation.
>
> (Deleuze and Guattari 1987: 12)

'Who left the door open?'

On 20 September 2004, the US news weekly *Time* published a special issue dedicated to the issue now known as border security. The cover story was titled 'Who left the door open?', and announced that the issue was to be devoted to 'the lack of national security at the United States' borders' (Barlett and Steel 2004). The general thrust of the special issue was that a mere three years on from the events of September 11, and despite the massive investment made in homeland security, 'sneaking into the US is scandalously easy – and on the rise'. As corroboration, *Time* estimated that 'the number of illegal aliens flooding into the US ... will total 3 million – enough to fill 22,000 Boeing 737–7000 airliners'. But this is not the only scandal reported. If these 'illegals' could once have been assumed to be nearly all Mexican, today 'a small but sharply growing number come from other countries, including those with large populations hostile to the US'. Having established the potential for danger at the border, the special issue proceeds to carry out a sort of audit of the damage and the risks associated with such a leaky border, and asks plaintively: 'why does the US fail to protect itself?' and 'is this the perfect cover for terrorists?'

The article is full of assumptions and assertions that a critical inquiry into migration today would surely want to interrogate – not least the idea that more intense forms of policing the state's borders are really conducive to the protection of its citizens, not to mention the lives of migrants. However, it is not the article but rather one particular map – one of a number of graphics accompanying the special issue – that I find interesting. Entitled 'Breaking point' (*Time* 2004), it seems intended to convey a sense of imminent crisis at the U.S.–Mexico border. There are a number of interesting features here. First, there is the fact that the graphic places the observer in terms of an imaginary and seemingly impossible viewpoint that is oblique to the landscape, as though the viewer were piloting a plane approaching the US Southwest. The southwestern section of the border is to the foreground while the vast landmass of North America rolls out towards the horizon. The earth's atmosphere is lightly etched in shades of blue on the horizon, contrasting sharply with the blackness of space beyond. It seems that 'illegal immigration' is happening not just in relation to US territory but within a quasi-planetary space – a slippage that Hardt and Negri (2000) would surely appreciate.

But another interesting feature of the map concerns its visual field which is largely dominated by geographical and natural features, such as deserts, mountain ranges and rivers. What geographers would call 'political' features are only faintly present. The US–Mexico border is certainly emphasized as a somewhat jagged line – drawn in red, just in case we miss the point. State lines and the occasional city are marked also. But much more prominent are the olive, grey and khaki shadings which convey a sense of the physical relief of this space; the lay of the land. In some respects it resembles a political topography rather than a political geography of 'illegal immigration' – a point I shall return to later.

There are other features that deserve to be mentioned. For instance, there are four boxes of text that draw our attention to particular sites along the border, and which elucidate the problems with 'immigration' occurring at those sites. Many of these are referenced and developed in the articles which make up the special issue. There is the small border town of Bisbee. Its tiny hospital 'may' be forced to close because of the cost of caring for 'illegal immigrants'. There are the ranches at the border losing cattle when fences are cut. There is the Tohono O'odham reservation whose facilities are overtaxed by the migrants, its land 'trashed'. And as if to capture the depth of the scandal of the leaky border we learn that not even the army is immune from disruption at the hands of the 'illegals'. Fort Huachuca may be a 'top-secret intelligence training ground' but it is also a 'thoroughfare for smugglers'. What these little boxes and their mini-dramas seem to be saying is this: Americans may be divided along lines of class, region, race and employment, but at least in the case of those citizens who populate the borderlands, there is commonality around one point: all experience a common suffering at the hands of 'illegal immigrants'.

Maps like this are common if not ubiquitous within press, television and Internet coverage of migration issues in general, and especially the type of migration that is given the problematic title of 'illegal immigration'. They also quite frequently accompany official reports and policy documents. Certainly it could be argued that such maps contribute in minor but not insignificant ways to the wider symbolic and semantic field within which political questions of human mobility are debated today. Yet such maps have been largely ignored by critical scholarship about migration. While there is now a sizeable literature concerning the political and social construction of immigration, this tends to concentrate on the production of identities at the level of written text and speech. The growing literature on securitization of migration is a case in point (Buonfino 2004; Ceyhan and Tsoukala 2002). For all its sophistication, this literature has tended to privilege the speech act as its model of analysis and pays scant attention to the visual mediation and construction of security situations (Williams 2003).[2]

Migration cartography

This chapter seeks to partially remedy this rather strange oversight by focusing on what I am calling the cartography of 'illegal immigration'. Simply put, it argues that we should take such maps more seriously. To this end, the chapter will treat these cartographic inscriptions as irreducible elements in their own right, and not merely pictorial decorations or illustrative features for textual practices. One of the principal aims of the chapter is to call attention to the phenomenon of migration cartography and to demonstrate that migration cartography merits considerably more critical attention than it has hitherto received.

It goes without saying that there are several ways in which we might frame such an analysis. One approach would be to examine migration map-making in relation to questions of the production and legitimation of state power and territoriality. In a recent work exploring various imaginings of the state, Mark Neocleous takes up the theme of how political rule is legitimated by the idea that every state, and 'its' people, has a 'home', namely, a particular territory. He identifies several ways in which the idea of territory as home is concretely produced. One of these is through a series of categorical distinctions that are inscribed in law but also popular imagination. These distinctions affirm the state as the home of the citizen in part by marking such identities as the refugee, the alien, and the vagabond as dis-placed and transgressive subjects.[3] Another technique is the map. Through its capacity to dominate the political imagination, this 'crucial political technology of space', Neocleous avers, is responsible for nothing less than legitimating 'the great movement of territorialization through which the whole earth has been turned into an object of state stewardship' (2003: 124). Here we might observe that the peculiarity of migration cartography is precisely that it combines these two techniques of domesticating the polity. For its essence is to graft a representation of outsiders onto an apparently objective depiction of 'the shape and territorial outline of the state' (Neocleous 2003: 123). Given the kinds of emotional and political effects it is thereby capable of generating, perhaps it should come as no surprise that migration cartography has come to occupy a prominent place within popular and official discourses about immigration.

While I will certainly touch on themes of territoriality, this is not the primary line of analysis I pursue in this chapter. Instead, I want to make a different reading of the phenomenon of migration mapping, one that relates quite closely to the theme of cultural political economy. This paper will argue that as a corollary to the study of the cultural constitution of the economic, it is also important to understand how cultural practices and artefacts can play a significant role in limiting, containing and sometimes suppressing public and political perceptions of the economic. Borrowing a term from Barry (2002) this is a phenomenon that I call anti-political economy.

My first major section explores some possible meanings of anti-political economy, and how it relates to cultural political economy. Here I distinguish between two possible interpretations of anti-political economy. The first, following Barry (2002), is about translating political controversies into technical objectives that might be pursued by relatively de-dramatized means within the space called 'the economy'. The requirement that construction companies observe certain building codes when fabricating houses or roads is an example of this sense of anti-political economy. Without standards, every new house would carry with it the potential of sparking local controversy or even public outcry on the grounds it was structurally unsound, too high so that it shadowed neighbouring properties, or perhaps not consistent with the prevailing architectural style of the neighbourhood. Standards, regulations and codes serve to limit political disagreement by 'placing actions and objects (provisionally) outside the realm of public contestation, thereby regularizing the conduct of economic and social life, with both beneficial and negative consequences' (Barry 2002: 271). This is not to say that the drafting of such regulations and codes is without political controversy. On the contrary, a passing familiarity with municipal politics indicates that a given proposal to change building or other codes will frequently be met with opposition from builders, environmentalists, community organizations, and so forth. But the point is that once agreed upon, standards and codes serve to lessen the likelihood of constant politicization by providing guidelines for technical and economic activity.

The second sense of anti-political economy relates to what I call the move of *non-identification*. Here it is a case of understanding how certain economic moments and identities can be suppressed by other discourses and systems of meanings, and rendered non-economic. A particularly gendered notion of 'housework' can serve as an illustration of the move of non-identification. For example, by casting domestic work as the natural task of 'housewives', and a social responsibility of women, patriarchal discourse lessens the possibility that a wide range of activities undertaken in and around the household will be regarded as productive activity taking place within 'the economy' (see Waring 1988).

In the subsequent sections I consider a series of examples of the cartography of 'illegal immigration'. Adapting Dalby and Ó Tuathail's (1998) useful typology of geopolitics, I identify three categories of representation within migration cartography: popular, official and radical. I argue that both the above interpretations of anti-political economy can prove useful in making sense of these cartographic practices, and the various ways in which they shape the meaning of key identities like 'immigration', 'state', 'economy' and 'territory'. Most of my examples illustrate processes by which something called 'illegal immigration' is, on the one hand kept at a certain distance (if not completely detached) from that which our societies recognize as 'the economic', while on the other, maintained in an intimate relationship with themes of territory and security. Nevertheless, I want to argue that if migration cartography is often put to work in anti-political ways, this is far from being inherent in the practice of mapping. This point is developed in a final section where I discuss an example of counter-mapping. This case suggests, if nothing else, that migration cartography is fast becoming a medium for critical, deconstructive and sometimes polemical interventions as well.

Before taking up the themes of anti-political and cultural economy, it is necessary to clarify my understanding of the 'cultural'. Obviously the fact that there exist multiple ways of interpreting the cultural is a thread running through this volume. But in what sense are migration maps cultural? I do not think we should look for any kind of general answer to this question. Much depends on how we define culture, just as it depends on the kind of map in question. Much also depends on the use to which a given map is put. Hence, it is a matter of understanding the particular ways in which a given type of map might be said to have cultural aspects. While there are many ways in which maps could be related to culture, here I mention the two which seem most relevant to my project.

First, certain kinds of maps could be considered as cultural in the sense that they can be related to notions of lived, everyday life. The ubiquitous weather maps which close out the nightly newscast fit this description. Often appearing as nothing more than a background, they form part of the texture of everyday life. In quite subtle and not always acknowledged ways, they mediate our experience of the world. Just think of how weather maps privilege and construct national space. As Black (1997: 12) observes, you might live in Kent in the south of England, but because of the banal nationalism of weather reporting, you will likely be told more about the weather in distant Westmoreland than in nearby Pas-de-Calais. In other words, weather maps can often play a part in the production of the region or the nation as imagined community. While nowhere near as ubiquitous as weather maps, my sense is that a great deal of migration cartography works in this way. Embedded in television news and magazine reporting, it operates at the level of everyday life where, in subtle and not so subtle ways, it contributes to the perception of a 'here' and 'there', an 'us' and a 'them'. Here, migration maps 'demarcate divisions between self and other', as Best and Paterson (Introduction, this volume) have put it; their effects readily translating into 'logics of inclusion and exclusion, good and evil, powerful and powerless'.

But the cultural is relevant in a second sense. This is where the cultural is associated with the claim that any social practice involves shared understandings, meanings and assumptions that may be specific to a group or a time. To put it simply, maps are shot through with cultural assumptions. Maps rely on these assumptions in order to produce meaning. These assumptions may operate at the level of the convention. For instance, there is the use of blue to signify water. But they may operate through less formal, less visible mechanisms. For instance, there is a powerful association within Western culture which links the above with the good or virtuous and the below with the base or profane. Think of the meaning of heaven and hell within Christian theology, or upstairs and downstairs, in the social world of the Victorian household. Perhaps it is due to the suspicion that this subtle spatial code permeates the mapping of Europe in relation to Africa that, as we will see in our example of radical cartography below, Hackitectura elects to invert many of its maps of the Mediterranean space (Pérez de Lama *et al.* 2006).

Anti-political economy and cultural political economy

In their Introduction, Best and Paterson argue that conventional as well as critical strands of political economy have tended to overlook the role which cultural processes, practices and phenomena play in shaping economic objects. 'Political economy, as conventionally understood, whether in neoclassical, public choice, institutionalist, statist, or Marxist terms, thus fails to fully explain its object because it abstracts political economy from its cultural constitution' (Introduction). They insist that a better understanding of the cultural – a term they recognize as subject to a considerable range of interpretation – will make for a more powerful version of political economy. It will illuminate, among other things, the role which culture plays in shaping economic domains and the actors as well as the activities which populate those domains.

This does seem a very valid and important point to make, even if it could be argued that something resembling cultural political economy is already well underway amongst certain political and economic anthropologists.[4] But rather than engage directly in the question of the cultural and its shaping of political economy, I want to explore what I see as a corollary of this hypothesis. This is to consider the place of cultural practices and formations in relation to anti-political economy. The project of cultural political economy should not confine its attention to the positive ways in which practices, objects and processes come to be considered as 'economic', or the role of the cultural in explaining economic transformations. In addition, this project needs to encompass the study of these practices, at once material and discursive, whose effect is to manage the distribution of the economic and its separation from the non-economic. Put differently, it needs to attend to the various ways in which the economic is contained, neutralized, displaced and in some cases made invisible. Paying attention to some of the everyday ways in which migration is mediated and made visible both at public and official levels, my study of migration maps is intended to illustrate this phenomenon of anti-political economy. But before I return to the maps, it is necessary to reflect a bit further on the idea of anti-political economy.

One place to start is with Ferguson's political anthropology of international development policy. Focusing on Lesotho, Ferguson describes development practice in terms of an 'anti-politics machine'. There are two aspects of this machine which he describes in terms of 'instrument-effects'. The first is 'the institutional effect of expanding bureaucratic state power' (Ferguson 2006: 273). This expansion happens despite the fact that nearly all development projects are deemed by academics as 'failures' since they rarely meet their stated aims of alleviating poverty. The second is 'the conceptual or ideological effect of depoliticizing both poverty and the state' (Ferguson 2006: 273). This effect is the move which turns political issues into technical matters. Poverty, inequality and starvation, become statistics and objectives to be mitigated. Instead of a conflict, one has administration. Foucault describes the modern prison system as a success despite the fact that it never managed to 'solve' the problem of crime. It is a success because in unplanned and only partially coordinated ways it has constituted a manageable and governable space of crime, populated by a discrete class of persons called the delinquent (Foucault 1977). In much the same way, Ferguson uses the machine metaphor to theorize development as a successful failure.

Rather like Ferguson, Barry (2002) is interested in these moments of translation. But Barry discusses technicalization more specifically in relation to themes of economic and environmental governance. Barry emphasizes a particular domain of technical practices which he calls 'metrology'. The legal requirement for cars to undergo periodic emissions test is a good example of this. The emissions test has anti-political effects. For instance, it allows political objectives, such as the promotion of better air quality, to be projected onto a host of sites situated well beyond the state apparatus, such as the used-car lot. Particular political debates about pollution can be translated into technologically mediated practices: has this car passed its emission test? Moreover, the possession of certification to this end will typically shape the market value of the car. In the spirit of actor-network theory, Barry shows that through testing and certification practices, a range of actors including buyers, sellers, mechanics and scientists, are enrolled in strategies of environmental governance, but through formally non-political mechanisms.

But Barry brings something else to the idea of anti-political economy. First, he insists that one should not denounce the anti-political in blanket terms. If disagreement is a fundamental and pervasive feature of human life, then anti-politics – understood as mechanisms to manage disagreement, and make collective life viable – is in fact quite necessary. Hence it is a matter of differentiating between different *forms* of anti-politics. There are anti-political forms which might be considered as respecting and promoting certain forms of democratic experience (e.g. rules concerning the political impartiality of the civil service), and those which do not (e.g. certain forms of state censorship). Second, regimes of metrology are not as robust as certain accounts of technicalization (including, perhaps, Ferguson's Foucauldian version) presume. They are often fragile because they are susceptible to politicization. Metrology can become a surface of politics in its own right. For instance, making 'illegal immigration' into something statistical may induce certain depoliticization effects since it encourages the idea that this 'thing' has a quasi-natural existence in the world (like annual rainfall), and as such, can be governed once we devise the optimal policy 'solution'. Yet, statistics can become a site of politicization in its own right, such as whenever questions get raised about their accuracy. But in addition, the field of such statistics can be extended – to count not only the rate of 'illegal entries' or 'apprehensions', but death at the border: the human toll exacted by particular regimes of immigration control. In such ways, the statistics of 'illegal immigration' becomes a field of struggle.

While my understanding of anti-political economy is particularly indebted to Barry's development of the theme, I think it is important to identify a second aspect of the field of anti-political economy. This is less about nullifying politics/ disagreement within the economy (e.g. the potential for political disagreement between vendor and buyer in the used car salesroom), or purifying it from political contamination, but more about all those situations when affairs are conducted in ways which refuse, fail, neglect or consciously repress the identification of things *as* economic. I propose to call this second aspect the *non-identification* of the economic.

A classic case of such non-identification concerns household work. Feminist scholarship and activism has, of course, a long and lively history of engagement on just this matter. Marilyn Waring's (1988) study of the UN's System of National Accounts makes the point particularly clearly at the level of institutional and statistical practices. This system, which became the template for national economic accounting practices on an international scale following the Second World War, served to establish official definitions of what was to count as economic activity and what would not, who was in the labour force, who was not, and so on. Hence Waring reveals an anti-political economy embedded at the level of economic theory and statistical practice itself. Equally significantly, because of the way it is embedded in official practices, she shows that this non-identification of the economic will be reproduced unknowingly and almost automatically nearly every time these statistics are used.

For my purposes, there are two points that can be taken from Waring's discussion of the institutional power to define the economic, and conversely the extra-economic. The first is that non-identification is an active process and not merely an absence of recognition. Hence, the location of the household outside the economy is mediated by the immense cultural work which renders household work as something else – for example, as 'care', that natural responsibility and competence of persons identified as mothers and wives. Second, the point is not that there is a true definition of the economic by which everything else can be measured. Rather, the identification and non-identification of the economic is always mediated by politics. If it becomes possible to identify certain patriarchal practices in terms of anti-political economy, this is because feminist political interventions have made it so, not because such practices are inherently anti-economic in their effects.

So I analyze anti-political economy along two lines: with one it is a matter of the techniques which nullify and displace political disagreement in the economy; with the other, those moves which suppress the identification of things *as* economic. With this point in mind, let us now turn more fully to the issue of migration cartography.

Migration cartography as anti-political economy

Migration cartography is certainly not new. There is a long tradition of charting the movement and settlement of peoples which spans the disciplines of history, geography, ethnology and demographics. For instance, it was in the late 1960s that Martin Gilbert, eminent British historian and official biographer of Churchill, authored a series of historical atlases offering geospatialized narratives of British, American, Russian and Jewish history. The fact that the latter atlas (Gilbert 1969) ranges from a map which geo-graphs the Exodus from 'Slavery to the Promised Land' (Map 1), to one charting the 'Return of Jews to Zion 1948–64' (Map 98), reveals that such apparently demographic exercises are quite adept at combining politics and anti-politics. The fact that two events of quite different historical and factual status can be represented using identical iconography, and located through the cartographic exercise upon a similar epistemological and geo-historical plane suggests at the very least that these older forms of migration cartography are certainly not always politically innocent.

But something is different and relatively new with regard to much of the migration cartography which interests me here. The social and political context in which migration maps are being produced and received seems to have changed. As research on 'securitization' has observed (Bigo 2002; Huysmans 2006), the political framing of migration issues, including the treatment of refugees, has moved its subject matter much more closely to the realm of security policy. This move has often been traced at the level of political rhetoric, exploring how politicians, media commentaries and policymakers frame migration as a security issue, an existential threat to the cultural integrity and political sovereignty of the nation, etc. However, the study of migration maps points to and illustrates aspects of a more prosaic process of securitization, one that occurs at the level of everyday graphics, images and inscriptions. We can speculate that these representations are rarely politically decisive or influential on a singular basis. It would be hard to point to this or that map and argue that it changed public opinion about immigration in some decisive way. Instead, whatever effect they do have on public perceptions – the estimation of which is, of course, complex and beyond my scope here – we might assume to occur through processes of iteration. It is surely through their everyday presence in the margins of newspaper reports, as the background to television news, or as a supplement to official reports that they help to produce a securitized political imagination of migration as well as the state.

Popular cartographies

Let us return for a moment to the *Time* (2004) map, 'Breaking Point'. Michel Foucher uses the term 'geostrategy' to refer to 'concrete practices in places that are analysed as theatres of operation, actual and potential. It thus considers spatial, physical and human configurations in terms of war and defence' (2001: 165). We can certainly discern powerful geostrategic themes structuring this map. The US is cast as a territory enclosed by a border, which is marked in red. The map spatializes a series of border incidents, incidents which collectively attest to the vulnerability of a system of defense. But the map also generates a sense of drama and unease in other ways. For example, the map is subtended by three jagged graphs, displaying different aspects of the 'volume' of 'illegal border crossings' over time and place. Jonathan Inda (2006) has noted how narratives about 'illegal immigration' almost always represent it as something 'growing', and frequently 'out of control'. Things always seem to be getting worse. In the case of 'Breaking Point' this impression of impending crisis is magnified through the juxtaposition of the red-lined border and the upward slope of the graph.

Other maps are even more explicit in the way that they locate migration processes within geopolitical space. In making this move, such maps largely suppress the economic connotations of migration. Foregrounding themes of territorial invasion, they negate the fact that much of the movement that is pejoratively designated as 'illegal' or 'people smuggling' could be considered as labour migration in a global capitalist economy (De Genova 2002).

Consider the simple little map entitled 'routes through Europe' which comes from the BBC's online news website (Figure 5.1). It was originally embedded within a story exploring why the UK had become a major destination for asylum seekers (BBC 2001). The map depicts Europe as a space of national borders. However, these borders are traversed by thick, arching lines which represent flows of asylum seekers converging on central and western Europe. These flows are shown to be heading to certain cities, such as Prague, Istanbul and Belgrade, destinations that seem to be highlighted as nodal points within networks of irregular migration. Certainly the map speaks to immediate political concerns. It was published in the midst of a particular 'crisis' of asylum-seeking, one that condensed around the figure of 'Sangatte', a temporary refugee center in northern France where migrants sheltered while waiting to cross the Channel to England. However, I think the map also works on other levels as well. Viewing its bold lines of movement it is hard not to detect echoes of those classical maps of warfare in which Europe features as a 'theatre' of military operations. But if such maps can forge historical connections evocative of games of war and statecraft, they can also establish resonances among other more contemporary phenomena,

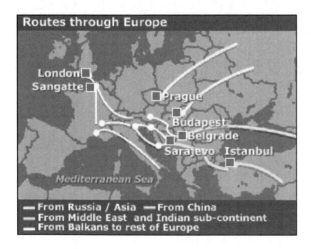

Figure 5.1 Routes through Europe.

Source: BBC (2001). Reproduced with kind permission from BBC news online.

many of which exist as the targets of metaphorical wars. For instance, it is not uncommon to see formally similar maps diagramming the transnational flows of illicit goods, weapons and drugs. It is quite likely that the 'security continuum' and the 'transfer of illegitimacy' – processes which Bigo identifies as profoundly structuring the political and governmental field of migration – are effected not just through the institutional and expert framing of things, but at the level of these little image-fragments.

Let us consider another map (Figure 5.2). This one utilizes data gathered by the Protection Project (2002) based at the School of Advanced International Studies at Johns Hopkins University. Its principal object is the depiction of 'trafficking routes' channelling vulnerable persons into the US. There are two points I want to make here. First, while we should not lose sight of the fact that 'trafficking' is itself far from being a neutral concept (Aradau 2004), it is worth noting how this map could be accused of perpetrating an act of visual exaggeration. Its makers note at the bottom that to count as a route there needs to be 'at least one documented case of trafficking of persons'. In other words, a route is not necessarily a well-worn pathway but nothing more than, at minimum, one documented case. Since the threshold for qualifying as a route is set so very low then it's hardly surprising that the map manages to portray human trafficking as an overwhelming and dramatic

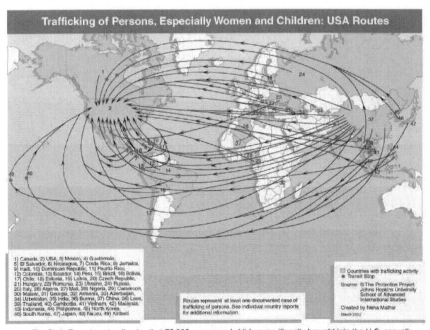

The State Department estimates that 75,000 women and children are illegally brought into the U.S. annually for forced prostitution and other forms of slave labor. Source: www.protectionproject.org

Figure 5.2 Trafficking of persons, especially women and children: USA routes.

Source: The Protection Project (2002). Reproduced with kind permission from The Protection Project.

phenomenon. In this case one could at least expect some differentiation in the depiction of the routes in terms of the incidence of trafficking.

My bigger point is not to note how such maps could be improved. Instead, it is to observe that this map, like the BBC one, conveys a powerful impression of Western, developed countries as being confronted by a set of forces which penetrate their borders. Especially in the case of the trafficking map, one gets the sense of a process of besiegement, of territories surrounded on all sides. It is not difficult to see how the politics of re-bordering, whether understood as the fortification of frontiers or the trend towards greater surveillance of mobile populations, follows almost logically from such representations.

Crucial to understanding the power of these and countless similar image-fragments, and their anti-political economy effects, is their selectivity. Nowhere in their vicinity do we see the other forces which might give them some context, whether lines of capital investment and disinvestment, flows of ideas and images, circuits of tourism and trade, or relationships of military influence. In the absence of these other connections, migration appears as an 'autonomous' force (Sassen 1998) emanating from the troubled 'borderlands' of the global system, and massing in and around its privileged heartland. In the absence of any representation of the multiple ties that interconnect global zones of wealth and poverty – for example, cultural ties carried over from the age of formal colonialism – the wealthy regions appear as innocent bystanders, as victims of malign forces. The point is not that maps ought to be comprehensive. Mapping, like other forms of diagramming, is necessarily a selective practice. 'A map is a show, a representation. What is shown is real, but that does not imply any completeness or entail any absence of choice in selection and representation' (Black 1997: 11). The point is not to lament the selectivity of the map but to recognize that such selectivity is deployed strategically, in ways that seem to resonate with public cultures of insecurity.

I have argued that the kinds of maps discussed thus far can be considered elements of anti-political economy because of how they objectify migration as a security question, and depict it as a game that plays itself out in and through a space that is primarily geo-territorial in nature. In the maps we have encountered, the geographical and the territorial is foregrounded while the socioeconomic barely registers. Furthermore, each depicts migration rather unambiguously as a force that converges upon the borders and territories of the wealthy nations. It seems to embody a threat that emanates from outside the state. That said, I do not want to suggest that these maps relentlessly convey an identical message. The field of migration cartography is far from homogeneous. Nor are its contents without certain forms of ambiguity. This much is evident when we turn to my final example of popular cartography: a map claiming to represent the journey of a single migrant, Marvin Hernandez, as he makes his way from San Salvador in El Salvador to Boston, Massachusetts.

Published in connection with a three part series in the online version of the *Arizona Daily Star* entitled 'Marvin's Journey: One Migrant's Tale' (Ibarra and Scott 2000), there are several things that are somewhat distinctive about this

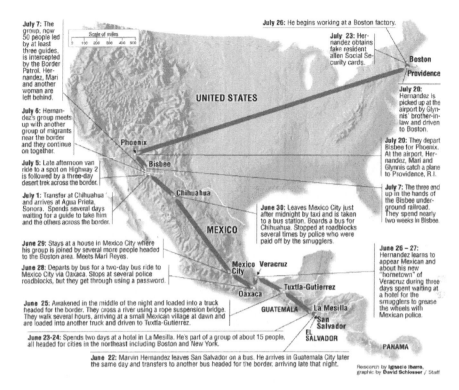

July 7: The group, now 50 people led by at least three guides, is intercepted by the Border Patrol. Hernandez, Mari and another woman are left behind.

July 6: Hernandez's group meets up with another group of migrants near the border and they continue on together.

July 5: Late afternoon van ride to a spot on Highway 2 is followed by a three-day desert trek across the border.

July 1: Transfer at Chihuahua and arrives at Agua Prieta, Sonora. Spends several days waiting for a guide to take him and the others across the border.

June 29: Stays at a house in Mexico City where his group is joined by several more people headed to the Boston area. Meets Mari Reyes.

June 28: Departs by bus for a two-day bus ride to Mexico City via Oaxaca. Stops at several police roadblocks, but they get through using a password.

June 25: Awakened in the middle of the night and loaded into a truck headed for the border. They cross a river using a rope suspension bridge. They walk several hours, arriving at a small Mexican village at dawn and are loaded into another truck and driven to Tuxtla-Gutierrez.

June 23-24: Spends two days at a hotel in La Mesilla. He's part of a group of about 15 people, all headed for cities in the northeast including Boston and New York.

June 22: Marvin Hernandez leaves San Salvador on a bus. He arrives in Guatemala City later the same day and transfers to another bus headed for the border, arriving late that night.

July 26: He begins working at a Boston factory.

July 23: Hernandez obtains fake resident alien Social Security cards.

July 20: Hernandez is picked up at the airport by Glynnis' brother-in-law and driven to Boston.

July 20: They depart Bisbee for Phoenix. At the airport, Hernandez, Mari and Glynnis catch a plane to Providence, R.I.

July 7: The three end up in the hands of the Bisbee underground railroad. They spend nearly two weeks in Bisbee.

June 26 – 27: Hernandez learns to appear Mexican and about his new "hometown" of Veracruz during three days spent waiting at a hotel for the smugglers to grease the wheels with Mexican police.

June 30: Leaves Mexico City just after midnight by taxi and is taken to a bus station. Boards a bus for Chihuahua. Stopped at roadblocks several times by police who were paid off by the smugglers.

UNITED STATES

Boston
Providence

Phoenix

Bisbee

Chihuahua

MEXICO

Mexico City   Veracruz

Oaxaca

Tuxtla-Gutierrez

GUATEMALA   La Mesilla

San Salvador

EL SALVADOR

PANAMA

Scale of miles
0   100   200   300   400   500

Research by **Ignacio Ibarra**,
graphic by **David Schlosser** / Staff

Figure 5.3 Map claiming to represent the journey of a single migrant, Marvin Hernandez.

Source: Ibarra *et al.* (2000). Reproduced with kind permission, the Arizona Daily Star.

map (Figure 5.3). First, there is the fact that we have here an instance where 'illegal immigration' is being represented at the level of the biographical. If previous maps showed migration as a transgressive practice of border crossing, here the level of detail is raised. The map documents events like the crossing of a river using a rope suspension bridge near a small Mexican village, and a three day trek across the desert to get to Bisbee, Arizona. In this way 'illegal immigration' starts to resemble a Homeric odyssey as the map geo-graphs the series of adventures and perils which Marvin encounters in the course of his journey. Far from demonizing the migrant – as the literature on securitization often presumes – this map seems to discern something faintly heroic in his quest.

Second, it is notable that the dangerous journey culminates with Marvin finding paid employment on the East coast. Three days after receiving fake resident alien social security cards, we are told, Marvin begins working in a Boston factory. Unlike some of the other maps, then, we do see here the recognition that migratory movements are bound up with the search, and the demand for paid employment – in this case within US manufacturing. That said, it is also notable that if the economy is accorded a place within this representation, it is one that is tightly circumscribed.

The economic is present, not as a realm of forces and processes of transnational trade, investment and communication, but only as an incident: the taking of illegal employment. Inasmuch as a map like this offers a kind of explanation of 'illegal immigration', the economic registers as just one moment amidst a world populated by smugglers, border patrols, corrupt police, and inhospitable terrains. In other words, the economic is not effaced but it is de-privileged: it registers as only one amongst many salient factors.

The final point I want to make here is somewhat more speculative. In discussing *Time* (2004) magazine's map of the US–Mexico border we noted how it locates unauthorized migration within a topographical space. Migratory movements were superimposed upon a map which was largely devoid of political features such as cities but instead much closer to being a physical geography. Much the same can be said of this depiction of Marvin's journey. Note, for instance, how the red line tracing Marvin's movements traverses mountains and deserts until it reaches Phoenix. This could perhaps be read as a move which naturalizes the territory of the state by embedding it in the landscape. But I think that it might be interpreted in a somewhat different manner, one that emphasizes the ambiguity of representation. Could we not read these political topographies of migration as speaking to the fact that for millions of people, migration has once again become an intensely embodied, strenuously physical activity – an affair conducted on foot, a dangerous passage negotiated across deserts and mountains, a perilous journey navigated over tempestuous waters? Could it be that these maps speak to ways in which the act of migrating once again requires the poor of the world to confront elemental forces, to negotiate the very contours of the earth? There was once a time when a state's delimitation of its territory was grounded in appeals to the idea of certain natural frontiers – a river, a mountain range, etc. (Pounds 1951). Such ideas have long since been abandoned. However, inasmuch as contemporary migrations like the one documented here involve a confrontation not just with the policing and security agencies of the state but with the terrain of the earth, perhaps there is a sense in which we are once more in the presence of the natural frontier.

Official cartographies

In my prior discussion I suggested that there are at least two possible interpretations of anti-political economy. The first is about translating political controversies into technical objectives that might be pursued by relatively de-dramatized economic and other means. The second is the move of non-identification, wherein economic moments and identities are suppressed by other discourses and systems of meaning. The maps I have discussed thus far tend towards this second position. At this point I want to consider one map that is much closer to this first position. That is, I want to consider the case of a map that appears to have a higher programmatic and governmental content, and a greater degree of instrumentality than the maps which typically appear in mass communication contexts.

Titled 'MTM Map on Mediterranean and African Irregular Migration Routes' (Figure 5.4), the map in question comes from a project called the Mediterranean

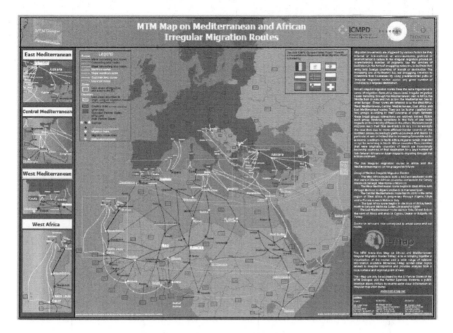

Figure 5.4 MTM map on Mediterranean and African irregular migration routes.

Source: ICMPD (2007). Reproduced with kind permission from ICMPD.

Transit Migration (MTM) Dialogue. The main architect of this project is the Vienna-based International Centre for Migration Policy and Development (ICMPD), but its partners include Europol and the EU's special agency for frontier controls, Frontex. ICMPD has been described as a 'think tank and an influential consultancy centre for the EU Ministers of Justice and Home Affairs' (see entry for ICMPD at http://www.transitmigration.org/migmap/home_map1.html). A part of its field of operations has involved the reinforcement of the external frontiers of Eastern Europe in conjunction with that region's gradual assimilation into the EU region's. In many ways, MTM is a project of immigration policy statecraft. It is seeking to enlist North African governments (dubbed 'Arab Partner States'), and other actors geopolitically coded as 'countries of transit' and 'origin', in Europe's ongoing campaign to police unruly migration flows – or what the EU in its more adversarial moments designates as its 'combat with illegal immigration'.

ICMPD's map can be fruitfully compared with some of the other maps we have discussed thus far. It is interesting in several respects. First, notice how Europe, represented as a largely undifferentiated blue mass, now recedes into the background. The focus has shifted somewhat from the space of destination, and even from the trans-European routeways identified in the BBC map, to Africa and to the Near and Middle East, to the in-between regions of transit. More and more, it seems, the routeway, and its subjective correlate, the migrant's journey (Figure 5.3), as much as the border, becomes an object of knowledge in its own right.[5]

Second, and following from this, the map presents the viewer with something we might call an analytics of the route. This was largely absent from the Protection Project's map (Figure 5.2). Here we encounter multiple kinds of line, allowing for the differentiation of media of movement (land, sea, air), and scales of movement (major, minor).

Third, where previously there were curved lines offering the impression of determined flows of population, here we are presented with something which appears more finely calibrated, diagrammatic and technical. The lines are straighter than before and distributed by a constellation of towns and cities. Movement plays itself out across a space of nodal places. The ensemble of the routes and the nodes comprises a network. If the project of European integration has often imagined itself positively in terms of a space of networks (Barry 1996), here we find one instance where a less benign face of the network appears, and where Europe imagines its limits rather than its extension, in terms of the network.

In what ways might this attempt to generate a scientific analysis of migration routes serve as an element within the technicalization of migration politics? Does this anti-political move, which displaces a whole series of possible political questions about the distribution of justice, citizenship and wealth under global conditions, go hand in hand with the attempt to co-opt the 'Arab Partner States' designated and colour-coded by the map, into international regimes of 'migration management'?

It is certainly important to challenge the political detachment which is claimed for maps like this one, and the larger projects of migration management to which they belong (see Düvell 2006). However, there is another dimension of mapping that I want to explore in this instance. Here a comparison with the cartography of colonialism is instructive for it speaks to the map as an *ethical* technology, concerned as much with establishing the right and fitness of certain authorities to govern distant peoples and places, as it is with the precise nature or geographical location of those persons and places. Mapping is, in this sense, about making ethical as well as territorial claims. Joyce has put this nicely in regard to official cartography's aspiration to construct British India as an object of rule. It illustrates that 'the practice and reception of instruments of governance may sometimes be of secondary importance: what seems to have mattered here ... was the creation of the illusion of a rational, and therefore governable, space, that of a mapped "India"' (Joyce 2005: 37).

In the case of ICMPD and other international agencies, we are not of course dealing with the aspiration to control territories or build empires but a somewhat more modest aim: to rationalize the management of migratory processes. But of this map in particular I think we can speak of two kinds of ambition at work. One is, as with the mapping of India, a case of justifying one's own fitness to govern. It is perhaps about being perceived as a serious and reputable agency within the crowded field of migration and security policy. Another ambition is more specific to the form and content of the map. Note the way in which it seems to resemble the plan of a transportation system, or a transit map. Perhaps, then, it also expresses the political dream that the unruliness and 'turbulence' (Papastergiadis 2000) of contemporary migration really could be channeled into rational, ordered pathways.

Counter-mapping

If migration mapping deserves to be taken more seriously and regarded as an irreducible element within contemporary politicizations and depoliticizations of migration, this is not just because popular media utilize these maps in their encounter with the complexity of migration. Nor is it because certain experts and agencies like ICMPD and IOM tasked with the work of 'managing' migration have found in the map both a means to rationalize their interventions, and affirm their status *as* experts in the competitive institutional field of migration security. Migration mapping is a lively phenomenon today not just because it offers something valuable to policy officials and mainstream media. It is also because migration cartography has been fashioned as an instrument of protest, a polemical intervention and even a heterotopian medium for a range of actors outside the space of public policy and its institutions. Developing in parallel with official cartographies of migration, various tactical cartographers, critical geographers, self-styled hacktivists and visual artists have improvised a practice of migration counter-mapping – what one video artist and theorist calls 'writing counter-geography' (Biemann 2003; see also An Architektur 2003; MigMap n.d.; Raley 2008). If the restless desires and energies associated with capitalism are constantly provoking new spaces and experiences which sometimes defy existing categories, it is this challenge of making such processes representable and intelligible which this alternative cartography seems to be taking up.(Figure 5.5).

This visualistic counter-geography of migration deserves to be the subject of study in its own right. It also needs to be seen in light of a wider turn within political activism and critical thought whereby mapping has become a critical practice for a range of movements and counter-publics (Crampton 2001; Mogel and Bhagat 2008). Lacking the space to do more than gesture towards such a project here I shall confine myself to the discussion of one map (Figure 5.5). Produced by the Spain-based collective Hackitectura, the English version of its title is 'Cartography of the Straits of Gibraltar: Borders and Migrations'. It is just one of a sizeable family of maps this project has made concerning the migration politics of the Straits of Gibraltar. The choice of this site is, of course, far from incidental. The Straits has long been considered a meeting point as much as a frontier between Europe and Africa. But like the US–Mexico border, this space has more recently become a frontline in the struggle to tame new processes of global migration.

Hackitectura's maps attempt to reference the multiple processes, regimes and agendas which co-exist, converge and clash at the space of the Straits – questions of work, territory, citizenship, technology, frontier controls, mobility, and much else. The fact that the map positions this particular geographical locale at its very center,

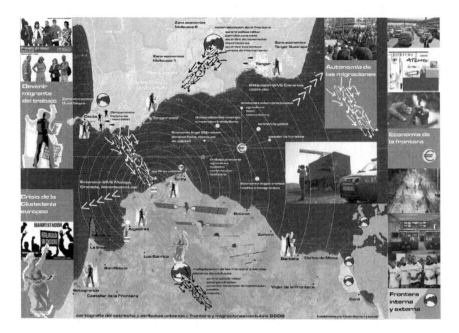

Figure 5.5 Cartography of the Straits of Gibraltar: borders and migrations 2006.

Source: Pérez de Lama *et al.* (2006). Reproduced with kind permission from hackitectura.

and the fact that all manner of networks, flows and processes are represented as traversing this symbolic frontier between Europe and Africa, suggests that the map is not interested in reproducing the old political lines of nations and continents. Instead, it strives to chart the emergence of strange new territories that confound these lines. For these map-makers, the Straits are an experimental encounter, a kind of 'laboratory-territory of the contemporary world' (Fadaiat 2005: 169). This ambition to map discordant and heterogeneous processes and spaces, to explore their combination, immediately marks it out from official cartographies which, as we have seen, are distinguished by the fact they reproduce the lines which organize and partition social knowledge about migration – a point I shall return to shortly.

There is so much going on in Hackitectura's maps that it is difficult to know where to start. Certainly we might mention how this map operates on one level as a work of parody. Notice how it flips cartographic convention on its head, placing North Africa 'above' and Europe 'below'. As such, and as I noted above, it might prompt us to consider how certain cultural assumptions about the good and the bad might be embedded in conventional mapping practices. Note also how it parodies the forceful lines which migration maps use to represent flows of population. In Hackitectura's version, these big vectors are replaced by a jumble of squiggly little arrows drawn in an almost childlike hand. Some of the lines are purposeful, others hesitate, turn back, or, quite ominously, even terminate in the sea. Each little line could be a biography in its own right. Or note how, on closer inspection, this map is written over other maps, and English terms inscribed over Spanish. Here we encounter the map as palimpsest. Whereas official mapping insists that the map unfolds across a blank space, these maps just add layer upon layer. Whereas official mapping may often erase other histories and geographies, Hackitectura brings the violence of mapping to the surface. There is no pretence to objectivity here, just as there is no suggestion that the maps are somehow uncontaminated by previous knowledges and uses. Instead, mapping is represented as a site of struggle in its own right, a struggle to dominate a space of authoritative representation. Hackitectura practices a 'living cartography' (Fadaiat 2005: 169) which insists upon its own provisionality.

Much more could be said about the parodic and subversive character of this map. But here I shall confine my comments to its relevance to the theme of anti-political economy. Here we can start by noting the extremely mixed, composite quality of the map. If it is a palimpsest it also resembles a work of bricolage. It harbors no aspiration towards systematicity or a uniformity of style that is so essential to the official map's credibility. Instead, heterogeneous elements, jagged forms and fragments are juxtaposed. There are advertisements for products, photographs showing uniformed officials (perhaps coast guards or police), posters for political demonstrations. Other photographs document additional aspects of this border complex that have no place within official cartography. They show a brown-skinned hand that works a sewing machine; a long line of traffic congested at a checkpoint; grainy night-time surveillance footage of border-crossers; and striking workers. Vivid symbols identify special sites of interest, but these are not of a tourist nature. The euro sign (€) identifies strategic locales in the growing economy of the borderlands, while a mini-version of the map of the Straits – the map within the map – signifies processes of internal and external frontier-ization. The overall effect is a bit like a school project where a group of students are asked to make a display exploring a particular topic. Each brings a clipping from home and pastes it onto the board, generating a unique play of interpretation.

In what ways could this map be said to challenge the anti-political economy of migration? One might answer this question by pointing to the very visible presence of economic processes and identities in the map. For instance, it depicts networks which gesture towards the connection between the licit and the illicit, and the co-dependence of local, global, European and 'underground' economies. So while it displays the processes of securitization and re-bordering at work in the region, it refuses to subsume the economic within the geopolitical – the move which, as we have seen, conventional maps do make. As we saw, Barry insists that the anti-political move to render a space of disagreement into technical, measurable and administrable forms is itself always susceptible to politicization, often in new and unpredictable ways. Hence, we might observe something similar here: that Hackitectura politicizes the anti-political regime of migration mapping by its insistence on the economic dimension and neoliberal capitalist uses of 'illegal immigration'.

However, I think such an interpretation, while valid in many respects, still misses something crucial. The key thing here is not merely the foregrounding of economic processes. For there is nothing inherently critical in pointing out that 'illegal immigration' is animated by market forces. Certainly this point is sometimes made as a response to anti-immigrantist claims. For instance, demands for migrants' rights and social justice often refute the popular image of the migrant as scrounger by pointing to the value, the 'invisible' economic contribution that illegal labour makes to a country's GDP. But just as often, the act of unauthorized migration is criticized on economic grounds – for instance, there is the often-heard complaint that migrants 'steal' jobs from 'native' workers, or depress the level of wages in the labour market. Clearly economically framed discussions can cut both ways.

If Hackitectura engages in a genuinely critical act, it is not merely by mobilizing the economic and insisting this is a political-economic as well as, or rather than, a security issue. It is not a matter of presenting one scientific discourse as essentially more truthful than another. For that move fails to problematize the organization of knowledge itself. If these kinds of map open up a critical space, it is in a different way: by exposing and at the same time transgressing the *purification* processes (Latour 1993), which enables discourse about 'illegal immigration' to function. Hackitectura seeks to represent something that finds no place in either the purified space of the geopolitical maps of trafficking, nor in economic (even certain political-economic) accounts of migration. A hodge-podge of pictures, graphics, symbols; the recycling and reuse of old maps to make something new; the juxtaposition of seemingly discordant fragments of technology, bodies, politics, machines and territory: this seems to point to an understanding of migration in terms of the assemblage – 'an ensemble of heterogeneous elements in contingent and provisional interrelationships' (Ong 2005: 259). This assemblage cannot be represented if one adheres to the conventions of the social sciences. For the organization of the social sciences, the lines which divide the economic from the geographical, from the political, and so on, are already internal to it.

Why is this significant? What political effects does it accomplish? Think back to the BBC and Protection Project maps. These typically represent illegal migration in terms of an interaction between passive and active entities. Western states are passive actors whose sovereign territory is violated by the intrusion of the active – the malicious external forces. The line always runs from a distant, outside place, through zones of transit, into the heart of the national territory. Under this view, and in much the same way that we have Ministries of Defence and not Ministries of Attack, Western states never *initiate*, they only *respond* to a prior 'incursion'. Migration policy, border control – these are cast as *re*-actions to a prior transgression.

Once we can see things in terms of an assemblage, a somewhat different picture is possible. There are two things to be said in this respect. First, the starting point is not two static and objective entities – be these the states of Spain and Morocco or the continents of Europe and Africa – existing in an external relationship with one another. Hackitectura take Deleuze and Guattari at their word because their performative practice starts 'in the middle, between things, interbeing, *intermezzo*' (Deleuze and Guattari 1987: 25). Their map reveals some of the many ways in which Europe and Africa fold into one another (Balibar 2004). There is no beginning or end, only the middle. For instance, take the case of border controls. These are totally invisible in many of the popular and official maps. Hence people smuggling appears in official representations only as a violent act perpetrated on victim-migrants and the states of destination (victim-states?). Yet smuggling only happens, it can only exist and thrive as an illicit form of 'travel agency' (Sharma 2003), because the thickening of borders has made it one of the only ways that refugees, for instance, can exercise the internationally sanctioned right of all politically threatened human beings to seek asylum. This is why it is so important that Hackitectura's assemblage represents migration *and* practices of border control, surveillance, investment and work as existing on the *same* plane, within the *same* space.

Second, by mapping from the point of view of the assemblage, Hackitectura says something important about contemporary capitalism and the character of work. Standard economic understandings of migration very much resemble the standard economic accounts of other things. There are forces of supply and demand, push and pull, incentives and disincentives. The global market is imagined as a 'hydraulic' system pushing and pulling its subjects around (Mezzadra 2004). But as David Harvey has recently reminded us, the textbook account of the economy is only one face of capitalist accumulation. Indeed, it is the benign and 'rational' face. There is another face which consists of all the 'predatory practices' which, far from belonging to a 'primitive' or 'original' stage of capitalism – as many Marxist accounts assumed – have a 'continuous role' and 'persistence ... within the long historical geography of capitalist accumulation' (Harvey 2004: 74). These predatory practices have been integral to the vitality of capitalism. They include the forcible appropriation of common land, slavery, as well as practices whose pedigree is more recent, such as biopiracy. But while Harvey doesn't mention it, a strong argument could be made that such a list should also include the political production of the illegal immigrant as a source of unfree and exposed labour (De Genova 2002; Moulier Boutang 1998). Locating its representation of migrant work within an assemblage comprising systems of surveillance, military and police personnel, free enterprise zones, and smuggling networks, Hackitectura unsettles the pure view of the economy, and reveals a regime of work shot through with relations of violence and force.

There is one final point to make. While an assemblage might be likened to a machine because of the interaction of its parts, and their translation of energy into certain outputs, it has none of the fixed attributes which we typically associate with the more conventional conception of machinery. Assemblages are provisional and contingent arrangements. The connections between their parts are not guaranteed. Bits are prone to flying off at unforeseeable moments and at unpredictable tangents. There is one symbol on the map that I have not yet mentioned. It seems to be the figure of Marianne. Of course, this figure first appeared at the time of the French Revolution as a symbol of liberty and citizenship. Yet Marianne was and remains a much-contested symbol. Revolutionaries had depicted her wearing a Phrygian cap, a cap that had been worn by freed slaves in Greece and Rome, but also by Mediterranean seamen and convicts in the galleys. In many representations of Marianne, such as busts in many town halls, the cap was deemed to be too seditious and replaced with a crown. The revolutionary force of Marianne was neutralized, her image sanitized and made more compatible with less democratic forms of rule. Marianne would thus seem to be a particularly suitable image to attach to this assemblage – a sign of potential future citizenships, but also citizenships without assurances.

Conclusion

This chapter has argued that the project of developing a more culturally attuned and informed version of political economy is a timely and important one. It has suggested that any discussion of the intersection of politics with cultural and economic phenomena should pay attention to those occasions when it is not so much the constitution of the economic which is at stake, but its suppression or displacement. The chapter has suggested the notion of anti-political economy as a useful starting point for investigations which examine the delimitation of the economic.

The argument has been illustrated by reference to the case of migration cartography. A secondary argument of the chapter is that these migration maps deserve to be an object of critical analysis in their own right, and that such analysis can enrich ongoing work on the visualization, securitization and geopoliticization of migration. It transpires that it would be inaccurate to describe migration cartography unequivocally as a practice of anti-political economy. In many cases it is, but not always. For migration mapping is, in fact, not adequately described as a singular instrument of power or ideology but more accurately a heterogeneous field comprising multiple political agendas, representations, interests and possibilities. Indeed, so rich and insightful are certain forms of migration counter-mapping that they can serve not just as case studies for scholarly analysis in political economy or migration and security studies, but as materials that might aid in the development of new and better concepts.

In a recent study oriented towards theorizing what he calls 'the turbulence of migration', Papastergiadis argues that contemporary forms of migration have become so complex and diverse that 'it is now almost impossible to map movement with a series of arrows, on a flat two-dimensional representation of the world' (Papastergiadis 2000: 24). If this is indeed the case, then we are faced with something of a conundrum. Why is it that migration mapping – which in many cases does indeed reduce migration to a series of arrows on a two-dimensional plane – should become a common representational practice just at a time when it should be in many ways outmoded? In showing that migration mapping can operate in multiple registers – official, popular, radical – and can find various political and anti-political applications, this chapter on the cartography of illegal immigration has offered one possible answer to this puzzle.

Notes

1 I am grateful to William Biebuyck and Oxana Golovkina for their assistance with research for this chapter, and to Canada's Social Sciences and Humanities Research Council for funding. The editors provided insightful comments on an earlier draft, as did participants at workshops in Ottawa, London and Minneapolis, where some of the themes were first worked out.
2 Certainly if we look beyond the social sciences narrowly conceived we do find a sustained engagement with questions concerning the visual representation and construction of human migration. Video artists, film-makers, curators, cultural and urban theorists are amongst those who are currently exploring the visual (and aural) field of migration. See, for example, Projekt Migration, a major initiative funded by Germany's Federal Culture Foundation, which included seminars and an exhibition in Cologne in 2005, and generated the impressive catalogue, *Projekt Migration* (Cologne: DuMont Verlag, 2005). That said, even amongst cultural and performative work, there has been little engagement with questions of mapping. One exception is the video work of Ursula Biemann. For instance, in *Contained Mobility* (Biemann 2004) she uses cartographic idioms to examine political controversies about human migration, subtly conveying how there is an ongoing geo-strategic re-coding of ports and other spaces of everyday commerce. More recently, see the excellent website MigMap, and its powerful 'virtual cartography of European migration policies' (www.transitmigration.org/migmap/home_ map1.html; accessed 18 September, 2008). Critical here is the fact that it is not migrants and population flows but the migration, security, humanitarian and policing agencies and their expert discourses that are located at the center of the mapping exercise.
3 Elsewhere I have suggested the name of domopolitics for the move that seeks to legitimate certain forms of migration policy in the name of the state as 'home' (Walters 2004). Domopolitics seems particularly useful for thinking about cases where the management of the state and the defense of society is not rationalized in explicitly bio-racial terms or even within a language of (national) culture, but instead through allusions to house-breaking and home invasion. In these circumstances the idea of border control comes to resemble a home alarm system or firewall (Walters 2006).
4 For example, see many of the excellent essays collected in Ong and Collier (2005).
5 A fuller discussion of this map would need to consider it in terms of a genealogy of migration governance. With certain exceptions (Inda 2006; Ngai 2004) this project remains undeveloped. One aspect of such a genealogy would surely be an account of the contingently formed and shifting objects and territories of migration governance. If so, then interventions such as ICMPDs will perhaps appear in connection with the birth of something new – a *dispositif* formed around the time, space, economy and culture of *transit*.

Bibliography

Aradau, Claudia (2004) 'The perverse politics of four-letter words: risk and pity in the securitization of human trafficking', *Millennium*, 33(2): 251–77.

An Architektur (2003) 'The geography of a border: Sangatte', available online at http:// www.anarchitektur.com/aa03_sangatte/aa03_sangatte.pdf (accessed on 18 September 2008).

Balibar, Etienne (2004) 'Europe as borderland', *Alexander von Humboldt Lecture in Human Geography*, University of Nijmegen, 10 November, available online at http://www.ru.nl/socgeo/colloquium/Europe%20as%20Borderland.pdf (accessed: 18 September 2008).

Barlett, Donald and James Steele (2004) 'Who left the door open?', *Time*, (September 20) 164(12): 51–63.

Barry, Andrew (1996) 'The European network', *New Formations*, 29: 26–37.

—— (2002) 'The anti-political economy', *Economy and Society*, 31(2): 268–84.

BBC (2001) 'Europe's asylum "soft touch"?', BBC News Online, 4 September, available at http://news.bbc.co.uk/2/hi/uk_news/1524588.stm (accessed 18 September 2008).

Biemann, U. (2003) 'Writing Counter-Geography', available on-line at http://www.geobodies.org/resources/_dI/Europlex_engl_txt_low?dI accessed: 16/10/09

Biemann, Ursula (2004) *Contained Mobility* (DVD).

Bigo, Didier (2002) 'Security and immigration: toward a critique of the governmentality of unease', *Alternatives*, 27(1) (supplement): 63–92.

Black, Jeremy (1997) *Maps and Politics*, Chicago, IL: University of Chicago Press.

Buonfino, Alessandro (2004) 'Between unity and plurality: the politicization and securitization of the discourse of immigration in Europe', *New Political Science*, 26(1): 23–49.

Ceyhan, Ayse and Anastassia Tsoukala (2002) 'The securitization of migration in western societies: ambivalent discourses and policies', *Alternatives*, 27: 21–41.

Crampton, Jeremy (2001) 'Maps as social constructions: power, communication and visualization', *Progress in Human Geography*, 25(2): 235–52.

Dalby, Simon and Gearóid Ó Tuathail (1998) *Rethinking Geopolitics*, New York: Routledge.

De Genova, Nicholas (2002) 'Migrant "illegality" and deportability in everyday life', *Annual Review of Anthropology*, 31: 419–47.

Deleuze, Gilles and Félix Guattari (1987) *A Thousand Plateaus: Capitalism and Schizophrenia*, London: Athlone Press.

Düvell, Franck (2006) 'Crossing the fringes of Europe: transit migration in the EU's neighbourhood', *Centre on Migration, Policy and Society Working Paper* 33, available at: http://www.compas.ox.ac.uk/publications/Working%20papers/WP0633-Duvell.pdf (accessed 18 September 2008).

Fadaiat (2005) 'Technological observatory of the Straits', available at http://straddle3.net/media/print/0609_fadaiat_book_txt.pdf (accessed 18 September 2008).

Ferguson, James (2006) 'The anti-politics machine', in Aradhana Sharma and Akhil Gupta (eds) *The Anthropology of the State: A Reader*, Malden, MA: Blackwell, pp. 270–86.

Foucault, Michel (1977) *Discipline and Punish: the Birth of the Prison*, London: A. Lane.

Foucher, Michel (2001) 'The geopolitics of frontlines and borderlines', in Jacques Lévy (ed.) *From Geopolitics to Global Politics: a French Connection*, London: Frank Cass, pp. 159–70.

Gilbert, Martin (1969) *Jewish History Atlas*, Arthur Banks (cartography), London: Weidenfeld and Nicolson.

Hardt, Michael and Antonio Negri (2000) *Empire*, Cambridge, MA: Harvard University Press.

Harvey, David (2004) '"The new imperialism": accumulation by dispossession', in Leo Panitch and Colin Leys (eds) *The Socialist Register 2004*, London: Merlin.

Huysmans, Jeff (2006) *The Politics of Insecurity*, London: Routledge.

Ibarra, Ignacio and Jeffry Scott (2000) 'Marvin's journey: one migrant's tale', *Arizona Daily Star* (online), 29 October, available at http://www.azstarnet.com/journey/day1.html (accessed 18 September 2008).

Ibarra, Ignacio, David Schlosser and staff (2000) 'Untitled', *The Arizona Daily Star*, 29 October, available at: http://www.azstarnet.com/journey/thejourney.gif (accessed 18 September 2008).

ICMPD (2007) 'MTM map on Mediterranean and African irregular migration routes', available at http://www.icmpd.org/fileadmin/ICMPD-Website/MTM/New-Map-MTM_Poster-Landscape_EN_v1.pdf (accessed 18 September 2008).

Inda, Jonathan (2006) *Targeting Immigrants: Government, Technology, and Ethics*, Oxford: Blackwell.

Joyce, Patrick (2005) *The Rule of Freedom*, London: Verso.

Latour, Bruno (1993) *We Have Never Been Modern*, Cambridge MA: Harvard University Press.

Mezzadra, Sandro (2004) 'The right to escape', *Ephemera*, 4(3): 267–75.

MigMap (n.d.) 'A virtual cartography of European migration policies', available at http://www.transmigration.org/migmap (accessed 18 September 2008).

Mogel, Lize and Alexis Bhagat (eds) (2008) *An Atlas of Radical Cartography*, Los Angeles: JOAAP Press.

Moulier Boutang, Yann (1998) *De l'esclavage au salariat : économie historique du salariat bridé*, Paris: Presses universitaires de France.

Neocleous, Mark (2003) *Imagining the State*, Philadelphia, PA: Open University Press.

Ngai, Mae (2004) *Impossible Subjects: Illegal Aliens and the Making of Modern America*, Princeton, NJ: Princeton University Press.

Ong, Aihwa (2005) 'Splintering cosmopolitanism: Asian immigrants and zones of autonomy in the American West', in Thomas Blom Hansen and Finn Stepputat (eds) *Sovereign Bodies: Citizens, Migrants, and States in the Postcolonial World*, Princeton, NJ: Princeton University Press, pp. 257–75.

Ong, Aihwa and Stephen Collier (eds) (2005) *Global Assemblages: Technology, Politics, and Ethics as Anthropological Problems*, Malden, MA: Blackwell.

Papastergiadis, Nikos (2000) *The Turbulence of Migration*, Malden, MA: Polity.

Pérez de Lama, José and Belén Barrigón Ferrero (hackitectura.net) with Javier Toret (2006) 'Cartografia del Estrecho de Gibraltar. Frontera y migraciones 2006 [Cartography of the Straits of Gibraltar: Border and migrations 2006]', available online at HTTP: http://mcs.hackitectura.net/tiki-browse_image.php?galleryId=20&sort_mode=created_desc&desp=25&offset=0&imageId=1149 (accessed 18 September 2008)

Pounds, Norman (1951) 'The origin of the idea of natural frontiers in France', *Annals of the Association of American Geographers*, 41: 146–57.

Protection Project (2002) 'Human rights report on trafficking in persons, especially women and children', Washington, DC: The Protection Project.

Raley, Rita (2008) 'Border hacks: the risks of tactical media' in Louise Amoore and Marieke de Goede (eds) *Risk and the War on Terror*, London: Routledge, pp. 197–217.

Sassen, Saskia (1998) *Globalization and its Discontents*, New York: New Press.

Sharma, Nandita (2003) *Travel Agency: A Critique of Anti_Trafficking Campaigns'*, *Refuge*, 21(3): 53–65.

Time (2004) 'Breaking Point [a map]', *Time.com*, available at http://www.time.com/time/covers/1101040920/map/ (accessed on 18 September 2008).

Walters, William (2004) 'Secure borders, safe haven, domopolitics', *Citizenship Studies*, 8(3): 237–60.

—— (2006) 'Rethinking borders beyond the state', *Comparative European Politics*, 4(2/3): 141–59.

Waring, Marilyn (1988) *If Women Counted: A New Feminist Economics*, San Francisco, CA: Harper Collins.

Williams, Michael (2003) 'Words, images, enemies: securitization and international politics', *International Studies Quarterly*, 47(4): 511–31.

6 Joyless cosmopolitans

The moral economy of ethical tourism[1]

Debbie Lisle

The return of Thomas Cook

As many historians and scholars of tourism have argued, travel turned into modern tourism on the 5 July 1841 when the teetotal preacher Thomas Cook organized a railway journey from Leicester to Loughborough so that over 500 people could attend a Temperance meeting (Inglis 2000: 14; Withey 1997: 135–6; see also Brendan 1991; Hamilton 2005; Swinglehurst 1974). The excursion was organized for Baptists and other individuals who had signed the Temperance pledge, and the destination was chosen 'exactly because Loughborough was dry and the whole family could go on a day's outing without fear of meeting drunks' (Inglis 2000: 47). It seems there was no stopping the preacher after that fateful summer's day in 1841: 'Cook's Tours' rapidly expanded to the seaside, the Continent, the Middle East, Egypt, America, and eventually around the world. Indeed, Cook's global expansion – facilitated by his development of the travellers' cheque – became the template for modern tourism in the twentieth century. Cook's inauguration of modern tourism offers us a stable point of origin from which we can compare our current progress: do our contemporary holidays reflect the same imperialist gaze that Cook's Tours did? Can we continue Cook's dream of 'democratising' travel by making it more affordable? What lessons can we learn from the successful 'branding' of Thomas Cook & Sons in the nineteenth century? For me, these Cook-inspired reflections too often neglect how the *moralizing* tone at the heart of Cook's enterprise continues to shape our experiences of travel. It would be easy – too easy, I think – to confine such moralizing to Cook's involvement in the Temperance movement. Certainly, as Withey argues, Cook built his tourism business using 'the same kind of moral fervour previously devoted to publishing Temperance tracts' (1997: 137). But such 'moral fervour' was only a small part of a much more comprehensive worldview in which Cook reproduced predominant, and often contradictory, Victorian values in the world of tourism. Cook's worldview – his ethical vision if you like – makes more sense when considered alongside other nineteenth-century philanthropists and reformers (e.g. Robert Owen) whose laudable egalitarian dreams were constrained by elitist values and Victorian morality. Initially, Cook appears to be an early class warrior because his organized excursions ran entirely counter to the elitist eighteenth-century Grand Tour that restricted the experience of travel to privileged aristocrats (Butcher 2003: 36–7; Withey 1997: 135–66). Indeed, Cook believed that 'everyone, rich and poor alike, had the *right* to travel', and he employed his particular brand of 'enthusiastic philanthropy' to make that experience possible for the working classes (Withey 1997: 138; Smith 1998: v).

I want to resist the easy championing of Cook's efforts to extend travel to the masses, and look instead at the limitations of his egalitarian dreams. His efforts to democratize travel were circumscribed – and indeed compromised – by his wider ethical vision that dictated what *kind* of travel was to be made available to 'the millions'. For Cook, travel – even for pleasure – was to be the improving and ennobling sort that promoted 'tolerance and Christian benevolence' (Withey 1997: 138). It was not just *any* kind of travel that Cook was offering to the masses – it was the kind that would improve and even civilize them in line with Christian values and Victorian morality. While such religious moralizing might seem distasteful to our secular, modern ears, it was not surprising in nineteenth-century Britain; indeed, the areas of health, religion, education and industry were all being transformed by various strategies of 'betterment'. Cook simply added travel to that mix: 'How to Behave' *whilst travelling* became one more set of stipulations about 'How to Behave' more generally in nineteenth-century Britain. What particularly interests me about Cook's effort to enlighten the masses through the experience of travel is its contradictory nature – the way he offered up the pleasures of travel to the masses, only to discipline the enjoyment of such pleasures. The echo of Foucault is loud and clear: all strategies that aim to emancipate and improve subjects – from the extension of healthcare and education to the extension of travel and leisure – are always also about disciplining, regulating and controlling those subjects (1990a, 1990b, 1992). And so it was with Cook's Tours. One was not simply let loose on the world, one was taught how to behave *properly* while travelling by adhering to Mr Cook's moral instructions, which were delivered either in person (if he was your guide and exemplar), or in his monthly *Excursionist* magazine and other press articles. My point is that Cook's efforts to bring travel to the masses cannot be understood as a simple or innocent propagation of egalitarian values; rather, such 'emancipating' practices must be examined for the way they constructed, disciplined and moralized the new subject position of the mass tourist. In this sense, Cook's Tours are politically significant because, like other biopolitical practices of the time, they aimed to transform the 'unruly' working classes of nineteenth-century Britain into cultured, enlightened and civilized subjects.

I start with Thomas Cook because I think the contradiction he originally embodied – that travel is for everyone, but only if it is the improving kind of travel – remains fundamental to the way we understand tourism today. Such moralizing is especially evident in debates over ethical tourism – certainly everyone should be able to travel, but only if they travel ethically. There is no doubt that the unrestricted growth of tourism around the world since Cook's time has caused serious problems, most notably the entrenchment of structural global inequality and the destruction of the environment. Indeed, efforts to redress these problems are being mobilized all over the place – in government departments, in the media, on Internet blogs, in academic circles, in NGOs, in industry 'codes of conduct' and above all, in consumer decision making. My concern is that the panic over *what to do* about the serious problems caused by tourism has produced a very powerful consensus in which ethical tourism is not only placed in opposition to modern mass tourism, but it has also become the magic solution that will alleviate all the problems caused by over a century of modern mass tourism. What I am most concerned with is how the consensus over ethical tourism has assimilated and neutralized the critical force of those who initially alerted us to the problems caused by tourism in the first place – political economists who warned of the structural inequalities exacerbated by the tourism industry; sociologists and cultural studies scholars who revealed the commodification of local cultures and the rise of consumerism; and environmentalists who documented tourism's contribution to climate change.

This chapter identifies and critiques the *normative* claims at the heart of the consensus over ethical tourism, and illustrates the power relations that are both instigated and effaced by such claims. As such, the chapter uses the case of ethical tourism to make a deliberate intervention in the wider debates about cosmopolitan ethics. Brassett and Bulley helpfully suggest that these wide-ranging debates take place between those who see value in identifying, strengthening and applying universal ethical norms that lead to emancipation (we might call these 'progressive cosmopolitans'), and those who call attention to the power relations embedded in such claims and point out how they enact 'effective silences' (we might call these 'critical cosmopolitans') (2007: 2; see also Beck 2002; Calhoun 2002; Cheah and Robbins 1998; Derrida 2001; Erskine 2002; Heater 2002; Molz 2005; Turner 2002; Vertovec and Cohen 2002). My argument is that the consensus over ethical tourism maintains itself by reproducing an account of ethics as advocated by progressive cosmopolitans. The dominant tradition of normative thinking that underscores this position assumes that ethics can simply be *added* to practices such as tourism to help us identify and censure damaging forms of tourism, and develop better forms of tourism for the future. I start from the position that the 'ethical' cannot be separated out in this manner; rather, it is always already embedded in the political, the economic, the cultural and the environmental. In refusing the predominant normative framing of the problem, this chapter draws on critical cosmopolitan thinkers to argue that the current consensus over ethical tourism (i.e. that it is the solution to all our problems) can only be maintained to the extent that it silences the problems, difficulties and consequences that ethical tourism itself produces. By deliberately uncovering and foregrounding such problems, this chapter aims not only to puncture the consensus over ethical tourism, but also to destabilize the wider progressive cosmopolitan agenda upon which that consensus rests. But the chapter has a wider concern as well: it forces us all to think more carefully and critically about what 'the ethical' in ethical tourism actually entails. For lurking within all of our political economies of tourism, our cultural analyses of its commodification, and our efforts to chart tourism's environmental damages, is a powerful – if unacknowledged – account of ethics. To demonstrate how a particularly normative account of ethics is currently shaping how we address the problems of tourism, the paper critically reads Smith and Duffy's (2003) comprehensive *The Ethics of Tourism Development*, and challenges their idea that 'doing good' on holiday can help us overcome entrenched cultural differences. My point is that whenever we buy into the seductive idea that ethical tourism is the magic solution to all of our problems, we are – whether we know it or not – reproducing this normative account of ethics. Allowing such an account to be reproduced uncritically means we become complicit in the power relations, hierarchies, exclusions and violence that the prevailing consensus over ethical tourism is currently enacting.

To foreground the work that ethics does in tourism, this chapter examines the *moral* economy of ethical tourism. If we understand an economy to be a system (large or small) within which differential values are ascribed to different practices, then the term *moral* economy adds an extra layer to that process of ascription by highlighting how value is saturated with assumptions about *virtue*. Using the concept of moral economy draws our attention to the way in which a prevailing discourse of virtue mobilizes and connects diverse subjects – economic, political and cultural subjects – through a particular understanding of how to be good. What I am interested in is how the current consensus over ethical tourism is held together by a discourse of virtue and driven by a particular notion of being good: not only does ethical tourism solve all the problems caused by mass tourism, it also makes you a better person and the world a better place. Certainly it is possible to examine the specific moral economies of other types of tourism. Indeed, every traveller – from the most predatory sex-tourist to the most earnest rainforest volunteer – operates within a moral economy that ascribes value to their actions. But what marks ethical tourism out from other forms of travel is that it has constructed and maintained a discursive monopoly on virtue that makes the consensus over ethical tourism easy to secure. By separating virtue from pleasure, this discursive monopoly encourages the virtues of ethical tourism and condemns the pursuit of pleasure endemic to mass tourism. Such mobilizations of virtue within tourism are nothing new; indeed, Thomas Cook saw travel as a civilizing and improving practice that 'broadened the mind and encouraged a thirst for knowledge, in the process breaking down barriers of class and nationality' (Withey 1997: 138). Travelling with Cook gave you clear instructions on how to be *good* while experiencing a holiday. Ethical tourism is simply a contemporary version of the same thing: it gives you instructions on how to 'be good' on vacation by redressing economic inequalities, respecting other cultures and protecting the environment.

To begin unravelling and politicizing such a tightly packed consensus, this chapter refuses such an easy separation of virtue and pleasure, and argues instead that virtue and pleasure circulate in more complex ways within the moral economy of ethical tourism. As Foucault has argued, the value judgements produced by a discourse of virtue are never aimed solely at the repression of pleasure – for this would be to reproduce an untenable separation between virtue and pleasure. Rather, he argues that a discourse of virtue sustains itself by continually producing, multiplying, disseminating and ultimately managing pleasure (1990a, 1990b, 1992). Thus, the disciplining effects of ethical tourism's moral economy (i.e. its instructions on how to be good and how to condemn those who are bad), cannot be divorced from the productive aspects of such an economy (i.e. the new possibilities for pleasure that appear within the discourse of virtue at particular places and times). I want to argue that we are currently witnessing just such a production within ethical tourism as virtue is being transformed into a perverse kind of pleasure. To illustrate the contemporary circulation of virtue and pleasure, this chapter examines the puritanical nature of ethical tourists and their ability to take pleasure in ascetic, pious and worthy forms of travel. By way of conclusion, I suggest that Michel Houellebecq's diagnosis of global tourism as bleak and even nihilistic in his novel *Platform* (2002) offers us a compelling alternative to the normative consensus currently framing ethical tourism (1990a, 1990b, 1992).

Visited to death

Modern mass tourism has been considered a problem of some sort since it began on that fateful day in 1841. Indeed, Butcher argues that mass tourism has always been denigrated by self-appointed guardians of proper, good and authentic 'travel', and we have seen a number of incarnations of the travel = good/ tourism = bad dichotomy since Cook's Tours began (2003: 33–49). But the recent privileging of ethical tourism as the only good form of tourism has constructed a powerful consensus between a number of disparate voices that seek to limit the growth of mass tourism. This consensus begins at the material level: without the proper infrastructure, the very tourist attraction that is bringing visitors (i.e. an ancient building, a pristine mountain) starts to erode – it is literally visited to death. In this sense, tourism is a victim of its own success. The consensus continues in the realm of political economy: the tourism industry continually exacerbates the global disparity of wealth and entrenches structural inequalities. Examples of this might include, for example, wealthy Western tourists who visit global resorts such as Sandals or Club Med in places like Jamaica or Senegal who see nothing outside of the gated resort, and whose money enhances the profits of the multinational owners rather than the local community. The argument here is that because tourism is primarily an *industry*, it operates through a fundamentally unjust global economy, and therefore reproduces the structural inequalities between wealthy tourist consumers and disempowered tourist workers. Such structural inequalities are also reproduced in the cultural realm as destinations cater to the short-term needs of tourists with economic power rather than the longer-term needs of the local community. This means that tourist sites all over the world – be they cities, nature reserves, museums or resorts – are all starting to resemble one another as destinations are commodified in order to serve the needs of a global travelling elite. The consensus over ethical tourism is most secure, however, in the litany of environmental damage that is caused by mass tourism (Hall and Gossling 2005; Holden 2000; Hunter and Green 1995). Holden helpfully categorizes tourism-related environmental damage into three main areas: resource usage (e.g. tourists getting clean water for showers while locals are deprived of drinking water), behavioural considerations (e.g. the dramatic increase of trekkers to Nepal has led to deforestation) and pollution (e.g. carbon emissions released by airplanes full of tourists jetting off for holidays) (2000: 64–107).

Unsurprisingly, such widespread agreement over the *seriousness* of the problems caused by mass tourism has prompted media workers, activists and academics to offer ethical tourism as the solution. 'Travel' sections in broadsheet newspapers regularly carry stories on ethical tourism, promote ethical tourism companies, stage 'Ethical Travel Awards' and even have links so that readers can offset their own carbon emissions. Traveller blogs such as the *Lonely Planet* 'Thorn Tree' travel forum have dedicated sections on ethical and responsible tourism (*Lonely Planet* 2008), and many activists are using blogs like 'Hospitality Ethics Pro Human Rights' to advocate for policy changes. Such efforts are supported by NGOs such as Tearfund and the London-based Tourism Concern who run specific media campaigns, pursue independent research, provide educational programmes and offer 'ethical' and 'green' travel advice in guidebook and webpage formats. Such enthusiasm from media and activist circles is matched by academics in tourism studies who are busy applying established ethical traditions to the case study of tourism (Fleckenstein and Huebsch 1999; Hultsman 1995; Macbeth 2005; Molloy and Fennell 1998; Payne and Dimanche 1996; Wheeler 1992). By far the most developed academic research on ethical tourism is in the area of 'Business Ethics and Marketing' which locates ethical tourism within the wider context of ethical consumerism and seeks to enhance this as a 'niche market' (Karwacki and Boyd 1995; Weeden 2002; Wheeler 1995).[2] This work resolves the seeming incompatibility between business and ethics by arguing that we *can* reconcile the drive for profit that underscores the tourist industry with our desire to treat hosts fairly, respect their cultures, and protect the environment. As Fleckstein and Huebsch argue, 'Being ethical is good business since being ethical enhances a company's profits, management effectiveness, public image and employee relations' (1999: 142). The global tourism industry and national governments have responded to this growing consensus by institutionalizing various 'codes of ethical conduct', the most prominent being the United Nations World Tourism Organization's 'Global Code of Ethics for Tourism' which was implemented in July 2001. It argues that tourism must do the following if it is to become more ethical:

- Contribute to mutual understanding and respect between peoples and societies.
- Operate as a vehicle for individual and collective fulfilment.
- Be a key factor in sustainable development.
- Contribute to the enhancement of the cultural heritage of humankind.
- Be a beneficial activity for host countries and communities.
- Take account of the obligations of stakeholders in tourism development.
- Work towards tourism as a human right.
- Protect the liberty of tourist movements.

- Protect the rights of the workers and entrepreneurs in the tourism industry.
- Implement the principles of the Global Code of Ethics for Tourism.

(UNWTO 2001: 1–8)

In addition, specific ethical codes have been developed by various professional groups within the industry as a whole (e.g. associations of tour guides, travel agents and independent tour operators). Although the implementation of such codes is made difficult by their voluntary nature, they have become important markers of aspiration for governments, businesses and tourism boards who use them to demonstrate that they are not only addressing the serious problems caused by tourism, but they are becoming more ethical in the process. For me, however, such codes are useful because they are an 'executive summary' of the key issues that hold the widespread consensus over ethical tourism together.

The problem with solutions

It is not surprising that within such a widespread consensus, voices that point out the *problems* with ethical tourism are rare. In development studies, however, such criticisms are starting to be articulated by those who question tourism's ability to fulfil the goals of development. Butcher, for example, illustrates the lingering colonialism of ethical tourism projects that construct non-Western cultures, peoples and nature as fragile entities that require *protection* from the evils of capitalist industry and Western consumerist values. He argues that by protecting 'traditional culture' and 'pristine nature' for their own pleasure and enjoyment, ethical tourists actually discourage larger (and much-needed) economic development projects that could benefit the local community and protect the environment. His point is not that sprawling resorts should always be chosen as a strategy of development, but that there is an opportunity cost involved when small-scale, 'ethical' and sustainable tourism projects are privileged over larger 'mass tourism' schemes that have the capacity to generate more income, jobs and economic growth. The problem is that in conducting their fight against mass tourism in developing societies (and its attendant evils of capitalism, consumerism, modernity and globalization), ethical tourists 'are doing the very thing they accuse western governments and companies of being responsible for – superimposing their own version of development, in this case one that is intensely critical of the modern project, onto societies crying out for the material benefits of modern societies' (Butcher 2003: 102). Butcher's work is a compelling examination of how the demands of ethical tourism are affecting development in places such as Belize, Ghana, India, Nepal and Zimbabwe, and it clearly demonstrates how 'morally superior alternatives' to mass tourism often reproduce the 'vicious circle' of fragility, dependency and poverty they are trying so earnestly to alleviate (2003: 56).

While Butcher's more empirically oriented work does not address the ethical and political claims inherent in the consensus over ethical tourism, his argument does provide an important starting place for my own efforts to challenge this consensus.

As does Smith and Duffy's (2003) *The Ethics of Tourism Development* which complements many of the empirical case studies analysed by Butcher with theoretical considerations of the main approaches to ethics. Smith and Duffy analyse tourism development through the lenses of moral relativism, hedonism, utilitarianism, cultural difference, virtues, rights and justice, and argue that despite claims to the contrary, many traditional accounts of ethics do not adequately address the inequalities so endemic in tourism development. For example, they demonstrate how utilitarian arguments privilege and protect majority claims at the expense of minorities, and can therefore be used to justify violence done to minority groups if it guarantees the greatest happiness for the most people. So while the 40 Ibaloi families who were displaced by the new Sheraton hotel in Addis Ababa suffered an injustice, this was ultimately justified because it is outweighed by the happiness of the thousands of guests who stay at the hotel, and the happiness of hundreds of locals who are employed by the Sheraton (Smith and Duffy 2003: 62–3). Smith and Duffy also critique the discourse of human rights that is articulated most powerfully in the numerous 'codes of ethical conduct' implemented by governments, NGOs and the tourism industry. While this discourse offers a more persuasive argument than utilitarianism, they point out that human rights can also act 'as a smokescreen to cover the ruthless and self-interested pursuit of policies aimed at furthering particular rather than universal human interests' (Smith and Duffy 2003: 79).

Smith and Duffy's comprehensive account of the ethical foundations of tourism development does not claim to offer a new ethical theory that will address the problems caused by mass tourism (2003: 166). This is fair enough – the book is more a critical survey than a polemic – but what I find interesting about their work is that an ethical alternative is always implicit in their critique. While they do not elaborate upon this alternative, it strikes me as an effort to push the limits of the progressive cosmopolitan framework that they are working within. Smith and Duffy acknowledge that 'the key problem for ethics seems to be that of understanding the other' (2003: 166), and after critiquing Rawlsian and Habermasian notions of social justice, they suggest that an 'ethics of care', or 'difference ethics', is the best foundation for ethical tourism. Drawing on Irigaray and Levinas – and paraphrasing Gadamer – they outline a more just relationship with the Other:

> This relation cannot be forced on the Other but requires us to develop a tactful response to their presence, one that helps us understand their difference to us and preserves a respectful distance. It avoids the offensive, the intrusive, the violation of the intimate sphere of the other.
>
> (Smith and Duffy 2003: 166)

As they rightly point out, this recalibration of difference has serious implications for notions of authenticity – something central to *all* forms of tourism including ethical tourism (Cohen 1988; Hughes 1995; MacCannell 1976, 1992; Wang 1999). Drawing on Levinas, they argue that the tourist's desire for *authentic* difference in the form of the exotic is nothing more than a projection of their own values, desires and expectations. Because they reduce everything to the same, and interpret the world through their own normative framework, tourists are unable to 'experience a genuine *ethical* relation with the Other' (Smith and Duffy 2003: 134). For Smith and Duffy then, the problems caused by mass tourism – its reproduction of structural inequality, its commodification of culture and its denigration of the environment – stem from the tourist's inability to construct and maintain a *respectful distance* from the Other.

By advocating tourism based on an 'Ethics of Care', Smith and Duffy imply that it is actually *possible* to have an ethical encounter with the Other so long as 'respectful distance' is maintained. This presents a difficulty: 'respectful distance' can only occur if it somehow neutralizes – or even forgets – all of the historically constituted power relations that exist between selves and Others in the moment of encounter. My point is that questions of power – and of historically constituted power relations – absolutely *cannot* be sidestepped in tourism encounters, no matter how 'respectful' the distance might be between selves and Others. Smith and Duffy suggest 'the fact that we cannot have a truly authentic experience of another culture, one that is pure and unaffected by our own cultural expectations, does not rule out the possibility of an ethical tourism based on respect for that culture' (2003: 132). Somehow, an 'ethics of care' creates the conditions for *genuine* encounters between hosts and guests which can 'blossom into something more: a real desire to preserve rainforests, to assist the poor of the South, and so on' (2003: 134). What troubles me with this claim is that it leaves ethical tourism – the kind that makes 'real' efforts to help the poor – free from critical scrutiny. Relying on notions of 'respect' and 'recognition' – absolute hallmarks of the progressive cosmopolitan agenda – does not neutralize or avert the ongoing work of power. Rather, such terms end up installing a false notion of equality between selves and Others, and in doing so, negate the difficult asymmetries that saturate all tourism encounters. So while I agree with much of Smith and Duffy's critique of how the conventional ethical foundations of tourism often entrench inequality, I would also want to apply such critical force to their preferred 'ethics of care' alternative. In the end, their notion of 'respectful distance' is not an alternative at all because it remains indebted to a progressive cosmopolitan tradition.

In their conclusion, Smith and Duffy argue that 'a genuine ethical tourism might seem almost impossible … and while a healthy scepticism of much ethical theory is certainly necessary, things may not be quite so bleak' (2003: 164). However, things *are* impossible, and indeed bleak – even those 'sensitive' tourism encounters that claim to maintain the 'respectful distance' produced within an ethics of care mobilize their own power relations, and we should not pretend otherwise. Arguing that the *best* forms of tourism invoke Levinas's notion of 'respectful distance', Irigaray's notion of *wonder* and Gadamer's belief in the *fusion of horizons* is to forget that these framings are *also* characterized by intractable tensions, struggles and disagreements that can *never* be finally resolved, redeemed or overcome (Smith and Duffy 2003: 112–13, 166). As with all ethical traditions that provide a finally-final solution to a problem, an 'ethics of care' installs its own norms, ideals, limits, hierarchies and exclusions. And this is precisely where the limitations of Levinasian ethics are revealed. As many scholars have argued, his account of the relational ethics between self and Other, and the possibility of 'respectful distance' that this creates, are part of the problem because in separating the ethical from the political, Levinas consistently downplays the work of power (Beardsworth 1996; Campbell 1999; Critchley 1992, 1999; Connolly 1993; Derrida and Dufourmantelle 2000). To foreground power relations in the tourist encounter, we require a mode of deconstruction in which there is no distinction between ethics and politics. This is what Foucault called *ethico-political critique* – an approach that traces the power relations that are produced in particular moral economies at particular points in history (Campbell 2005; Simons 1994). This approach speaks directly to my project: it allows me to identify and trace the power relations that are produced by the contemporary moral economy of ethical tourism, and to show how the progressive cosmopolitan tradition currently bolstering the consensus over ethical tourism is intent on silencing those power relations. So where Smith and Duffy end, I want to begin – not with a new form of ethics, or a new 'solution' to the problem of mass tourism, but with an *ethico-political critique* that foregrounds the power relations that are being produced by ethical tourism.

The pleasures of virtue

As students of Foucault will know, the best way to identify power relations is to locate the subject positions that sustain them, and to trace the behaviours and affects that these subjects produce. One of the great silences contained within the consensus over ethical tourism is that it can only be sustained if it produces powerful feelings of guilt in tourists. Indeed, we only *become* ethical tourists because we are told that our selfish pursuit of pleasure whilst abroad causes harm to others – it entrenches economic inequalities between hosts and guests, it commodifies culture, and it contributes to the destruction of the environment. All of the arguments marshalled by advocates of ethical tourism are aimed at making us feel guilty at how our affluence negatively affects – and indeed, is built on the shoulders of – those in the Third World. Embracing ethical tourism (and ethical consumerism more generally) is the perfect solution: it allows us to maintain our current affluent lifestyles (including that much-needed holiday) whilst alleviating those disturbing feelings of guilt. We no longer have to feel bad about our acts of consumption because these acts have been transformed into *doing good for others* as a way to make us *feel good about ourselves*. This production of guilt – and its alleviation – is central to the moral economy of ethical tourism because it names *pleasure* as the experience which must be moralized and subject to condemnation. We know that pleasure is one of Urry's major categories in his taxonomy of modern tourism: 'Places are chosen to be gazed upon because there is an anticipation, especially through daydreaming and fantasy, of intense pleasures, either on a different scale or involving different senses from those customarily encountered' (1990: 3). We also know that the pursuit of pleasure through tourism has always been a primary object of 'moral detestation' and 'expressions of censure' (Berry 1994; Chard 1999: 47; Inglis 2000: 55–73). But what we always seem to forget is that the condemnation of pleasure only works if it succeeds in making the subject feel guilty enough to change their ways. For Chard, the production of guilt has undoubtedly changed our behaviour: while the Romantics threw off the religious and moral constrains of their time to pursue hedonistic pleasures abroad, the current moralization of tourism 'affirms the position of the traveller as the subject of more modest demands, seeking out carefully regulated pleasures' (Chard 1999: 47, 213).

Guilt, of course, is not just about the condemnation and regulation of pleasure – it is also about the mobilization of virtue. As Foucault has argued with regards to sexuality, virtue and pleasure can never be separated because pleasure is virtue's silent – and necessary – other (1976, 1984a, 1984b). He refutes the 'repressive hypothesis' which assumes that a discourse of virtue successfully prohibited and silenced sexuality through much of the eighteenth and nineteenth centuries. The notion that Victorians were uniformly prudish and straight-laced with regards to sexuality is a fiction. What was actually happening at the time was a production, multiplication and dispersion of discourses of sexuality such that the pleasures of sex became a 'problem' to be solved in the spheres of health, policing, marriage, education, law, etc. (Foucault 1976: 18). While Foucault's analysis of the 'regime of power-knowledge-pleasure' focuses specifically on the production of sexuality, it also tells us a great deal about the discursive construction and circulation of virtue and pleasure within the moral economy of ethical tourism. As the initial production of guilt suggests, the discourse of virtue can be disciplining – it can condemn, denounce and punish those subjects who partake in the damaging pleasures offered by mass tourism. But the discourse of virtue is also about the production, multiplication and dispersion of pleasure. In the case of ethical tourism, it rewards those who take pleasure in virtue itself – those who enjoy ascetic, sanctimonious and worthy forms of travel. This seems a strange contradiction, for how can one *take pleasure* in being virtuous?

In *The Genealogy of Morals* (1996), Nietzsche explores this contradiction by showing how pleasure can be taken in ascetic forms of life:

> an ascetic life is a contradiction in terms ... a green and cunning gaze is directed against thriving physiological growth, especially against its expression, beauty, joy; while a pleasure is felt and *sought* in failure, atrophy, pain, accident, ugliness, arbitrary atonements, self-denial, self-flagellation, self-sacrifice. All this is paradoxical to an extreme: we find ourselves confronted here with a contradiction which wills itself as a contradiction, which derives *enjoyment* from this suffering and even becomes increasingly self-assured and triumphant.

> (1996: 97)

Foucault develops this idea further and argues that whenever subjects achieve mastery over their desires and pursue asceticism in any form, they are experiencing a 'pious' form of pleasure. In *The History of Sexuality, Volume II*, he explains in detail how, as subjects, we are always doing battle with ourselves – we are always in training to be moderate and virtuous, and therefore we are always seeking victory over our innate desires and pleasures (1992: 62–77). Indeed, to be virtuous and behave ethically, it is necessary to adopt a 'combative attitude towards the pleasures' (1992: 66). Both Nietzsche and Foucault reject the traditional idea that pleasure is derived from hedonism and argue instead that it is derived from moderation, self-control and asceticism. This form of self-discipline goes hand in hand with a more public kind of pleasure derived from discovering and revealing the transgressors of established ethical norms. Indeed, Foucault describes the pleasure to be had from 'knowing that truth, of discovering and exposing it, the fascination of seeing it and telling it, of captivating and capturing others by it, of confiding it in secret, of luring it out in the open – the specific pleasure of the true discourse on pleasure' (1990a: 71). What this exposure ultimately enables, of course, is a negative judgement of those who are not able to successfully control and discipline their desire for pleasure. As Nietzsche argues, 'the ascetic treats life ... as a mistake which one rectifies through action – indeed, which one *should* rectify: for he *demands* that one should follow him, he imposes wherever he can his *own* evaluation of existence' (1996: 96). Following on from this, I want to argue that ethical tourists are the new ascetics. They engage in an agonistic battle with themselves in order to master their desires for exotic pleasure that erupt most explicitly when they are away from the more familiar surroundings of work and home. And by making virtue *pleasurable* through asceticism, ethical tourists are able to secure their identities by castigating those mass tourists who are unable to properly self-discipline.

This ascetic subject begins to make sense when we look at the opposition between pleasure and work that has traditionally framed the experience of tourism. The concept of the 'pleasure periphery' positions the Third World as the leisure playground for wealthy Western tourists so that pleasure, leisure and relaxation are located elsewhere, while denial, work and austerity are located at home (Butcher 2003: 102; Inglis 2000: 59; Turner and Ash 1975; Urry 1990: 19–20). Many sociologists have traced the effects of globalization upon this traditional spatialization of pleasure, arguing that a deterritorialization of the 'pleasure periphery' goes hand-in-hand with a deterritorialization of the labour market (Lash and Urry 1993; Rojek 1995). In other words, as the distinction between home and away began to disappear, so too did its attending distinction between work and pleasure. Such deterritorializations have enabled, rather than frustrated, ascetic ethical tourists who can now shape their holidays through a familiar *work ethic*. By experiencing pleasure only in the active doing good for others, ethical tourists effectively put the *travail* (heavy labour) back into the experience of travel.[3] Reinscribing the relationship between virtue and pleasure through a work ethic highlights the puritanism underscoring ethical tourism. Indeed, ethical tourists are now being branded through the more general marketing term of 'New Puritan' or even 'Neo-Crom' (harkening back to the seventeenth-century rise of Puritanism under Oliver Cromwell). While academics have largely ignored the construction of New Puritans, it has, unsurprisingly, been embraced by marketing consultants. As the Future Foundation reports, ethical forms of consumerism like eco-tourism are part of a wider 'Assault on Pleasure' that is forcing companies to respond to increased calls for regulation and legislation by consumers (2005). One of the primary characteristics of the New Puritan subjectivity is, of course, 'a new distribution of guilt' in which life is framed by the urge 'not to do things, not to indulge' (Future Foundation 2005: 2). If the Future Foundation is correct, then the rise of the New Puritans will have a serious effect on the tourism industry: 'by 2015, global tourism could be in decline because taking a flight to Costa Rica is considered a terribly irresponsible thing to do' (Siegle 2005: 18). They document that in 2005 long-haul flights and vacations to 'environmentally sensitive' sites (e.g. the Parthenon, Machu Picchu) remain unregulated, but by 2010 it is predicted that tourism will be one of the most heavily regulated sectors in the global economy (Future Foundation 2005: 12–13). It is not hard to hear the echo of this New Puritanism in the many 'codes of ethical conduct' advocated by governments, NGOs and the tourism industry. Indeed, such explicit prohibitions of 'bad' behaviour and exhortations to 'good' behaviour are reminiscent of religious doctrines based on a denial of earthly pleasures and a duty to God – only now such modes of discipline are being applied in a wholly secular context. For me, the rise of New Puritanism is significant because it is the clearest indication that virtue and pleasure have collapsed in the moral economy of ethical tourism.

Pleasure extended

One of the people to seriously question the ascetic and puritanical nature of ethical tourism is writer Michel Houellebecq. In his novel *Platform* (2002), Houellebecq punctures the smug confidence of ethical tourists by exposing their hypocrisy. *Platform* is about Michel, a disaffected middle-class civil servant who meets Valerie on a package tour to Thailand. The two of them embark on a tender relationship that includes dangerous sex, S&M and swinging, and eventually they start a holiday company to provide sex tourism for wealthy Europeans. As Michel explains, their company's resorts are necessarily located in a number of Third World destinations:

> You have several hundred million Westerners who have everything they could want but no longer manage to obtain sexual satisfaction: they spend their lives looking, but they don't find it and are completely miserable. On the other hand, you have several billion people who have nothing, who are starving, who die young, who live in conditions unfit for human habitation and who have nothing left to sell except their bodies and their unspoiled sexuality. It's simple, really simple to understand: it's an ideal trading opportunity. The money you could make is almost unimaginable.
>
> (Houellebecq 2002: 242)

In the end, Valerie is killed when one of their holiday resorts in Thailand is blown up by Islamic terrorists.[4] While the issues of race, politics and cultural difference are at the heart of Houellebecq's narrative, they are not, for me, the most interesting aspects of *Platform*. Houellebecq uses the example of sex tourism to demonstrate the hypocrisy of the normative claims traditionally used to justify the global expansion of Western consumerist values. In doing so, Houellebecq asks a number of significant questions: why is the global sexual economy subject to such legal regulation and moral censure? Would it not be better – indeed, more *ethical* – to legitimate the global practice of sex tourism in order to give Third World sex workers a fair deal? Houellebecq's point is that if we are really so concerned with making our consumption habits ethical, then that concern must extend into *all* of our habits, even those – like sex tourism – that we find distasteful.

Houellebecq's target is not sex tourists, but rather his Western, middle-class, left-leaning readership. Indeed, the overwhelming feeling produced by this book is discomfort, and that is largely due to the ethical orientation of Houellebecq's main character, Michel. As Ní Loingsigh argues, the reader is desperate to find some kind of resistance to Michel's proposition of ethical sex tourism – to find some moment of redemption – but Houellebecq, for the most part, refuses (2005: 86).[5] The one character who takes up a clear position against sex tourism – Josiane – is portrayed as self-righteous, duplicitous and ideologically inconsistent. When a number of her middle-class companions on the Thailand package tour admit to having sex with Thai prostitutes, she is outraged – she shrieks her disgust at them, throws her food across the table and storms out of dinner. Josiane, you see, considers herself not only a traveller, but an ethical one at that. The hypocrisy of any supposedly 'ethical' resistance to sex tourism is further revealed when Michel discusses *The White Book* – his underground guidebook that, 'under the pretence of denouncing sexual tourism, ... gave all the addresses, country by country' and offered detailed recommendations of the best places for paedophilia, etc. (Houellebecq 2002: 78–9). Such hypocrisy is finally sealed when the multinational conglomerate that owns Michel and Valerie's sex tourism company (and is fully cognisant of its activities) makes a public statement after the terrorist attack destroys the resort in Thailand: 'The Aurore Group, a signatory of the world charter for ethical tourism, in no way sanctions such activities; those responsible will be punished' (Houellebecq 2002: 340). As a reader, these moments of duplicity are recognizable and often hilarious – but they leave us with an unpalatable choice: either take up a position against sex tourism and align yourself with deranged ethical tourist zealots like Josiane, or accept Houellebecq's cynical universe where ethical claims always have political consequences. For the Western, middle-class, left-leaning readership predisposed to take up an ethical position against Michel, this is a stark choice. For Houellebecq, of course, it is not.

Much of the anxiety experienced by readers of *Platform* centres on the character of Michel: he is both 'like us' (e.g. he watches game shows, he reads bestsellers, he goes to art galleries, he is concerned about poverty) and, of course, he is emphatically *not* like us (e.g. he is a sex tourist, and he promotes sex tourism). This ambiguous representation exposes the limits of 'our' own ethical horizons, and the point at which the tolerance, recognition and respect we profess to offer the world cannot be extended. In the end, Michel must be declared *not* 'one of us' – which is why many readers initially responded to the novel through 'a rhetoric of outrage' that presented Michel – and by extension Houellebecq – as 'sinful' and their own outraged readings as 'virtuous' (Ní Loingsigh 2005: 87). For me, the fury over *Platform* demonstrates what happens when the hypocrisy of 'our' conventional and supposedly undisputable ethical coordinates – the very coordinates sustaining ethical tourism – are exposed. His novel is so disturbing because he makes the ideological opposition to sex tourism hugely problematic. If the reader insists on self-righteously condemning sex tourism, then 'the reader, like the tourist, is being told where to go and is being cynically manipulated in order to confirm the novel's portrayal of the *type* of individual that would challenge its content' (2005: 86). The only way to avoid being the *type* of individual so ridiculed in *Platform* is to accept Houellbecq's challenge to 're-examine with honesty and humility the processes involved in forming value judgements and moral positions' (Crowley 2002: 16; Ní Liongsigh 2005: 87).

Virtue on vacation

In the end, today's ethical tourism is not so very different from Thomas Cook's first excursion. Whilst he advocated Temperance, we advocate ethical behaviour. While he wanted to make tourism available for the masses, we do so only to the extent that such tourism enshrines equality and protects other cultures and the environment. *Some* form of mass tourism has always been denigrated, and while Thomas Cook's Tours were initially frowned upon because they democratized what was previously an elite and aristocratic practice, we now direct our moral censure at any form of travel that does not re-brand itself as 'ethical'. What interests me mostly is the seduction of such judgements – the delight at being able to morally condemn others and the impossibility of resisting the promise of virtue. This is precisely the seduction that the consensus over ethical tourism encourages. Its normative – and apolitical – account of ethics suggests that the entrenched power relations of cultural difference can be reconciled, redeemed, and most importantly, overcome. I argue that such incommensurabilities must be paid attention to, remembered and lived with. Indeed, all tourism encounters – even supposedly 'ethical' ones – are saturated with the existing power relations endemic to cultural difference, and are continually generating new subject positions that enact new power relations (e.g. the ascetic ethical tourist who takes a smug form of pleasure in 'doing good' and punishing the 'guilt-free pleasure seekers' who shun their way of life (Siegle 2005: 18)). What we require, it seems to me, are more *agonistic* and *ambivalent* understandings of tourist encounters that force us to confront our *permanent complicity* in the structures of inequality, injustice and violence we spend so much of our time trying to alleviate. One way out of the normative cul-de-sac is offered by Derrida's conception of hospitality; indeed, there is much critical work to be done using notions of encounter, ambivalence and hospitality to re-imagine the traditional account of host–guest relations as framed by tourism studies. In the end, perhaps we should all book 'responsible' holidays, pursue ecotourism and volunteer to protect the rainforest – but we should *not* make the mistake of thinking that these activities make us more virtuous or ethical than anyone else. More to the point, we should not make the mistake of thinking that because these activities are branded 'ethical', they exist outside of relations of power – that they somehow allow *innocent* and *unscripted* cultural encounters to take place.

Notes

1 The author would like to thank Paul Smith, the archivist at the Thomas Cook travel company, for an informal discussion about Thomas Cook's ethical vision; Jacquie Best and Mat Paterson for useful editorial comments; David Dwan for demanding questions and help on conceptual precision; Susan McManus for critical insight and theoretical encouragement; and finally, Naeem Inyatullah for a challenging conversation about bleakness, hope and Houellebecq.

2 According to the *Ethical Consumerism Report (2007),* UK consumers spent £103 million on responsible tourism operators in 2006, a two per cent increase from the previous year (The Cooperative Bank 2007). Wheeden cites a survey in which '27% of UK tourists stated that a company's ethical policy was of high importance to them when choosing with which operator to travel' (2000: 143; see also Goodwin and Francis 2003).

3 An interesting – and relatively unexamined – formulation of this kind of asceticism can be found in those who spend their vacations volunteering to save rainforests, plant trees, work at orphanages and build hospitals (Santos and McGehee 2005; Simpson 2004).

4 Written before 9/11 and the Bali bomb in 2002, Houellebecq's story is eerily prescient, and unsurprisingly, it was his unapologetic views about Islam, as articulated in the French press, that received all the media attention. Indeed, a number of Islamic organizations sued Houellebecq for incitement to religious and racial hatred, but the author was soon acquitted of all charges (Rushdie 2002; Webster 2002).

5 As Naeem Inyatullah points out, *Platform's* bleakness is redeemed by Michel's love for Valerie. In this sense, Valerie (rather than Michel) is the centrepiece of the book: like other successful Western career women, she *takes* pleasure, but she also *gives* pleasure like the 'pre-modern' Thai prostitutes she employs. She is the *ideal* in *Platform* because she constructs a 'false mediation between 1st and 3rd worlds' (pers. comm., July 2007).

Bibliography

Beardsworth, R. (1996) *Derrida and the Political,* London: Routledge.

Beck, U. (2002) 'The cosmopolitan society and its enemies', *Theory, Culture & Society,* 19(1&2): 17–44.

Berry, C. (1994) *The Idea of Luxury: A Conceptual and Historical Investigation,* Cambridge: Cambridge University Press.

Brassett, J. and D. Bulley (2007) 'Ethics in world politics: cosmopolitanism and beyond?', *International Politics,* 44: 1–18.

Brendon, P. (1991) *Thomas Cook: 150 Years of Popular Tourism,* London: Elek Press.

Butcher, J. (2003) *The Moralization of Tourism: Sun, Sand ... and Saving the World?* London: Routledge.

Calhoun, C. (2002) 'The class consciousness of frequent travellers: toward a critique of actually existing cosmopolitanism', *South Atlantic Quarterly,* 101(4): 869–97.

Campbell, D. (1999) 'The deterritorialization of responsibility: Levinas, Derrida and ethics after the end of philosophy', in D. Campbell and M. Shapiro (eds) *Moral Spaces: Rethinking Ethics and World Politics*, Minneapolis, MN: University of Minnesota Press, pp. 29–56.

—— (2005) 'Beyond choice: the onto-politics of critique', *International Relations*, 19(1): 127–34.

Chard, C. (1999) *Pleasure and Guilt on the Grand Tour: Travel Writing and Imaginative Geography 1600–1830*, Manchester: Manchester University Press.

Cheah, P. and B. Robbins (eds) (1998) *Cosmopolis: Thinking and Feeling Beyond the Nation*, Minneapolis, MN: University of Minnesota Press.

Cohen, E. (1988) 'Authenticity and commodification in tourism', *Annals of Tourism Research*, 15(3): 371–86.

Critchley, S. (1992) *The Ethics of Deconstruction: Derrida and Levinas*, London: Blackwell.

—— (1999) *Ethics, Politics, Subjectivity: Essays on Derrida, Levinas and Contemporary French Thought*, London: Verso.

Crowley, J. (2002) 'French kisses … and the rest: *Platform* by Michel Houellebecq', *The Observer*, Review, 11 August: 16.

Connolly, W. (1993) 'Beyond good and evil: the ethical sensibility of Michel Foucault', *Political Theory*, 21(3): 365–89.

Derrida, J. (2001) *On Cosmopolitanism and Forgiveness*, London: Routledge.

Derrida, J. and A. Dufourmantelle (2000) *Of Hospitality (Cultural Memory and the Present)*, R. Bowlby (trans.), Stanford, CA: Stanford University Press.

Erskine, T. (2002) ' "Citizen of nowhere" or "the point where circles intersect"? Impartialist and embedded cosmopolitans', *Review of International Studies*, 28(3): 457–78.

Fleckenstein, M. P. and P. Huebsch (1999) 'Ethics in Tourism – Reality or Hallucination?', *Journal of Business Ethics*, 19(1): 137–42.

Foucault, M. (1990a) *The Will to Knowledge: The History of Sexuality Volume I*, R. Hurley (trans.), London: Penguin.

—— (1992) *The Use of Pleasure: The History of Sexuality Volume II*, R. Hurley (trans.), London: Penguin.

——(1990b) *The Care of the Self: The History of Sexuality Volume III*, R. Hurley (trans.), London: Penguin.

Future Foundation (2005) *The Assault on Pleasure: How the marketing / communications community should review and respond to modern attempts to regulate or restrict consumer enjoyment of brands and products*, London: Future Foundation.

Goodwin, H. and J. Frances (2003) 'Ethical and responsible tourism: consumer trends in the UK', *Journal of Vacation Marketing*, 9(3): 271–84.

Hall, C. M. and S. Gossling (2005) *Tourism and Global Environmental Change*, London: Routledge.

Hamilton, J. (2005) *Thomas Cook: The Holiday Maker*, Strand: Sutton Publishing.

Heater, D. (2002) *World Citizenship: Cosmopolitan Thinking and its Opponents*, London: Continuum.

Holden, A. (2000) *Environment and Tourism*, London: Routledge.

'Hospitality Ethics Pro Human Rights' (2008) [Web Log] http://www.tourismethicsplus. blogspot.com/ (accessed on 13/03/08)

Houellebecq, M. (2002) *Platform*, Frank Wynne (trans.), London: William Heinemann.

Hughes, G. (1995) 'Authenticity in tourism', *Annals of Tourism Research*, 22(4): 781–803.

Hultsman, J. (1995) 'Just tourism: an ethical framework', *Annals of Tourism Research*, 22(3): 553–67.

Hunter, C. and H. Green (1995) *Tourism and the Environment: A Sustainable Relationship?* London: Thompson Learning.

Inglis, F. (2000) *The Delicious History of the Holiday*. London: Routledge.

Karwacki, J. and C. Boyd (1995) 'Ethics and ecotourism', *Business Ethics: A European Review*, 4(4): 225–32.

Lash, S. and J. Urry (1993) *Economies of Signs and Space*, London: Sage.

Lonely Planet (2008) 'Lonely planet – sustainable travel', available at http://thorntree. lonelyplanet.com/categories.cfm?catid=42 (accessed 13 March 2008).

Macbeth, J. (2005) 'Towards an ethics platform for tourism', *Annals of Tourism Research*, 32(4): 962–84.

MacCannell, D. (1976) *The Tourist: a New Theory of the Leisure Class*, London: MacMillan.

—— (1992) *Empty Meeting Grounds: The Tourist Papers*, London: Routledge.

Molloy, D. C. and D. A. Fennell (1998) 'Codes of ethics and tourism: an exploratory content analysis', *Tourism Management*, 19(5): 453–61.

Molz, J. G. (2005) 'Getting a "flexible eye": round-the-world travel and scales of cosmopolitan citizenship', *Citizenship Studies*, 9(5): 517–31.

Nietzsche, F. (1996) *On The Genealogy of Morals*, Douglas Smith (trans.), Oxford: Oxford University Press.

Ní Loingsigh, A. (2005) 'Tourist traps confounding expectations in Michel Houellebecq's *Plateforme*', *French Cultural Studies*, 16(1): 73–90.

Payne, D. and F. Dimanche (1996) 'Towards a code of conduct for the tourism industry: an ethics model', *Journal of Business Ethics*, 15(9): 997–1007.

Rojek, C. (1995) *Decentring Leisure: Rethinking Leisure Theory*, London: Sage.

Rushdie, S. (2002) 'A platform for closed minds', *The Observer* 28 September, available at http://books.guardian.co.uk/review/story/0,12084,799748,00.html (accessed 17 May 2007).

Santos, C. A. and N. G. McGehee (2005) 'Social change, discourse and volunteer tourism', *Annals of Tourism Research*, 32(3): 760–79.

Siegle, L. (2005) 'Just say no', *The Observer* (Magazine), 23 October: 18–24.

Simons, J. (1994) *Foucault and the Political*, London: Routledge.

Simpson, K. (2004) ' "Doing development": the gap year, volunteer-tourists and a popular practice of development', *Journal of International Development*, 16(5): 681–92.

Smith, M. and R. Duffy (2003) *The Ethics of Tourism Development*, London: Routledge.

Smith, P. (1998) 'Introduction', in Paul Smith (ed.) *The History of Tourism: Thomas Cook and the Origins of Leisure Travel* (Vol. 1), London: Routledge, Thoemmes Press and the Thomas Cook Archives.

Swinglehurst, E. (1974) *The Romantic Journey: the Story of Thomas Cook and Victorian Travel*, London: Pica Editions.

The Cooperative Bank (2007) 'Ethical consumerism report 2007', available at http:// www.co-operativebank.co.uk/servlet/Satellite?c=Page&cid=1170748475331& pagename=CB/Page/tplStandard&loc=ll (accessed on 25 January 2008)

Turner, B. S. (2002) 'Cosmopolitan virtue, globalization and patriotism', *Theory, Culture & Society*, 19(1&2): 45–63.

Turner, L. and J. Ash (1975) *The Golden Hordes: International Tourism and the Pleasure Periphery*, London: Constable.

UNWTO (n.d.) 'Global code of ethics for tourism', available at http://www.unwto.org/code_ethics/pdf/languages/Codigo%20Etico%20Ing.pdf (accessed 3 May 2007).

Urry, J. (1990) *The Tourist Gaze: Leisure and Travel in Contemporary Societies*, London: Sage.

Vertovec, S. and R. Cohen (2002) *Conceiving Cosmopolitanism: Theory, Context and Practice*, Oxford: Oxford University Press.

Wang, N. (1999) 'Rethinking authenticity in tourism experience', *Annals of Tourism Research*, 26(2): 349–70.

Webster, P. (2002) 'Calling Islam stupid lands author in court', *Guardian*, 18 September, available at http://books.guardian.co.uk/news/articles/0,6109,794084,00.html (accessed 17 May 2007).

Weeden, C. (2002) 'Ethical tourism: an opportunity for competitive advantage?', *Journal of Vacation Marketing*, 8(2): 141–53.

Wheeler, M. (1992) 'Applying ethics to the tourism industry', *Business Ethics: A European Review*, 1(4): 227–35.

—— (1995) 'Tourism marketing ethics: an introduction', *International Marketing Review*, 12(4): 38–49.

Withey, L. (1997) *Grand Tours and Cook's Tours: A History of Leisure Travel, 1750–1915*, London: Aurum Press.

Part 4

Cultural futures of political economy

7 Cultural political economies of the war on terror

Louise Amoore and Marieke de Goede

The old 'just war' line doesn't quite hold with terrorists under foreign sovereignty. Not that that's exactly what I'd call it, not in places like Afghanistan or Somalia. In any case, the problem is worldwide. London, Cape Town, Malaysia ... this kind of terrorism is transnational, fluid. Its structure is the whole globe.

(Foden, 2002: 69)

Introduction: what happened to globalization?

In Giles Foden's 2002 novel *Zanzibar*, fictional CIA expert Jack Queller represents a lone voice drawing attention to Al Qaeda's global and dispersed nature among a security establishment looking for the sovereign embodiment of enemies in the form of rogue states and evil civilizations. Queller's recognition of the diversity of Islam and his experience with US funding of Al Qaeda when they were both fighting the Soviets make him more readily disposed to see Al Qaeda at work in unexpected locations around the globe, including, potentially, Western cities. *Zanzibar's* plot revolves around the bombings of the US embassies in Nairobi and Dar-es-Salaam. Queller's understanding of the threat posed by Al Qaeda's diffuse nature puts him on the bombers' trail, but he is not able to gather sufficient support in the intelligence community to act pre-emptively to stop the bombings. According to its cover, *Zanzibar* was 'eerily prescient' about the threat posed by Al Qaeda to the daily life of contemporary globalization. Muses Queller toward the end of the novel: 'That was one of the frightening and unusual things about al-Qaida [*sic*] – the way it could slip to and fro, over relatively long periods of time, between the routines of everyday life and business and the extraordinary world of a terror organization, whose very purpose was to subvert the everyday' (Foden 2002: 309).

Almost a decade after the 2001 attacks, however, Queller's voice would no longer seem to be such a lone one. Security analyses drawing out the globally dispersed and particularly unpredictable nature of Al Qaeda have proliferated. Not only is Al Qaeda's 'new terrorism' supposed to be more deadly and dangerous than older, national-separatist movements, it is also thought to be particularly transnational in its organization and its fund-raising structures. According to Paul Wilkinson (2007: 7) of the St Andrew's Centre for the Study of Terrorism and Political Violence, for example: 'Bin Laden's Al Qaeda network is more of a global movement than a traditional tight-knit terrorist organization. From open sources we estimate that it has a presence in at least 60 countries … What is clear is that their network makes Al Qaeda the most widely dispersed transnational terrorist movement in the history of modern terrorism'.

In contrast to the burgeoning literature that emphasizes the new globalization of terrorism, political economy literature post-9/11 seems to have taken a turn away from analysing globalization in theory and practice. To many observers, 9/11 spelled the end of globalization as we knew it, effecting the violent return of the sovereign state and intensive border control while dispelling the era of fluid, networked political economies. On 28 September 2001, Morgan Stanley Chief Economist Stephen Roach seemed to set the tone of the debate when he argued in the *Financial Times* that 9/11 could spell the end of globalization. Roach (2001: 20) wrote: 'Terrorism puts sand in the gears of cross-border connectivity and the result threatens the increasingly frictionless world of globalization. The tragic events of September 11 have, in effect, levied a new tax on such flows. The security of national borders will now have to be tightened'. Many political economists share at least some of Roach's concerns. In their book *The Rebordering of North America*, for example, Peter Andreas and Thomas J. Biersteker (2003: 9) examine the impossible demands placed on intensified US border practice after 9/11, and argue that 'it may do more to inhibit legitimate travel and trade than terrorists'. For Biersteker (2002), at least, there are also positive elements to re-bordering after 9/11: in his analyses of terrorist finance, Biersteker welcomes renewed political will to re-regulate global financial flows.

To some extent, these opposing views of globalization illustrate a curious division of academic labour that seems to be emerging post 9/11. In this division of labour, political economists continue their research with little attention to the security practices authorized after 9/11, seemingly leaving the war on terror and its manifold political-economic practices to the field of security studies. Conversely, security analysts, including those broadly associated with the field of 'critical security studies', tend to foreground analyses of sovereignty and states, and fail to deploy the insights and conceptual tools developed by more than a decade of analysis of the economies of globalization. More precisely, security studies has not fully grasped the importance of the manifold economic practices at work within the war on terror, and the many ways in which sovereign security decisions are taken in hybrid public–private spaces.[1]

This chapter seeks to cut through this emerging division of labour, and argues that political economists have critical insights to offer to the analysis of 9/11 and its concomitant new business practices. In the name of the war on terror, the proliferation of transnational expertise and private authority, which characterizes globalization for many analysts, continues unabated. In fact, many private firms, including business consultants and transnational banks, are now directly implicated in the management of borders and the monitoring of financial flows (see, for example, Amoore 2006; Sparke 2008). Such an implication is more complex, however, than a simple outsourcing of security or, indeed, a straightforward business motivation for war-mongering, may suggest. In this chapter, we engage the question of the interconnectedness between globalization and sovereignty, or business and security, post 9/11. We examine how emerging new business practices depend upon cultural understandings of threat and uncertainty, most notably the discourse of the 'New Terrorism' as foretold by Foden's fictional CIA analyst Queller. Furthermore, we theorize the specific imaginations at work in the deployment of commercial data for contemporary practices of securitisation, and demonstrate how these transcend the apparent split between globalization and sovereignty. First, however, it is important to understand how terrorism became understood as the 'dark side of globalization' in the years after 9/11, and how this understanding worked as a first step to rescue the implicit 'bright side' of globalization.

The dark side of globalization

This chapter deploys a lens of 'cultural political economies' in order to examine the manifold ways in which security and economy fold and blend into each other in the context of the war on terror. A cultural economy here is understood to be a 'complex system' including material and non-material elements, such as threat perceptions, software modelling, security consulting, financial product innovation, military technologies and law enforcement actions, which 'profoundly [affects] the social and geographical structure of daily life' (Campbell 2005: 945). David Campbell's thorough examination of the cultural politics of the SUV seeks to address the interconnections between 'what appear as individual consumer preferences for certain vehicles' and 'their geopolitical effects' (2005: 945). In such exploration, Campbell argues, it is indispensable to understand the cultural practices of desire and fear that work to produce particular constellations of car-buying and oil-demand in this moment in US history (also Paterson 2000). In this reading, it would be impossible to separate out 'culture' from 'materiality', as it involves a reconceptualization of 'materialism so it is understood as interwoven with cultural, social and political networks' (Campbell 2005: 951; cf. de Goede 2006; Best and Paterson, Introduction, this volume). As such, this chapter's exploration of the cultural economies of the war on terror should not be understood to be addressing the cultural *dimension* of practices of security. Instead, we offer an analysis of the complex constellation in which economic opportunity and security imaginations become fused, with the ability to have profound effects on the material fabric of everyday life.

It is important, then, to understand how the threats of terrorism became culturally rendered in relation to globalization. After brief conceptualizations of terrorism as the resurgence of a pre-modern era, espousing pre-modern values, the adage that Al Qaeda *itself* embodies modernity became widely accepted. More precisely, in the wake of 9/11, terrorism became coined as the 'dark side of globalization' (Rumford 2001). As early as 21 September 2001, Richard Haass, Director of the

White House Office of the Policy Planning Staff, said in remarks to the National Defense University:

> International terrorism epitomizes a dark side of globalization ... The al-Qaida network alone operates in over 60 countries. It is connected together by the communication technologies emblematic of our era – cellular and satellite phones, encrypted email, Internet chat rooms, videotape, and laser disks. Its members travel from continent to continent with the ease of any business traveler or vacationer.... And in their hands the airplanes that connect families and businesses became human guided missiles that cruelly snuffed out thousands of innocent lives.
>
> (Haass 2001)

Haass' comments are remarkably similar to the reasoning of capitalism's critic John Gray, whose (2003a) book *Al Qaeda and What it Means to Be Modern* did much to popularize the idea that the terrorist threat embodies modernity rather than challenging it. Gray (2003: 74) writes: 'As capital has gone global, so has crime. Nearly everywhere, the irregular armies and political organizations that practise the new forms of warfare are linked with the global criminal economy'. In particular, the idea that globalization's benefits, in the form of travel, communication and cosmopolitanism, offered unprecedented and unexpected opportunities for those with evil intentions has become popular in media and policy discourse. A recent article in *Foreign Policy* posits this as *the* global problem of the twenty-first century, and writes:

> The bad news of the 21st century is that globalization has a significant dark side. The container ships that carry manufactured Chinese goods to and from the United States also carry drugs. The airplanes that fly passengers nonstop from New York to Singapore also transport infectious diseases. And the Internet has proved just as adept at spreading deadly, extremist ideologies as it has e-commerce.
>
> (Weber *et al.* 2007: 49)

Such conceptualizations seem to entail injunctions to a new governing and perhaps even a 'rolling back' of globalization. To some extent they seek to effect just that: a number of authors in the debate, including Gray, display a real anxiety about globalization. In debates about terrorism finance, for example, some of the leading authors, including Italian economist Loretta Napoleoni, have been embraced by the alter-globalization left, for drawing attention to the underbelly of global capital flows and calling for its renewed regulation (e.g. Napoleoni 2007). Such arguments seem to confirm the views of those who regard 9/11 as the end of globalization as we knew it, and a return to re-bordering and national sovereignty.

However, constituting terrorism as the dark side of globalization can also be read as a first step in rescuing the implicit 'bright side' of globalization. This rescue revolves around the articulation of 'our way of life' as that which must be defended against the threat of terrorist annihilation, and yet also that which contains its own means of protection. As Richard Johnson (2002) suggests in his discussion of the Bush–Blair call to 'protect our way of life', invoking Raymond Williams' notion of culture as 'ways of life' that give meaning to the fabric of our world (1962: 312, see also Davies, Chapter 2, this volume), the cultural practices of daily life have become a call to arms. Recall in the aftermath of 9/11 how the routines of daily life were called up as a source of resilience. 'We were told to shop', says Susan Willis, 'shop to show we are patriotic Americans. Shop to show our resilience over death and destruction' (2003: 122). The London bombings on 7 July (7/7) met with similar celebrations of the 'vibrant and resilient city, getting back to normal, going back to work, getting back on the Tube'. Such articulations of our 'way of life', as well as its delineation from the 'incomprehensible' way of life of the terrorist, work to save (parts of) globalization from new injunctions to govern.

However, such articulations of 'our way of life' can also be understood to give a particular meaning to globalization. Rather than rescuing particular pre-existing elements thought to be part of an already present phenomenon called globalization, the articulation of our way of life under threat newly inscribes globalization with particular meanings and values (cf. Coutin *et al.* 2002). In this sense, we could argue that such deployments are profoundly *performative* (Butler 1993). What can be seen to be emerging conceptually, then, is the imagination of two worlds of globalization: one populated by legitimate and civilized groups whose normalized patterns of global travel, communication and business behaviour are to be secured; and another populated by illegitimate and uncivilized persons whose suspicious patterns of behaviour are to be targeted and apprehended. In order that the licit and legitimate world of profitable movements of money, goods and people may remain an alluring and enduring prospect, then, control over the illicit world of terrorism, trafficking or illegal immigration must be made credible. As William Walters (2006: 197) argues, new bordering practices work less as 'iron curtains', and more as 'firewalls, differentiating the good and the bad, the useful and the dangerous, the licit and the illicit ... immobilizing and removing the risky elements so as to speed the circulation of the rest'.[2]

In this paradigm of a duality of globalization, the apparently paradoxical emergence of the new globalization of terror networks versus the new return of sovereignty is reconciled. At the same time, the *meaning* of globalization – the way of life to be secured and protected – did not necessarily pre-exist 9/11, but is constituted through the very discourses that claim to rescue it. In this sense, globalization is a thoroughly cultural practice, and the next section will examine in more detail the cultural mediations on which the emerging contemporary business practices of security rest.

Cultural mediations of the new terrorism

We have argued that the contemporary landscape of globalization constitutes neither an unproblematic continuity of neoliberalism, nor an unequivocal return of the sovereign state, but the cultural imagination of two worlds that need to be separated, sorted and secured against each other's presence. It is in these processes of separation and security that significant new business practices are at work, entailing complex new interplays of public and private; governmentality and sovereignty. Not reducible to a sheer '*privatization* of means for establishing and securing force, law and order' (Rosén 2008: 77, emphasis added), these new business practices fuse the public and the private in what we will call a 'complex assemblage' (Connolly 2004). Before turning to a more detailed analysis of this complex assemblage, however, it is important to understand how particular visualizations of the terrorist threat underpin the commercial opportunities here arising.

The articulation that casts terrorism as the dark side of globalization entails a particular imagination of the nature of the terrorist threat. The 'new terrorism' is thought to be fluid, globally dispersed, unpredictable, but uniquely destructive in intention and consequence. Rather than assessing the truth-value of such imaginations, we are interested in the politico-cultural work here performed. Culture, as Derek Gregory (2004: 11) explains 'is never a mere mirror of the world', we can never simply hold up the looking glass of culture to shed new light on contemporary economy or society (also Best and Paterson, Introduction, this volume). Rather, 'culture involves the production, circulation and legitimation of meanings through representations, practices and performances that enter fully into the constitution of the world' (Gregory 2004: 11). We regard the cultural constitution of a particular understanding of the contemporary threat to be indispensable to, and inseparable from, the material practices of everyday security and economy that have developed since 9/11 (cf. Campbell 1992; Dillon 2007). It is only through its articulation in academic research, popular culture and policy papers, that the discourse of the new terrorism was able to acquire its material significance.

The introduction to this chapter noted Giles Foden's fictionalization of a 'fluid, dispersed' Al Qaeda, with extraordinary powers to 'subvert the everyday'. Current discourses of the 'New Terrorism' do much to corroborate this image of a fluid but uniquely destructive terrorist network. According to Wilkinson, the New Terrorism distinguishes itself based on three factors: its 'universalistic ideology', 'world wide network of operational and preparative cells', and the 'nature and scale of the violence [it] employs' (2003: 3–4). Writes Wilkinson (2003: 2):

> New Terrorism groups are based on transnational networks of cells, preparative cells, affiliated groups and support networks, have multinational composition, and do not need to rely on a state sponsor for securing funding [and] weapons ... and specialise in suicide no-warning attacks ... aimed at inflicting large-scale loss of life.

Such conceptualizations (see also Haass 2001) have become increasingly important in understandings of recent attacks in Europe, where the recognizable 'others' of illegal immigrants, Al Qaeda members or known 'extremists' could not readily be implicated. For example, intelligence commentator Aidan Kirby (2007: 415–16) understands the 2005 7/7 London bombers to have been a 'self starter cell', 'an autonomous clique whose motivations, cohesiveness, and ideological grooming occurred in the absence of any organized network or formal entry into the jihad'. Kirby (2007: 426) recommends the deployment of sociological theory in counterterrorism, to foster a better understanding of social processes of alienation and group dynamics. Such emphasis on the proliferation of domestic terrorists who may be 'among us' fosters the emergence of a more mobile norm against which multiple others can be pre-emptively identified.

What is remarkable about the New Terrorism discourse is not that it exists in policy circles – indeed, it draws upon much longer established articulations of threat, security and netwar that have been advanced by military think-tanks such as the RAND Corporation since the Cold War (see DerDerian 2001). What is remarkable is the extent to which this discourse remains unchallenged in critical academic engagement with the war on terror. Sociologist Karin Knorr Cetina (2005), for example, offers a reading of terrorist networks as 'global microstructures', that has many affinities with Wilkinson's vision. According to Knorr Cetina, Al Qaeda has a 'lightness' of organization, that is able to manifest 'patience' and 'preparedness' on a global scale (2005: 215, 219). Gregory (2004: 50), by comparison, confirms that Al Qaeda is a 'network of networks with neither capital nor center, so that its "radical non-territoriality" renders any conventional military response problematic'. He goes on to criticize the 'cartographic performances' that reduced the dispersed Al Qaeda threat to a 'bounded locus of transnational terrorism' (Gregory 2004: 50). In the immediate aftermath of 9/11, this bounded locus became Afghanistan, imagined to be a sovereign state rather than the destitute landscape that it already was, according to Gregory.

What Gregory does not acknowledge, however, is how precisely the understanding of Al Qaeda as a 'network of networks' *itself* entails spatial and cultural imaginations that foster particular security responses. It is the very discourse of the new terrorism itself that underpins a new politics of what we call 'data wars', whereby commercial data on the minutiae of everyday life – such as ATM transactions, passenger data, shopping records – are deployed to visualize bodies-in-movement and pre-empt potential threats. If the 'new' terrorist threat[3] is conceptualized as a 'global microstructure', or a 'network of networks', patiently waiting to strike, security interventions that seek to identify and target the nodal points of such networks become seemingly logical. In short, the very possibility of sovereign decisions based on mobilities rests upon a calculability that is authorized by a particular imagining of globalization. Sovereign decision is precisely extended and not diminished by globalization.

Consider, for example, the conclusions drawn by the UK Intelligence and Security Committee in its enquiry into the London bombings of July 2005:

> Steps are now being taken to develop a more proactive approach to identifying threats in the UK … The potential value of *** and *** as a means for

identifying new threats has been highlighted to the Committee. The fact that the 7 July group was in contact with others under Security Service investigation has emphasized the potential for new threats to be identified through the examination of information and contact networks relating to existing targets.

(UK Intelligence and Security Committee 2006: 35–6)

Despite its blacking out of the specific policies here recommended, it becomes clear from the text that the analysis of 'contact networks' of suspects is to become a key strategy to pre-emptively 'pick up unknown terrorist activities and plots'. The analysis of such contact networks can be based on personal observation, but more often relies upon the redeployment of already commercially available data, including telecommunications and financial data, in security practice.

The visualization of the globally dispersed terrorist network, then, entails *its own* practices of territorialization in which the spaces of suspicion come to be located among the millions of transactions that characterize everyday communication and commerce. With the 'new terrorist' thought to be especially elusive, authorities are turning to complex algorithmic data-analysis programs to 'join the dots' of suspect activities. Most often derived from the residue of daily life left in the patterns of travel, financial and consumer transactions, these abstracted items of data become the nodal points that, when joined in association with other items, are assumed to become an indisputable visualization of a person. It is here that commercial techniques of marketing are redeployed to the security domain. It is here that the globalized worlds of consulting and commerce enable and legitimate controversial security decisions, while simultaneously fostering booming business practices. It is to a more detailed analyses of such data-mining techniques that we now turn.

Data wars: economies of attention

In the specific and situated deployment of commercial data for security inter- ventions, culture embodies and advances a visual economy. In this sense, the practice of data-mining, as it migrates from commercial to security contexts, can be regarded as a cultural economy not only because it embodies a specific culturally mediated understanding of terrorist threat, but more importantly because it deploys a particular mode of visualization. Such visual economy is understood as a means of apportioning, segregating, and singling out 'objects of interest' for our collective attentions (Cuff 2003). How do ways of life come to be known and recognized as such? How is a 'normal' way of life settled out, and how does it identify deviations from norm? As in the contemporary profiling of consumers in the marketplace – where the as-yet-unencountered unknown consumer is the holy grail sought via fragments of data on their conduct and behaviour – so in the war on terror the as-yet-unknown terrorist is rendered knowable through the fractured bits and bytes of a way of life. As the art historian Jonathan Crary has demonstrated through his careful and detailed genealogies of attention in the modern world, objects and people come to our attention via 'strategies of isolation and separation' (1999: 3). Understood in this way, the sovereign lines that are drawn in contemporary security practice are absolutely and quite literally also *economic*: they are lines that segregate and divide, 'dividing practices' that render ways of life economic, make them amenable to management, trading or exchange.[4]

To consider cultural political economies of the war on terror, then, is not simply a matter of uncovering the cultural dimension of already settled out political strategies. As Crary argues, the significance of attention and attentiveness to the world is not merely cultural, not confined in its implications to the histories of visual culture. Rather, modes of attention and attentiveness are also acutely material – central in modern times to the way that ways of life, culture and cultural difference are made governable. What we see, how we see, what is made visible, how visualization occurs – these are not simply the cultural dimensions of a material life, but instead they are the very essence of an economy of culture. That is to say, practices of attention themselves embody an economy – a means of representing and acting on the world such that it can be apportioned, segregated, annexed, exchanged or interchanged. As Crary writes on attentiveness, it is 'not primarily concerned with looking at images but rather with the construction of conditions that individuate, immobilize, and separate subjects, even within a world in which mobility and circulation are ubiquitous' (1999: 74). In this sense, practices of attention are one specific means of instituting the dividing practices at the heart of contemporary techniques of government. In short, while contemporary practices in no way substitute for past practices of division and enumeration, they do classify in novel and more finite ways that are worthy of critical attention.

In the immediate aftermath of 9/11, and in the complex of practices that came to be known as the war on terror, an enemy was identified whose probable future actions were already visible in the traces of life left in existing data. Giving evidence at a US Congressional hearing only five months after 9/11, IBM's federal business manager testified that 'in this war, our enemies are hiding in open and available information across a spectrum of databases' (Intelligent Enterprise 2002: 8). Technology consultants and IT providers such as IBM have made the generation of probabilistic association rules the forefront of homeland security practices. The idea is that locating regularities in large and disparate patterns of data can enable associations to be established between apparently 'suspicious' people, places, financial transactions, cargo shipments and so on (Ericson 2007). Rules of association are produced by algorithms – models or 'decision trees' for calculation (Quinlan 1986). In effect, algorithms precisely function as a means of directing and disciplining attention, focusing on specific points and cancelling out all other data, appearing to make it possible to translate *probable* associations between people or objects into *actionable* security decisions. In 2003, for example, a US joint inquiry concluded that 'on September 11, enough relevant data was resident in existing databases', so that 'had the dots been connected', the events could have been 'exposed and stopped' (Joint Inquiry 2003: 14). It is precisely this 'connecting of dots' that is the work of the algorithm. By connecting the dots of probabilistic associations, the algorithm becomes a means of foreseeing or anticipating a course of events yet to take place:

> This is a lesson we learned from September 11. After-the-fact reviews of the hijackers' travel reservations showed that we might have been able to uncover the plot if we'd had better computer systems and better access to travel data … *We didn't connect those dots before 9/11, but we should have.* We learned that lesson, and now ATS allows us to look for these links.
>
> (Baker 2006, emphasis added)

The December 2006 US institution of a computer-based screening program called Automated Targeting System (ATS), deployed to screen international travellers at all air, land and sea borders, illustrates the work of the algorithm in pre-emptive security practice. Originally developed for the purpose of screening cargo and container shipments into US ports – assigning a risk score to all imports in advance of their arrival at the border – ATS was exported to the domain of mobile people to enable the 'identification of previously unknown areas of note, concern or pattern' (Baker 2006: 9). Far from a system of border controls that inhibits the idea of a fully globalizing world, ATS governs by utilizing the spatialities and temporalities of a globalizing world. As Stuart Baker explained the system, it would be capable of singling out high risk individuals for security attention, while simultaneously offering a 'faster service for most travellers' (Baker 2006). The trappings of a life lived in the circuits of the global economy – credit card records, air miles, money transfers, travel records and so on – become the data for algorithmic security decisions.

So, how does the algorithm become integral to the imagining of a securable and yet globalized world? In effect, the algorithm appears to make possible the conversion of *ex post facto* evidence in the war on terror into a judgement made in advance of the event. The significant point here is that diverse data points or specified 'pixels' in a digital image are drawn together in association, producing a recognizable whole. Though the visualized image may bear no resemblance to the actual way of life of the person depicted, this scarcely matters because the digital alter ego becomes the *de facto* person. As the US Inspector General concluded in his survey of government applications of algorithmic techniques, 'association does not imply a direct causal connection', but instead it 'uncovers, interprets and displays relationships between persons, places and events' (Department of Homeland Security 2006: 10). It is the specific visualization of threat, then, that marks out the algorithm as a distinctive mode of calculation – to be displayed on the screens of border guards, stored on subway travel cards, shared between multiple public and private agencies. In this sense, the algorithm produces a screened visualization of suspicion, on the basis of which 'other' people are intercepted, detained, stopped and searched.

The origins of algorithmic techniques for visualizing people lie, perhaps not surprisingly, in commercial techniques for imagining the consumer. In the early 1990s IBM mathematicians began to work on using barcode data on consumer purchases to project probabilistic judgements about the ways of life of the customer in a given scenario (cf. Agrawal *et al.* 1993). The point here was not to be able to *predict* future patterns on the basis of past data, indeed the commercial clients categorically did not want predictability or to capture an already predictable customer. Instead, the dream was to visualize the impulse buyer, the capricious lifestyle of the unknown consumer who might be drawn into the targeting of the marketers. Though the uncertainties of future patterns are not treated as strictly knowable, they are seen to be at least amenable to pre-emptive decision making based on the visualized person. It is precisely this model of pre-emptive visualization of an unknown person that is now running through the logics of security practice, indeed IBM's same team is now leading the 'mathematical sciences role in homeland security' (BMSA 2004), with IBM prominent contractors on Heathrow airport's MySense biometrics program and on the trials for the UK's e-borders Semaphore and Iris programs (Department of Homeland Security 2006; Computing 2004: 1).

As a means of segregating and delineating attention in contemporary security practice, then, algorithmic techniques for making visible mobile people, and indeed products, goods and money, embody what Samuel Weber calls a 'target of opportunity', a competitive 'seizing' of 'targets that were not foreseen or planned' (2005: 4) such as one would find also in the commercial marketplace:

> However different the war on terror was going to be from traditional wars, with their relatively well-defined enemies, it would still involve one of the basic mechanisms of traditional hunting and combat, in however modified and modernized a form: namely 'targeting'. The enemy would have to be *identified* and *localized*, *named* and *depicted*, in order to be made into an accessible target ... None of this was, per se, entirely new. What *was*, however, was the mobility, indeterminate structure, and unpredictability of the spatio-temporal *medium* in which such targets had to be sited ... In theatres of conflict that had become highly mobile and changeable, 'targets' and 'opportunity' were linked as never before.
>
> (Weber 2005: 3–4, original emphasis)

Samuel Weber's key point of discussion is the theatre of war, though his argument sheds significant light on the cultural economies that we depict here. The *identification, localization, naming* and *depiction* of mobile targets is, in this conjoined public–private war, conducted in and through daily life, in advance of any possible future strike or intervention. The targeting of unknown people is, put simply, becoming a matter of both positioning in the sights (targeting and identifying) and visualizing through a projected line of sight (pre-empting, making actionable). Algorithmic 'decision trees' draw even the most overloaded sensory domains into apparent management: the busy and noisy border crossing is stilled on the border guard's screened list of 'selectees' to single out for further attention; the crowded subway ticket hall quietly selects anomalous smartcard data and intercepts at the barrier; the RFID data from a football fan's swipecard transmits an automatic signal to the local police. From the visualization of a mobile citizen of the global economy is derived the possibility to act on that person. 'Ideally, I would like to know', said Michael Chertoff, 'did Mohamed Atta get his ticket paid on the same credit card. That would be a huge thing. And I really would like to know that in advance, because that would allow us to identify an unknown terrorist' (*New York Times* 2003).

In fact, of course, the algorithmic 'decision trees' do not take decisions at all, they merely defer decision into a calculation that is pre-programmed.[5] As such, the sovereign decisions of the war on terror do not strictly become privatized or outsourced to the commercial sector (Avant 2005; Leander 2005). The authorisation of the risk-based algorithmic ways of thinking that we have considered here defies a clear sovereign–commercial distinction. We prefer to use the concept of 'complex assemblage' to understand how the deferral of security decisions into calculative risk models produce new spaces of governing in the war on terror. An assemblage is understood as an apparatus of governing that exercises power at multiple sites and through diverse elements, that work in conjunction but may also encounter friction (Connolly 2004: 35). In this sense, the concept of the assemblage cuts through the distinction between globalization and sovereignty, or political economy and security, that we noted at the outset of this chapter. Instead, it offers an appreciation of the way in which 'neither state authorities, corporate elites, [nor] market mechanisms ... possess sufficient foresight to govern the world intentionally as a system', while all governing entities are 'nonetheless enabled, contained and restrained by the larger world assemblage in which [they are] set' (Connolly 2004: 35). Thus, the concept of an assemblage allows us to cut through the public–private distinction, in order to take into account diverse actors and spaces in the new exercise of security decisions: both the risk analysts and the models they build, both the security experts and the imagination they deploy, both the mid-level bureaucrat and the law they exceed. Only in this manner may we begin to delineate the cultural political economy of the war on terror, and the many new commercial security practices at work.

Conclusion: cultural political economies of violence

Political economists, one might say, have never really fully got to grips with the idea of violence. They might point to the inequalities of the global political economy, the injustices of the export processing zone or supply chain, the gendered rendering of the worlds of globalization. But they never actually get to the 'real' bodies. If violence in our contemporary world must imply blood on the floor, a tangible and touchable visceral world of Guantanamo Bay and Abu Ghraib, then what can the researchers of global financial flows and market algorithms really have to say of any crucial importance? Surely, the argument might go, it is the world of sovereign acts of violence and security that is in most urgent need of critical attention? And yet, as we have suggested, the world of commercial targeting and market decision is not so very far away from the world of state targeting and security decision. It is not sufficient, we have argued, to consider the violent acts of terror or counter-terror as an anomalous disturbance to the much more normal patterns of globalization. As Slavoj Zizek has put it, visible violence is 'seen as a perturbation of the "normal", peaceful state of things' when, in fact, there is an 'invisible violence' that sustains the normal run of things 'against which we perceive something as violent' (2008: 2). Understood in these terms, it is routinized acts of violence that support the visible bright side of globalization, that sustain the very 'norm' in the normal run of things, critical political economists have, for some time, pointed to the mundane and prosaic violences of everyday worlds of globalization. The globalization that is re-made to be compatible with the war on terror, as we have shown, is not so much perturbed as enabled by ordinary and continuing violent acts of segregation, apportioning and division (see also Amoore and de Goede 2008).

To point to the co-existence of the cultural imagination of globalization and an apparent post-9/11 world to be secured, however, is not to endorse the concept of a 'darker' and more dangerous reverse face of some already existing phenomenon called globalization. As we have argued, culture is never simply a mirror of the world, there can never be merely cultural 'dimensions' of global political economies. Instead, work has to be done to visualize and bring into being – to perform – the sovereign and commercial players and practices of globalization. Like the hero on the stage who must always be joined by the heinous villain – the better to fully realize both the full heroism and villainy of the piece – the parts are performed together in an assemblage that fully allows for cohesion *and* friction. The visualization of a permanent set of security uncertainties that can be folded into the otherwise normal globalized world of risk calculations – at borders, in the financial system, inside the supply chain – reorders the economies of attention in our world in ways that bring the visceral violences of the war on terror 'renditions' in close proximity to the mundane and casual violences of the data rendered in the political economies of globalization.

Notes

1 But see Leander (2005) and Avant (2005).
2 For more about the deployment of risk practice in the war on terror, see Amoore and de Goede (2008).
3 For a challenge to the newness of the 'new' terrorism, see Duyvesteyn (2004).
4 In common with others who have sought to push economy 'beyond economism' – that is, beyond *the* economy as a pre-discursive, pre-political and self-evident material reality – economy is used here to denote a field of intervention and a specific means of rendering political life governable (de Goede 2003; Miller and Rose 1990). 'The art of government', writes Foucault, 'is essentially concerned with answering the question of how to introduce economy – that is to say, the correct manner of managing individuals, goods and wealth within the family – how to introduce this … into the management of the state' (1991: 92). Foucault finds in economy a continuity of the art of governing the state, such that the 'very essence of government' has come to mean 'the art of exercising power in the form of economy' (1991: 93).
5 For Jacques Derrida, a decision is not a decision if it simply redeploys calculative practices in order to decide. A decision cannot, in Derrida's reading, be determined by

the acquisition of knowledge, for then it is not a decision but 'simply the application of a body of knowledge of, at the very least, a rule or norm' (1994: 37). An apparent decision taken on the basis of what is 'seen' evidentially, via the calculations of experts, or in the screened results of algorithmic visualization, is not a decision at all. 'The decision, if there is to be one', writes Derrida, 'must advance towards a future which is not known, which cannot be anticipated' (1994: 37).

Bibliography

Agrawal, Rakesh, Tomasz Imielinski and Arun Swami (1993) 'Mining association rules between sets of items in large databases', SIGMOD Proceedings: 914–25.

Amoore, Louise (2006) 'Biometric borders: governing mobilities in the war on terror', *Political Geography*, 25(3): 336–51.

Amoore, Louise and Marieke de Goede (2008) 'Transactions after 9/11: the banal face of the preemptive strike', *Transactions of the Institute of British Geographers*, 33(2): 173–85.

Andreas, P. and T. J. Biersteker (eds) (2003) *The Rebordering of North America: Integration and Exclusion in a New Security Context*, New York: Routledge.

Avant, Deborah (2005) 'Private security companies', *New Political Economy*, 10(1): 121–31.

Baker, Stewart (2006) *Remarks*, Center for Strategic and International Studies, Washington, 19 December, available at http://www.dhs.gov/xnews/speeches/sp_1166557969765. shtm "accessed October 11 2009".

Biersteker, T. J. (2002) 'Targeting terrorist finances: the new challenges of financial market globalization', in K. Booth and T. Dunne (eds) *Worlds in Collision: Terror and the Future of Global Order*, Basingstoke: Palgrave.

BMSA (2004) *The Mathematical Sciences' Role in the War on Terror*, National Academies Press.

Butler, Judith (1993) *Bodies That Matter: On the Discursive Limits of 'Sex'*, London: Routledge.

Campbell, David (1992) *Writing Security: United States Foreign Policy and the Politics of Identity*, Minneapolis, MN: University of Minnesota Press.

Campbell, David (2005) 'The biopolitics of security: oil, empire and the sports utility vehicle', *American Quarterly*, 57(3): 943–72.

Connolly, William (2004) 'The complexity of sovereignty,' in J. Edkins, V. Pin-Fat and M. J. Shapiro (eds) *Sovereign Lives: Power in Global Politics*, London: Routledge, pp. 23–40.

Computing (2004) 'Government confirms IBM's semaphore win', *Computing*, 3(November): 1–3.

Coutin, Susan B., Bill Maurer and Barbara Yngvesson (2002) 'In the mirror: the legitimation work of globalization', *Law and Social Inquiry*, 27(4): 801–43.

Crary, Jonathan (1999) *Suspensions of Perception: Attention, Spectacle, and Modern Culture*, Cambridge, MA: MIT Press.

Cuff (2003) 'Immanent domain: pervasive computing and the public realm', *Journal of Architectural Education*, 57(1): 43–9.

de Goede, Marieke (2003) 'Beyond economism in international political economy', *Review of International Studies*, 29(1): 79–97.

de Goede, Marieke (ed) (2006) *International Political Economy and Poststructural Politics*, London: Palgrave.

Department of Homeland Security (2006) *Survey of DHS Data Mining Activities*, Washington, DC: Office of the Inspector General.

DerDerian, James (2001) *Virtuous War*, Boulder, CO: Westview Press.

Derrida, Jacques (in conversation with Richard Beardsworth) (1994) 'Nietzsche and the machine', *Journal of Nietzsche Studies*, 7: 7–65.

Dillon, Michael (2007) *Politics of Security: Towards a Political Philosophy of Continental Thought*, London: Routledge.

Duyvesteyn, Isabelle (2004) 'How new is the new terrorism?', *Studies in Conflict & Terrorism*, 27: 439–54.

Ericson, Richard (2007) *Crime in an Insecure World*, Cambridge: Polity.

Foden, Giles (2002) *Zanzibar*, London: Faber and Faber.

Foucault, Michel (1991) 'Governmentality', in G. Burchell, C. Gordon and P. Miller (eds) *The Foucault Effect: Studies in Governmentality*, Chicago, IL: Chicago University Press, pp. 87–104.

Gray, J. (2003) 'The era of globalization is over', *New Statesman*, 24 September: 25–7.

Gray, J. (2003a) Al Qaeda and What It Means to Be Modern, London: Faber and Faber.

Gregory, Derek (2004) *The Colonial Present: Afghanistan, Palestine, Iraq*, London: Blackwell.

Haass, Richard N. (2001) 'The Bush administration's response to globalization', Remarks to the National Defense University, Washington, 21 September 21, available at http://www.state.gov/s/p/rem/5508.htm "accessed December 1 2008".

Intelligent Enterprise (2002) 'For want of a nail', 5(7): 8.

Johnson, Richard (2002) 'Defending ways of life: the (anti-) terrorist rhetorics of Bush and Blair', *Theory, Culture and Society*, 19(4): 211–31.

Kirby, A. (2007) 'The London bombers as "self starters"', *Studies in Conflict and Terrorism*, 30: 415–28.

Knorr Cetina, K. (2005) 'Complex global microstructures: the new terrorist societies', *Theory, Culture and Society*, 22(5): 213–34.

Leander, Anna (2005) 'The power to construct international security: on the significance of private military companies', *Millennium Journal of International Studies*, 33(3): 803–26.

Miller, Peter and Nikolas Rose (1990) 'Governing economic life', *Economy and Society*, 19(1): 1–31.

Napoleoni, Loretta (2007) 'Terrorism financing in Europe', in Jeanne K. Giraldo and Harold A. Trinkunas (eds) *Terrorism Financing and State Responses*, Stanford, CA: Stanford University Press, pp. 171–184.

New York Times (2006) 'Officials seek broader access to airline data', *New York Times*, August 23: 3.

Paterson, M. (2000) 'Car culture and global environmental politics', *Review of International Studies*, 26: 253–70.

Quinlan, J. R. (1986) 'Induction of decision trees', *Machine Learning*, 1: 81–106.

Roach, S. (2001) 'Back to borders', *Financial Times*, 28 September.

Rosén, Frederik (2008) 'Commercial security: conditions of growth', *Security Dialogue*, 39(1): 77–97.

Rumford, Chris (2001) 'Confronting "uncivil society" and the "dark side of globalization": are sociological concepts up to the task?', *Sociological Research Online*, 6(3), available at http://www.socresonline.org.uk/6/3/rumford.html (accessed 2 June 2008).

Sparke, Matthew (2008) 'Fast capitalism/slow terror: cushy cosmopolitanism and its extraordinary others', in Louise Amoore and Marieke de Goede (eds) *Risk and the War on Terror*, London: Routledge.

UK Intelligence and Security Committee (2006) *Report into the London Terrorist Attacks on 7 July 2005*, London.

US Joint Inquiry (2003) *Report of the Joint Inquiry into the Terrorist Attacks of September 11, 2001*, Washington, DC: House Permanent Select Committee on Intelligence (HPSCI) and the Senate Select Committee on Intelligence (SSCI).

Walters, William (2006) 'Border/control', *European Journal of Social Theory*, 9(2): 187–203.

Weber, Samuel (2005) *Targets of Opportunity: On the Militarization of Thinking*, New York: Fordham University Press.

Weber, Steven, Naazneen Barma, Matthew Kroenig and Ely Ratner (2007) 'How globalization went bad', *Foreign Policy*, January–February: 49–54.

Wilkinson, Paul (2003) *Observations on the New Terrorism*, Foreign Affairs Committee, June, available at http://www.st-andrews.ac.uk/intrel/research/cstpv/pdffiles/Foreign%20Affairs%20Commission.pdf "accessed December 1 2008".

—— (2007) 'The challenge of international terrorism and its implications for the rule of law and human rights', *Commonwealth Ministers Reference Book*, available at http://www.st-andrews.ac.uk/~wwwir/research/cstpv/journals/articles/commonwealthministersreferencebook2007.pdf "accessed December 1 2008".

Williams, Raymond (1962) *The Long Revolution*, Harmondsworth: Penguin.

Willis, Susan (2003) 'Old glory', in S. Hauerwas and F. Lentricchia (eds) *Dissent from the Homeland: Essays After September 11*, Durham, NC: Duke University Press.

Zizek, Slavoj (2008) *Violence: Six Sideways Reflections*, London: Profile Books.

8 Cybernetic capitalism and the global information society

From the global panopticon to a 'brand' new world

Maxime Ouellet

> Welcome. Welcome to a brand new day. A new way of getting things done.
> Welcome to a place where maps are re-written and remote villages are included.
> A place where body language is business language. Where people subscribe to
> people not magazines, ... Welcome to a network where anyone can be famous ...
> Where businesses are born, countries are transformed. And where we are more
> powerful together than we ever can be apart.
> Welcome to the human network[1]
>
> (Cisco Systems advertisement, 2007)

This advertisement for Cisco Systems – the world's primary supplier of network
solutions for the Internet – suggestively illustrates the new economic imaginary
linked to information and communication technologies (ICTs) and to the emergence of a 'global information society'. Such ads suggest that ICTs will create
a new, inclusive networked world in which everybody can become 'celebrities'
through online self-broadcasting. They will also make capitalism more 'human'
and will empower individuals in the face of institutions like the state, which we
are told possess excessive power. We will thus enter a 'brand new world', a global
information society, networked in form, where social problems will be resolved
through improved communication.

Debates about what is 'new' in capitalism abound in the social sciences.
Analyses portraying economic, social, political and cultural transformations
in Western societies have proliferated since the 1960s: society is variously
described as 'postindustrial', 'information-based, 'postmodern', 'networked', and
'knowledge-based'. Most of these analyses maintain that social relations are being
restructured through a fundamental transformation towards an economy in which
information and knowledge have become the principal factors of productivity.
Simply put, we are supposedly witnessing an 'information revolution' generated
by ICTs.

The central idea that will be developed in this chapter is that the 'novelty' or
the 'revolutionary' character of what is called the age of information (Castells
1996) is cultural rather than technological. The rise of neoliberal ideas and their

implementation in the 1980s were both founded on a 'new economic imaginary' designed to legitimize a hegemony in crisis and to produce a different kind of economic individual. Through a cultural approach to international political economy, I will use the concepts of hegemony (Cox 1987), governmentality (Foucault 2004) and the 'new spirit of capitalism' (Boltanski and Chiapello 1999) to demonstrate the ways in which this new economic imaginary endeavours to produce subjects that are adaptable and adapted to the current conditions of capital accumulation. The cultural approach developed in this analysis will focus on the various mediations between this imaginary and material practices.

This argument will be developed in three parts. First, I will explore how the emerging new economic imaginary is the result of the convergence of neoliberalism and cybernetic theory. Neoliberalism is based on an epistemological shift in which economic analysis entails the study of the optimal distribution of information through the price system. Cybernetic theory, the science of social regulation and the optimization of information resources, shares certain similarities with neoliberal economic theory that are central to an understanding of the 'information society'. Second, I will examine the manner in which various social forces have transformed the *spirit of capitalism*, suggesting that we are witnessing a convergence of democracy and the market into a 'global democratic marketplace'. This new *spirit of capitalism* is a crucial legitimating discourse for cybernetic capitalism. Finally, I will discuss the way this 'global democratic marketplace' imaginary is transforming subjectivities through a new form of 'spectacular' governmentality. I will analyse more specifically how ICTs – which some have argued promote the emergence of a global panopticon (Gill 1995) – are also fostering a 'brand' new world that can be understood as a new more flexible regime of domination.

The 'information society' as a new economic imaginary based on the convergence of neoliberalism and cybernetics

While the idea of an information society emerged first in sociology (Bell 1973; Castells 1996), there has in recent years been increased interest in the concept in international political economy (IPE), where some have defined it as an economic imaginary (Palan and Cameron, 2004). We can see this for example in the neo-Marxist accounts of Jameson (1991), Harvey (1989), and Hardt and Negri (2000) with their arguments about postmodernism as a cultural logic of capitalism or as an empire, and in critical and neo-Gramscian accounts of communications in IPE (Comor 1998; Deibert 1997; Davies 1999). We can also see it in liberal accounts like that of Rosenau (1992), where ICTs are constitutive of 'governance without government' or where they contribute to the 'soft power' of the US (Nye 2004). While some Marxist critics (Woods 1997; May 2002) suggest the need to be wary of claims of 'novelty' and understand these changes as part of capitalist development rather than a departure from it, what is nevertheless important is to take seriously the symbolic power of culture to shape a broad social imaginary.

Culture – understood as a structured ensemble of symbolic mediations – always relates to a social imaginary that works to constitute both social and economic relations (see Introduction and Chapter 7, this volume). From this perspective, the economy cannot be understood without an economic imaginary. As Cornelius Castoriadis explains:

> No society can exist without the organization of the production of its material life and of its reproduction as society. However, these organizations are not and cannot be dictated inescapably by natural laws or by rational considerations ... Nevertheless, it is economy that displays in the most striking way – precisely because it claims to be integrally exhaustively rational – the domination of the imaginary at all levels.
>
> (Castoriadis 1975: 219, 236)

Hence, social realities cannot exist without ideologies, where ideologies are understood not only in terms of 'false consciousness masking objective reality', but more importantly as discourses of justification that act to legitimize the contradictions in a given social order. Analyses dealing with the advent of a global information society hint at a transformation of the manner in which the capitalist economy is perceived – a shift towards a new ideology of communication (Breton and Proulx 2002) – which can best be understood as a kind of cybernetic capitalism.

This ideological transformation originates in a convergence between neoliberal economic thought and the cybernetic theory of communication. The discourse of the 'information society' shares certain similarities with neoliberal economic theory. Most of the authors who have dealt with the information society (Bell 1973; Castells 1996; Negroponte 1995; Toffler 1970) affirm that ICTs allow for an increase in the amount of information available to individuals and ensure its optimal allocation. According to Bill Gates (1995), these technologies will usher in a new phase of 'friction-free capitalism', that is the attainment of perfect market competition in which both buyers and sellers have access to complete information. The interconnection of the world through ICTs will thus facilitate decision-making processes through the more efficient production, distribution and consumption of information. In short, ICTs will allow markets to conform to the rules put forward in neoclassical economic literature, in which markets operate under conditions of perfect information (Comor 2002). According to other scholars, ICTs enable a cyber-democracy sustained by a global civil society, which can now create a Habermasian global public sphere (Lipschutz 1999; Falk 2000; Shaw 1994). The convergence of market and cybernetic theories thus creates the possibility for a convergence of market ideology with democracy.

These analyses all present technology as a determining factor in society. Instead, the phenomena they discuss must be studied from a cultural angle in order to avoid falling into technological determinism. Through their cultural approach to economics, Miller and Carrier (1998) use the concept of 'virtualism' to demonstrate that economic practices are being progressively transformed in an effort to replicate the abstract models conceived by economists. Hence, the discourse of 'the information society' can be considered as an abstraction – understood as an economic imaginary – which seeks to *produce something real* by transforming individual and collective subjects into rational actors.

'Virtualism' parallels the epistemological mutations generated by neoliberal thought in its aspiration to alter the object of economic analysis. The epistemological revolution underpinning neoliberalism consists of applying the microeconomic paradigm of the firm to economic agents. In neoliberal thought, individuals are no longer considered solely as consumers who can express their preferences in the market, but also as self-responsible entrepreneurs, who must pursue their 'utility preferences' by exchanging information via the market's communicational process. By 'managing' his or her life as an enterprise does, the individual subject thus progressively resembles the *homo economicus* imagined by neoliberal economists. As Hayek (1945) suggests, the fundamental economic problem is not so much the optimal reallocation of scarce resources but rather the efficient use of knowledge and information.[2] Hayek rejects the classical conception of the market as a space of perfect information; the market is no longer justified through optimal wealth distribution (which would require perfect knowledge), but rather through the provision of optimal information in complex and uncertain situations. Value therefore comes from information *about* information. Thus, according to Hayek, it is impossible for a centralized authority to obtain all available information and thus ensure efficient resource allocation. The efficiency criterion means leaving economic decisions to individual entrepreneurs who, though they may not understand the economic system as a whole, have the necessary information in their field of expertise to make optimal decisions. According to Hayek, the price system is the best means to communicate information. Through an analogy between the price system's role in the market and a telecommunication system, he almost prophetically heralds the emergence of the 'information society' decades prior to the coining of the term, maintaining that technology allows for an efficient and optimal distribution of information:

> In abbreviated form, by a kind of symbol, only the most essential information is passed on and passed on only to those concerned. It is more than a metaphor to describe the price system as a kind of machinery for registering change, or a system of telecommunication which enables individual producers to watch merely the movement of a few pointers, as an engineer might watch the hands of a few dials, in order to adjust their activities to changes of which they may never know more than is reflected in the price movement.
>
> (Hayek 1945: 528)

Inspired by Hayek, neoliberalism epistemologically redefines the object of economic analysis to focus on the study of the optimal distribution of information and thus creates a first convergence between economic and cybernetic thought.

Cybernetics – defined as the science of social regulation and of the optimization of information resources, in short, of control and of communication

(Wiener 1961) – gives the concept of communication its modern meaning. Cybernetics focuses on the capacity of machines to analyse information coming from an external environment, as well as on their ability to make decisions consistent with goals determined through a feedback process that allows systems to regulate themselves. Cybernetics also attempts to explain human behaviour by asserting that each being can be defined through the information exchanges it maintains with its environment. The word cybernetic, invented by Wiener, comes from the Greek word *kubernetes*, which means 'pilot' or 'rudder'. It thus shares the same roots as the word government: 'the art of managing and of running highly complex systems' (Lazar, 1992: 35). Thus, a second convergence between cybernetics and neoliberalism can be observed; as Foucault (2004: 228) explains, whereas economics since Adam Smith had consisted of the analysis of production, exchange and consumption, neoliberalism focuses more on the management of human behaviour and 'the strategic programming of individuals'.

The goal of the study of cybernetics is to prevent entropy (social disorder) towards which modern societies are held to be inexorably moving. This entropy may be mitigated by reducing the 'noise' that disturbs communication between individuals. This noise reduction is achieved through the improvement of communication, which is made possible by, among other things, the 'new thinking machines' (Lafontaine 2004), i.e. computers.

From the neoliberal perspective, making capitalism communicational or cybernetic involves attempts to reduce the 'noise' which prevents the price system – understood here as a system for communicating information – from functioning efficiently. As Lyotard (1984: 5) explains: 'The ideology of communicational transparency, which goes hand in hand with the commercialization of knowledge, will begin to perceive the state as a factor of opacity and noise.' Nevertheless, the analogy between cybernetics and neoliberalism remains paradoxical in that Wiener himself – who invented the theory of cybernetics – saw the commodification of knowledge and information as one of the sources of entropy.

Certain authors go further in thinking about the logic of the market as a communication system. Pennington (2003) and Wohlgemuth (2005) maintain that the market, through the price system, is an institution that allows for more deliberation than does politics and proposes a convergence between the conception of market as developed by Hayek and the concept of communicational rationality developed by Habermas. The latter defines communicational rationality as the highest form of rationality, which allows individuals engaging in a discussion that is free of constraints to reach a consensus on the common good (Habermas 1984). This consensus is established in the public sphere, and must be on the basis of a set of criticizable axioms that are evaluated according to the criterion of validity. For Habermas, the intersubjective process required in order to reach a consensus about the validity of specific claims takes place in the sphere of culture (the lifeworld). According to certain neoliberals, for the Habermasian ideal of communication to be efficiently achieved, it is essential to depoliticize a maximum number of social questions and to let them be regulated through the market (Pennington 2003; Wohlgemuth 2005). Politics, in this perspective, thwarts the efficiency of communicational rationality upon which the price system rests. According to the neoliberals, politics constitutes a 'noise' in communicational terms, which prevents the market from efficiently exchanging information.

The reconstruction of hegemony: towards a 'global democratic marketplace'

Any broad social imaginary becomes concrete through its articulation with specific symbols (Castoriadis 1975: 190). In the case of the new economic imaginary based on the convergence between cybernetics and neoliberal theory, these symbols emerged towards the end of the 1960s, following a triple crisis – economic, cultural, and political – experienced by Western democracies.

Neo-Gramscians have suggested that one of the principal interpretations of this crisis was that given by the Trilateral Commission, which saw the principal problem to be one of 'governability'. The Commission sought to construct a neoliberal world order under US leadership (Gill 1990). They saw ICTs as a crucial strategy to revive the US economy (Comor 1998; Schiller 1984), and thus to reconsolidate an ailing American hegemony (Sum 2003). The neo-Gramscian approach, which focuses on the hegemony of relations of production in a given world order, can be combined with a cultural approach focusing on the symbolic dimension of culture to show how the new economic imaginary is materialized in the discourses and practices of various social actors. Through a discussion of the notion of the *spirit of capitalism*, we will see how an alliance of heterogeneous social forces has attempted to legitimize cybernetic capitalism by fostering a convergence between democracy and the market that takes the form of a 'global democratic marketplace'.

The transnational managerial class and the new spirit of capitalism

The reconfiguration of the economic imaginary on which the ideology of communication is based was accomplished in a context of crisis through an alliance between the 'new right' and the 'new left', embodied in what Barbrook and Cameron (1996) call 'the Californian ideology'. Born in Silicon Valley, the Mecca of the 'new economy', this Californian ideology was built on the values of radical democracy taken from the counter-cultural movements. By insisting on decentralization, multiplicity, plurality, and identity fragmentation, these movements rejected traditional forms of institutional authority (parental, educational, state) that were considered to be constraints on individual emancipation. Inspired by McLuhan's (1989) writings on the global village among other things, some members of the hippy movement saw ICTs as an opportunity to create a Jeffersonian democracy in which individuals could express themselves freely in cyberspace. Anti-statism, combined with a faith in technological progress, reconciled the radical critics of the new left with the reactionary thought of the right (see Figure 8.1). The similarities between the discourse of Al Gore on the project of *Global Information Infrastructure* (GII), and that of Newt Gingrich,

Figure 8.1 This Intel advertisement illustrates the conjuncture between the counter-culture of the 'new left' (the hippies), with that of the neoconservative right (Christ). It can also be interpreted as an example of the new economic imaginary seeking to enchant technology in order to render capitalism more attractive.

neoconservative politician, reveal this convergence between the left and the right. According to Al Gore (1994) 'the GII will be a metaphor for democracy itself' by 'enabling each citizen – the human equivalent of the self-contained processor – to have the power to control his or her own life'. Likewise, Newt Gingrich affirms that the Internet is breaking up the gigantic social institutions of the industrial revolution and leading people back 'to something that is – strangely enough – much more like Tocqueville's 1830s America' (Gingrich 1995: 57).

This Californian ideology is part of what Boltanski and Chiapello (1999) call the *new spirit of capitalism*. For Boltanski and Chiapello, Weber's *spirit of capitalism*, formally just an account of the ideas and ethos which animate people in capitalist society, is to be understood more as an ideology through which capitalism legitimizes itself, despite the fact that capitalism constitutes an absurd system that requires the subordination of workers and binds capitalists themselves in an endless process of accumulation (Boltanski and Chiapello 1999: 41).

The 'new' *spirit of capitalism* was the discourse of justification that emerged during the 1980s and 1990s to provide a new basis of legitimation for the evolving mode of production. For example, the theory of network society put forth by Manuel Castells (1996), which can be understood as a theoretical synthesis of the various discourses on the information society, morally sanctions the new forms of capital accumulation. In this vein, the *Wall Street Journal* summarises the remarks of a specialist working for a high-technology firm:

> By linking innovation to broader shifts in the way people live, Mr. Castells bestows meaning on activities that some high-tech people fear are driven only by greed. 'People want somebody to come along and say what they're doing is all right—and say it with a bit more substance than they might,' says John Gage, chief scientist at Sun Microsystems Inc.
>
> (Zachary, 1998, p.B1)

Boltanski and Chiapello (1999) show that the concept of the network, which is at the centre of the *new spirit of capitalism*, was invoked by certain managerial authors in response to critiques of capitalism. These counter-cultural critiques of the 1970s deplored the bureaucratic and centralized nature of a mode of regulation that hindered the emergence of autonomous subjects. Through the various characteristics attributed to it (horizontal, egalitarian, participatory), the concept of the network expels the notions of power and of antagonism from the way social relations are understood. The analysis of the contemporary political economy in terms of the *spirit of capitalism* is a useful starting point for understanding the shifts in discourse and management practices (see Thrift, Chapter 9, this volume, for a specific example of this). This analysis must also be applied to other social institutions, since the ideology of communication has spread over all spheres of society and seeks to reconstruct world order in its own image.

According to Cox (1987), it is possible to perceive the emergence of a new transnational managerial class that exercises control over transnational corporations. This managerial class has its own organic intellectuals, to use the Gramscian expression, at its disposal. They work primarily through what Thrift calls the 'cultural circuits of capital' (Thrift 2005). Their task consists of instigating and constantly repeating new norms and values in order to make capitalism more 'sexy' and more human. Simply put, this task entails building a new economic imaginary that is more attractive than the existing one – considered to be too bureaucratic, hierarchical, and impersonal – in order to increase the cultural capital of companies and of capitalist practices through the introduction of ICTs. The discourse of the 'information society' has thus been promoted by an alliance of various forces, including bankers and industries operating in the information and communication sectors,[3] neoliberal politicians, technology gurus, and management theorists.

Among these organic intellectuals are people such as Nicholas Negroponte, Kevin Kelly, Bill Gates, George Gilder, Alvin Toffler, Daniel Bell, Peter Drucker,

Tom Peters, Thomas Friedman, Walter Wriston, and Manuel Castells. According to Peter Drucker, a management guru, the boundary dividing the intellectual from the manager is dissolved in the age of information, because each needs the other in order to produce 'useful' knowledge (1993: 230). Despite their disparate origins, all share the same ideology, that of communication, and see the advent of a new economy through ICTs. According to Kevin Kelly, founder of *Wired* magazine:

> Because communication – which in the end is what the digital technology and media are all about – is not just a sector of the economy. Communication is the economy ... The new economy is about communication, deep and wide. ... Communication is the foundation of society, of our culture, of our humanity, of our own individual identity, and of all economic systems.
>
> (Kelly 1999, p.5)

This belief in the democratic virtues of communication is part of what Thomas Frank (2001) calls 'market populism'. According to these organic intellectuals markets are far more democratic than elected governments; the market thus becomes a 'global democratic marketplace'.

The global democratic marketplace: a result of the convergence of ICTs and finance

The discourse promoted by the organic intellectuals of cybernetic capitalism was important in legitimizing the deregulation of telecommunications and financial sectors – both pillars of the 'new economy' – during the 1980s and 1990s. This was done part through the appropriation of the anti-bureaucratic critique of the 'new left' and of its faith in the opportunity for emancipation represented by ICTs. Deregulated telecommunications networks were supposed to bring about the development of perfect communication by allowing for universal access, cooperation, transparency, and efficiency (Mansell 1993: 7–8).

The deregulation of the telecommunications sector – combined with networking, computerization and the deregulation of the financial sector – has enabled the promoters of this neoliberal imaginary to talk about a 'global democratic marketplace'. For example, for Thomas Friedman (2000: 139), the deregulation of finance and telecommunications consists of a democratization process where the financial sphere becomes the public sphere and where individuals become 'super-empowered individuals'. Similarly, Walter Wriston, former president of Citicorp,[4] asserts that technology has transformed the 'gold standard' into the 'information standard', making it possible for markets to constantly 'vote' on governments' fiscal, diplomatic, and monetary policies (quoted by Hamilton 1986: 30–2). Others suggest that the democratization of finance which this deregulation is held to bring about builds on the 'pension-fund socialism', where workers finally own the means of production through their pension funds, already created by the expansion of pensions during the Fordist era (Drucker 1976).

Drucker (1993) also maintains that because a knowledge worker is owner of his knowledge, he can carry it with him wherever he pleases. This assertion arises from an individualistic and meritocratic vision of work where relations between autonomous individuals replace older hierarchies (May 2002). Nevertheless, this vision produces real effects in the symbolic structuring of social relations. Once adopted by political institutions, this belief generates an imperative to adapt to emerging conditions of production and to transform workers into flexible subjects in order to ensure state and enterprise competitiveness. This in turn results in a rejection of the state's responsibility for under-employment, which is instead blamed on the lack of qualifications and the inflexibility of workers themselves.

For the boosters of the new economy, the application of network metaphors to financial markets serves to realise Drucker's ideas about 'pension-fund socialism' and 'shareholder democracy'.[5] According to the director of the *Wired* magazine, Kevin Kelly:

> Networks promote this equity culture. The ownership of organizations is distributed and decentralized into a thousand points ... When you invest in a mutual fund, you invest in hundreds of thousands of other people's work ... This is network equity ... The workers of America really do collectively own the means of production ... This network equity is made possible by the same network technology – shrinking chips and expanding communications – that creates wealth in the first place.
>
> (Kelly 1999, p.157)

The transformation of finance through the introduction of ICTs is closely connected to transformations in the media brought about by the same technologies.[6] One reading of these transformations is that they signal the advent of a Habermasian public sphere for financial capitalism (Germain 2004). However, this interpretation ignores the power relations that pervade in the public sphere. The connections between finance – which refers to the economic universe – and the media – which refers to the democratic and political universe – involves a convergence in the information circulating within them, as it passes through the same channels (ICTs and the Internet). The merging of the financial universe with that of the media generates a convergence of *symbolic* nature; they now operate with the same logics drawn from the world of cybernetics, namely those of technical efficiency, operability, and control, as well as the logic of spectacle drawn from the media world. The spectacle, as will be developed further below, thus becomes a means of legitimating and governing cybernetic capitalism.

The transformation of the public sphere into a cultural industry has already been criticized by Habermas (1984, 1989) as a colonization of the 'lifeworld' (the sphere of culture) by the system (the sphere of economic and political power). This reproduction of the Marxian distinction between the sphere of culture and that of economy is no longer tenable – if it ever was. Indeed, we can also observe a colonization of the system by the 'lifeworld' in as much as this 'speculative public sphere' emerging from the fusion between the power of money and that of communication occurs in such a way that 'the discourse of money becomes money itself' (Leyshon and Thrift 1997: 21). Nevertheless, the sorts of communication going on in this transformation are rather different to those imagined by Habermas. Obviously, it is not communicational rationality, born of an enlightened discussion, as Habermas theorized that presides in these two spheres, but rather opinion, noise rumour and spectacle that dominate the 'global democratic marketplace'. The speculative logic that animates practice in the financial sphere transforms the potential for transparent communications into opacity.

From the global panopticon to a 'brand' new world

> What we have seen and said is that information technology has demolished time and distance, But instead of increasing the power of government and, thus, validating Orwell's image that Big Brother watched our every move, that proposition has been stood on its head and we have all wound up watching Big Brother.
>
> (Walter Wriston 1997, p.172)

> On January 24th, Apple Computer will introduce Macintosh
> And you'll see why 1984 won't be like 1984
>
> (Apple advertising slogan, 1984)

According to Castoriadis (1975: 41) culture creates the norms and values that shape human subjectivity. Imaginaries are thus reproduced in social and cultural practices. These practices both constitute and are constituted by particular subjectivities emanating from the modalities of power specific of a given society. In other words, the cultural transformations previously analysed also entail changes in individual subjectivities and in power relations. This section will consider how the rhetoric of the 'global democratic marketplace' and its various elaborations in terms of inclusive and participative global networks have political consequences: they lead to a project to restructure power relations through measures aiming to transform subjectivities, in order to adapt them to the conditions of accumulation in cybernetic capitalism.

The global information society project: toward a spectacular governmentality

Gill (1995) claims that with the spread of ICTs a 'global panopticon' has emerged: the surveillance capacities of ICTs are used by transnational capital to ensure the power of the new world order, which he describes as 'disciplinary neoliberalism'. Nevertheless, it seems that the Orwellian nightmare described by Gill also has a complementary aspect – that of the 'brand new world' being constructed through the 'global information society' project. Gill's criticism of disciplinary neoliberalism presents power as an oppressive force that operates uniformly and crushes the subjects' aspirations. Although Gill's critique is well founded, it must be augmented with a Foucauldian analysis of the ways in which liberal governmental power actually works to govern through liberty, recognizing and adjusting to subjects' desire for emancipation while simultaneously using that liberty to attain its own goals (Miller and Rose 1990). Specifically, although Gill's notion of disciplinary neoliberalism correctly analyses the way in which the market exerts its power on states and individuals, it understates the epistemological transformation generated by neoliberalism. Neoliberalism transforms capitalism's logic into a cybernetic system of social regulation maintained by communication. In cybernetic capitalism, information becomes the constitutive principle of society itself. This transformation, which situates communication at an ontological level, modifies the organization of power relations in more complex ways than simply an increase in surveillance.

This reconfiguration of power relations is apparent in the global information society project. Following the work on the *Global Information Infrastructure* (GIS-GII) headed by Al Gore, many international organizations (the World Bank, the G8, the OECD, the UN, the International Telecommunication Union (ITU), and so forth) have published reports written by groups of experts and have organized summits focused on the 'global information society'.

The main preoccupation evoked by these experts is the creation of a 'digital divide' between 'information rich' and 'information poor'. The focus on the digital divide can be understood as a strategy aimed at reviving capital accumulation by including and connecting as many as possible of those individuals and communities currently excluded from the networks. This project appears at first sight as a political project 'without politics', since the responsibility of developing the infrastructures required to connect the world is delegated to the private sector. However, this project constitutes an extension of the political in that it restructures the relations of power within society (Lemke 2004: 23). These international organizations work to transform power relations by producing new subjectivities through 'empowerment' measures. These measures designed to improve the connectivity of the excluded or the 'information poor' are developed through public–private partnerships, taking the form of networks that include representatives of large communication firms (such as Microsoft, AOL, Cisco, and so forth), the government, and civil society.[7]

This private sector role in governance can be seen as a means of extending the transnational corporations' influence into developing countries and of ensuring capital accumulation in the new financialized accumulation regime (Boyer 2000). At the same time, a reconstruction of authority in accordance with managerial principles is also occurring (Hansen and Salskov-Iversen 2005). Public–private partnerships are the ideal solution for the global extension of the emerging communicational imaginary. A good example is the *Global Knowledge Partnership* – a network for the exchange of best practices, know-how and expertise concerning management and the use of ICTs with the goal of increasing the capacities of developing countries.

Power in cybernetic capitalism reveals itself when subjects are transformed as they become connected to the network. This subjective transformation is effected through the assimilation of the managerial modes of organization by civil society and individuals. Through network connections, subjects transform themselves into self-entrepreneurs who manage their lives as a business. Integral to this reorganization of power relations is the notion of spectacle. A company's performance, for example, is based both on its economic and its dramatic performance. In order to attract investment in the 'global democratic marketplace', companies must permanently stage spectacles through what Tsing calls 'spectacular accumulation' (Tsing 2004). In a financialized economy, profits must be imagined even before they can be made. Thus, the primary means used consists of the construction of a brand image, a theatrical feat, and of a reputation, all of which enable the company to gain in financial value.

This is not a new phenomenon. It has already been critically analysed by institutionalist authors such as Veblen (1963), who developed the concept of intangible assets based on the owners' 'good will', and also by Keynes, who developed the analogy between stock market speculation and a beauty contest.[8] The re-financialization of the economy since the collapse of the Bretton Woods agreement, financial deregulation, and the increase of stock market assets through the proliferation of pension funds have certainly amplified this phenomenon. What is new, however, is the fact that the practice of 'branding' now applies not only to companies, but also to states and to individuals. Thus, it becomes one of the means of subject formation used by power in this regime of spectacular accumulation.

Jodi Dean (2002) refers to this mode of subject formation as 'celebrity drive'.[9] This process of subject formation works through self-advertisement, visibility, and recognition. In short, it works through the 'spectacularisation' of the self. Simply put, those who do not communicate do not exist. As the management guru Tom Peters (1997: 83) explains in his book *The Brand Called You*: 'Big Companies understand the importance of brands. Today, in the Age of individuals, you have to be your own brand. Here's what it takes to be CEO of Me Inc'.

Workers must therefore use ICTs as a 'self-marketing' tool. It is by considering this process of subject formation that we can best understand the measures of empowerment being developed by international institutions. For these organizations, ICTs are tools for self-marketing and for the development of individuals' own social, human, and reputational capital. As tools, they would for instance allow small farmers in Africa to connect to the web in order to sell their produce, according to the G8 Dot Force.[10] A successful life is thus presented as a simple matter of developing individuals' reputational capital through technology and permanent online education.

International organizations' efforts to foster the inclusion and 'empowerment' of the excluded thus can be understood as a new form of governmentality. A parallel may be drawn between capitalism's spectacular logic as described by Guy Debord (1969) in *The Society of the Spectacle* and the concept of governmentality developed by Michel Foucault (2004). For Debord, the spectacle works through the tyranny of the image,[11] which both unifies and expands the system of domination, thus making it difficult to distinguish between traditionally opposed categories (private and public, in and out, reality and its representation, true and false). In the spectacle, the appearance and staging of reality become *more real than reality.*

The Foucauldian concept of governmentality seeks to explain the articulation between discourses and concrete practices of power. Although it works through rather than against a discourse of freedom, governmentality is nonetheless a modality of power attempting to ensure order by using the freedom of others and oneself to achieve specific goals. The spectacular logic of capitalism associated with the 'global information society' project hence entails the creation of new subjects and of new practices of power in an effort to guide and to direct the conduct of others and itself. Thus, the spectacle is part of a shift in accumulation practices and of legitimation strategies at the centre of cybernetic capitalism.

By appropriating the counter-cultural critique from the 1970s, the 'global information society' project launches a new governmentality that can be described as 'spectacular'. Here, subjects are enjoined to engage in a constant communicative and branding exercise in order to thrive. The subject of cybernetic capitalism is thus distinguished from the autonomous modern subject in that rather than defining itself by its reflexive capacity to act upon its external world, it does so by its ability to self-regulate according to the information received from its environment. The individual defines him or herself by a capacity to communicate and adapt, since in cybernetics all beings are defined by the nature of the information exchanges they maintain with their environment (Wiener 1961). Understanding the spectacle in terms of governmentality means that it also entails governing at a distance; that is, it entails a technique that atomises individuals and encloses them within their own private space in ways that engender their adaptability in relation to capital's requirements. According to some, interactive devices connected to ICTs enable people to break from the spectacle's passive logic of unidirectional communication. It would be more accurate to suggest, however, that with the new means of communication, the spectacle instead is transformed into an 'interpassive' spectacle where a technological fetishism deprives us of our 'authentically passive experience', preparing us for 'frenetic, and mind numbing activity' (Zizek 2003: 109).

This process of subject formation occurs for states as well as for individuals. A set of new knowledges, specifically that of benchmarks, has emerged by which states can be compared and compare themselves in relation to this 'new beauty contest'. For example, the Network Readiness Index,[12] a measuring tool developed through collaboration between the Institut Européenne des Affaires, the World Bank and the World Economic Forum, aims to determine the countries in which the introduction of ICTs presents the greatest profitability potential. Another index, the Anholt-GMI Nation Brands Index[13] presents itself as the primary analytical tool allowing the measurement of each country's power in step with a series of criteria founded on perceptions of 'global public opinion' as far as cultural, political, human, commercial, and investment potential of the states' trademarks are concerned.

The 'branding' practice of companies and individuals is thus extended to the state, aiming to commodify its attributes with the goal of attracting capital and qualified labour in an 'information society' (Van Ham 2002). Adopting similar discursive strategies, commercial trademarks and states compete to ensure the citizen-consumers' allegiance. As Thomas Friedman explains:

> Countries now face the same challenge vis-à-vis their customers in the global marketplace – the members of the electronic herd. Countries used to brand for tourism. But that is not enough anymore. As we move into a world where everyone has the same hardware and everyone is being forced to get the same software to go with it, a country's brand, and the unique bond it can build with its foreign investors, becomes even more important.
>
> (2000: 244)

Conclusion

Cybernetic capitalism and its logic of spectacular governmentality blur the conceptual categories upon which modernity was founded. State and enterprise, public and private, media and market, citizens and consumers seem to converge in a permanent, networked, global system. Having spread over all sectors of society, the ideology of managerial communication initiates a deregulation of conceptual frameworks – paralleling those of telecommunication and finance – which might be, according to Gilles Deleuze and Felix Guattari, the prelude to the establishment of what they term 'societies of control':[14]

> Finally, the most shameful moment came when computer science, marketing, design, and advertising, all the disciplines of communication, seized hold of the word concept itself and said: 'This is our concern, we are the creative ones, we are the *ideas men*! We are the friends of the concept, we put it on our computers.' … The simulacrum, the simulation of a package of noodles, has become the concept; and the one who packages the product, commodity, or work of art has become the philosopher, conceptual persona, or artist. How could philosophy, an old age person, compete against young executives in a race for the universals of communication for determining the marketable form of the concept …?
>
> (1994: 10–11)

This appropriation of critique has already been described by certain critical theorists, such as Marcuse (1968), who criticized the repressive force of advanced capitalist societies capable of reconciling opposed forces with the system. According to him, the union of opposite categories (private–public, society–state, liberty–domination) implies the emergence of a new form of totalitarianism that transforms these concepts into empty words. The 'global information society' project, which operates by producing a rhetorical fusion of capitalism and democracy, thus creates such a totalitarianism that seems capable of self-reproduction through a process of auto-referential communication. Luhmann (1999) calls this process of auto-reproduction, *auto-poiesis*.[15] Looking at the technological fetishism animating the 'global information society' project, it seems pertinent to consider whether this auto-referential process might be 'auto-techno-poietic' (Valentine 2000).

The global information society project endeavours to build a global society founded on communication, a society to which individuals and states must adapt by engaging in self-marketing in order to be included. This 'auto-techno-poietic system' obscures the political nature of the economy by co-opting counter-hegemonic forces through their commodification. The understanding of the market as a cybernetic system thus neutralizes the political, reducing it to a question of techno-economic management.

Adaptation becomes the mantra of this neo-Darwinian process, which works through a 'survival of the fastest' logic. Nevertheless, a fundamental paradox exists at the very basis of this project, namely the aporia of inclusion in societies of control, expressed as: 'being included, but profoundly ignoring why' (Haesler, 1995: 74). This paradox calls for a consideration of the normative dimension of a social project in which there are no goals other than those of technical efficiency. Although this system seems stable and self-reproducing, it is nonetheless founded on an economic imaginary and must be continuously reproduced through social practices. A cultural approach to international political economy must therefore reveal the contingent and political nature of the founding economic imaginaries of social life, or it contributes to the reification of cybernetic capitalism.

Notes

1 http://www.cisco.com/web/thehumannetwork/index.html
2 Information and knowledge are used interchangeably by Hayek as do most neoclassical authors. This haziness surrounding the concept of information is also present in the conceptualization of the information society.
3 For a study of the converging interests of the financial and informational sectors, see Hamelink (1983).
4 Citicorp was one of the first banks to use computer systems in its activities.
5 Despite what these organic intellectuals think of cybernetic capitalism, the ideal of pension-fund socialism and of shareholder democracy is far from being achieved. In fact, neoliberalism has accentuated social inequalities. The re-financialization of the economy has profited only an infinitesimal fraction of the population. This overclass owns the majority of the stocks on the stock market and profits from them, whereas for the majority of the workers, salary constitutes the main source of revenue. Duménil and Lévy (2004) thus maintain that 1% of the American population's most wealthy class now owns 16% of the country's total revenue. Meanwhile, 90% of families with the lowest revenues have experienced a stagnation of their purchasing power, whereas that of the 0.01% most wealthy has quadrupled. For a critique of the notions of shareholder democracy and pension-fund socialism, see O'Sullivan (2000) and Lordon (2000).
6 For an analysis dealing with the analogy between the media and finance, see Thrift *et al.* (2004) and Thrift (2001).
7 The ICT Task Force, founded by the UN in order to solve the digital divide problem following the Millennium Summit for the eradication of poverty, has some of cybernetic capitalism's organic intellectuals among its members, including Nicholas Negroponte and Manuel Castells.

8 Veblen (1963) defined intangible assets as immaterial elements of wealth evaluated and capitalized according to the evaluation of potential gain which their property might procure. The most common form of these intangible assets, according to Veblen, appears in the form of a venture's reputation, or 'good will', in which publicity plays a fundamental role. Through an analogy between speculation and a beauty contest, Keynes explains the fallacious nature of the conception of markets which suggest that prices reflect the value of the real economy. Contestants would have to choose the picture that most resembles the average evaluation of all the contestants. According to this type of evaluation, what matters is not determining which face is the most beautiful, but rather anticipating collective opinion (Orlean 2000).

9 In its 'Human Network' advertisement discussed above, Cisco welcomes us to a world in which everyone can become a celebrity.

10 The Digital Opportunities Task Force (DOT Force) was launched by the G8 government leaders to look at how Information and Communication Technology (ICT) can bring digitally enabled opportunities to developing countries and help bridge the widening global socio-economic divide. Companies such as *Accenture, Hewlett Packard, Siemens, Telesystem, Thomson and Toshiba,* represented the private sector in this public-private initiative.

11 Regarding the role of the image – or visuality – in economy see Aitken, Chapter 3, Walters, Chapter 5 and Amoore and de Goede, Chapter 7 in this volume.

12 http://www.weforum.org/pdf/gitr/rankings2007.pdf

13 http://www.nationbrandindex.com/

14 On the notion of societies of control, see Deleuze (1990) and Hardt and Negri (2000).

15 Regarding the links between international political economy and Luhmann's auto-poiesis theory, see Daly (2004).

Bibliography

Barbrook, Richard and Angus Cameroon (1996) 'The Californian ideology', *Science as Culture*, 26(1): 44–72.

Bell, Daniel (1973) *The Coming of Post-industrial Society; a Venture in Social Forecasting*, New York: Basic Books.

Boltanski, Jean-Luc and Ève Chiapello (1999) *Le nouvel esprit du capitalisme*, Paris: Gallimard.

Boyer, Robert (2000) 'Is a finance-led growth regime a viable alternative to Fordism? A preliminary analysis', *Economy and Society*, 29(1): 111–45.

Breton, Philippe and Serge Proulx (2002) *L'Explosion de la communication à l'aube du XXe siècle*, Montréal: Boréal.

Cameron, Angus and Ronen Palan (2004) *The Imagined Economy: State, Globalization and Poverty*, Sage: London.

Carrier, James G. and Daniel Miller (eds) (1998) *Virtualism: A New Political Economy*, New York: Berg.

Castells, Manuel (1996) *The Rise of the Network Society*, Cambridge, MA: Blackwell.

Castoriadis, Cornelius (1975) *L'institution imaginaire de la société*, Paris: Édition du Seuil.

Cisco Systems, *The Human Network*, available at http://www.cisco.com/web/thehuman network/index.html (accessed 17 May 2007).

Comor, Edward A. (1998) *Communication, Commerce and Power: The Political Economy of America and the Direct Broadcast Satellite, 1960–2000*, London: Palgrave Macmillan.

—— (2002) 'When more is less: time, space and knowledge in information societies', in R. Mansell, R. Samarajiva and A. Mahan (eds) *Networking Knowledge for Information Societies: Institutions & Intervention*, Delft: Delft University Press, pp. 239–44.

Cox, Robert W. (1987) *Production, Power and World Order: Social Forces in the Making of History*, New York, Columbia University Press.

Daly, Glyn (2004) 'Radical(ly) political economy: Luhmann, postMarxism and globalization', *Review of International Political Economy*, 11(4): 1–32.

Davies, Matt (1999) *International Political Economy and Mass Communication in Chile: National Intellectuals and Transnational Hegemony*, New York: St Martin's Press.

Dean, Jodi (2002) *Publicity's Secret: How Technoculture Capitalizes on Democracy*, Ithaca, NY: Cornell University Press.

Debord, Guy (1969) *La société du spectacle*, Paris: Buchet/Chastel.

Deibert, Ronald J. (1997) *Parchment, Printing, and Hypermedia: Communication in World Order Transformation*, New York: Columbia University Press.

Deleuze, Gilles (1990) 'Post-scriptum sur les sociétés de contrôle', *Pourparlers*, Paris: Éditions de Minuit, pp. 240–7.

—— and Felix Guattari (1994) *What Is Philosophy?*, New York: Columbia University Press.

Drucker, Peter (1976) 'Pension fund "socialism"', *The Public Interest*, 42(Winter): 3–46.

—— (1993) *Post-capitalist society*, New York: HarperBusiness.

Duménil, Gérard and Domique Lévy (2004) 'Neoliberal income trends. Wealth, class and ownership in the USA', *New Left Review*, 30(November–December): 105–33.

Falk, Richard (2000) 'Global civil society and the democratic prospect', in Barry Holden (ed.), *Global Democracy: Key Debates*, New York: Routledge, pp. 162–78.

Frank, Thomas (2001) *One Market Under God: Extreme Capitalism, Market Populism and the End of Economic Democracy*, London: Secker & Warburg.

Friedman, Thomas L. (2000) *The Lexus and the Olive Tree: Understanding Globalization*, New York: Anchor Books.

Foucault, Michel (2004) *Naissance de la biopolitique: cours au Collège de France, 1978–1979*, Paris: Seuil/Gallimard.

Gates, Bill (1995) *The Road Ahead*, New York: Viking.

Germain, Randall D. (2004) 'Globalizing accountability within the international organization of credit: financial governance and the public sphere', *Global Society*, 18(3): 217–42.

Gore, Al, (1994) 'Remarks prepared for delivery by Vice President Al Gore', International Telecommunications Union, 21 March, available at http://www.ifla.org/documents/infopol/us/goregii.txt (accessed 3 December 2006).

Gill, Stephen (1990) *American Hegemony and the Trilateral Commission*, New York: Cambridge University Press.

—— (1995) 'The global panopticon? The neoliberal state, economic life, and democratic surveillance', *Alternatives*, 20(1): 1–49.

Gingrich, Newt (1995) *The Renew America*, New York, Harper Collins.

Habermas, Jürgen, (1984) *The Theory of Communicative Action*, Boston, MA: Beacon Press.

—— (1989) *The Structural Transformation of the Public Sphere: An Inquiry into a Category of Bourgeois Society*, Cambridge, MA: MIT Press.

Haesler, Aldo (1995) *Sociologie de l'argent et postmodernité*, Genève: Librairie Droz.

Hamelink, Cees J. (1983) *Finance and Information: A Study of Converging Interest*, Norwood: Ablex Publishing Corporation.

Hamilton, Adrian (1986) *The Financial Revolution*, Middlesex: Penguin.

Hansen, Hans Krause and Doris Salskov-Iversen (2005) 'Remodeling the transnational political realm: partnerships, best-practice schemes, and the digitalization of governance', *Alternatives*, 30(2): 141–64.

Hardt, Michael and Antonio Negri (2000) *Empire*, Cambridge, MA: Harvard University Press.

Harvey, David (1989) *The Condition of Postmodernity*, Cambridge: Basil Blackwell.

Hayek, F. (1945) 'The use of knowledge in societies', *American Economic Review*, XXXV, 4(September): 519–30.

Jameson, Frederic (1991) *Postmodernism, or The Cultural Logic of Late Capitalism*, Durham, NC: Duke University Press.

Kelly, Kevin (1999) *New Rules for the new Economy*, New York: Penguin Books..

Lafontaine, Céline (2004) *L'empire cybernétique: des machines à penser à la pensée machine*, Paris: Seuil.

Lazar, Judith (1992) *La science de la communication*, Paris: Presses universitaires de France.

Lemke, Thomas (2004) 'Marx sans guillemets: Foucault, la gouvernementalité et la critique du néolibéralisme', *Actuel Marx*, 36: 13–26.

Leyshon, Andrew and Nigel Thrift (1997) *Money Space: Geographies of Monetary Transformation*, London: Routledge.

Lipschutz, Ronnie D. (1999) 'From local knowledge to global environmental governance', in M. Hewson and T. J. Sinclair (eds) *Approches to Global Governance Theory*, Albany, NY: University of New York Press, pp. 259–83.

Lordon, Frédéric (2000) *Fonds de pension, piège à cons? Mirage de la démocratie actionnariale*, Paris: Raisons d'agir.

Luhmann, Niklas (1999) *Politique et complexité*, Paris: Les Éditions du Cerf.

Lyotard, Jean-François (1984) *The Postmodern Condition: A Report on Knowledge*, Minneapolis, MN: University of Minnesota Press.

Mansell, Robin (1993) *The New Telecommunication: A Political Economy of Network Evolution*, London: Sage.

Marcuse, Herbert (1968) *One Dimensional Man; Studies in the Ideology of Advanced Industrial Society*, Boston, MA: Beacon Press.

May, Christopher (2002) 'The political economy of proximity: intellectual property and the global division of information labour', *New Political Economy*, 7(3): 317–42.

McLuhan, Marshall (1989) *The Global Village: Transformations in World Life and Media in the 21st Century*, New York: Oxford University Press.

Miller, Daniel (1998) 'Conclusion: a theory of virtualism', in James G. Carrier and Daniel Miller (eds) *Virtualism: A New Political* Economy, New York: Berg, pp. 161–86.

Miller, Peter and Nikolas Rose (1990) 'Governing economic life', *Economy and Society*, 19(1): 1–31.

Negroponte, Nicholas (1995) *Being Digital*, New York, Knopf.

Nye, Joseph S. (2004) 'The information revolution and American soft power', in *Power in the Global Information Age: from Realism to Globalization*, New York: Routledge, pp. 81–96.

Orléan, André (2000) 'L'individu, le marché et l'opinion: réflexions sur le capitalisme patrimonial', *Esprit*, Novembre: 51–75.

O'Sullivan, Mary (2000) 'Le socialisme des fonds de pension, ou 'plus ça change ...': financement des retraites et corporate governance aux Etats-Unis', *L'année de la régulation*, No. 4, Paris: La Découverte, pp. 47–88.

Pennington, Mark (2003) 'Hayekian political economy and the limits of deliberative democracy', *Political Studies*, 51(4): 722–39.

Peters, Tom (1997) 'The brand called you', *Fast Company*, 10: 83, available at http://www.fastcompany.com/online/10/brandyou.html (accessed 4 April 2007).

Rosenau, James (1992) *Governance without Government: Order and Change in World Politics*, New York: Cambridge University Press.

Schiller, Herbert (1984) *Information and the Crisis of Economy*, Norwood: Ablex.

Shaw, Martin (1994) *Global Society and International Relation*, Cambridge: Polity Press.

Sum, Ngai-Ling (2003) 'Informational capitalism and U.S. economic hegemony', *Critical Asian Studies*, 35(3): 373–98.

Thrift, Nigel (2001) 'It's the romance, not the finance that makes the business worth pursuing: disclosing a new market culture', *Economy and Society*, 30(4): 412–32.

Thrift, Nigel (2005) *Knowing Capitalism*, London, Sage Publication.

Thrift, Nigel, Gordon L. Clarck and Adam Tickell (2004) 'Performing finance: the industry, the media and its image', *Review of International Political Economy*, 11(2): 289–310.

Toffler, Alvin (1970) *Future Schock*, New York: Random House.

Tsing, Anna (2004) 'Inside the economy of appearances', in Ash Amin and Nigel Thrift (eds) *The Blackwell Cultural Economy Reader*, Oxford: Blackwell, pp. 83–100.

Valentine, Jeremy (2000) 'Information technology, ideology and governmentality', *Theory, Culture & Society*, 17(2): 21–43.

Van Ham, P. (2002) 'Branding territory: inside the wonderful worlds of PR and IR Theory', *Millenium: Journal of International Studies*, 31(2): 249–69.

Veblen, Thorstein (1963) *The Engineers and the Price System*, New York: Harcourt, Brace & World.

Wiener, Norbert (1961) *Cybernetics; or, Control and Communication in the Animal and the Machine*, New York: MIT Press.

Wohlgemuth, Michael (2005) 'The communicative character of capitalist competition: a Hayekien response to the Habermassian challenge', *The Independent Review*, 10(1): 83–115.

Woods, Ellen Meiskins (1997) 'Modernity, postmodernity or capitalism?', *Review of International Political Economy*, 4(3): 539–60.

Wriston, Walter B. (1997) 'Bits, bytes, and diplomacy', *Foreign Affairs*, 76(5): 172–82.

Zachary, Pascal G. (1998) 'A philosopher of the web is a hit in Silicon Valley', *The Wall Street Journal*, 1 October: B1.

Zizek, Slavoj (2003) 'Fétichisme et subjectivation interpassive ', *Actuel Marx*, 34: 99–109.

9 A perfect innovation engine

The rise of the talent world

Nigel Thrift[1]

Introduction

In a recent issue of *The Economist* (2006), the argument was put straightforwardly: talent is the world's most valuable commodity and it is getting ever harder to find. Can it be that a world populated by six billion people is suffering from a shortage of talent? How have we come to a point where a culture might think like this? What does such thinking signify? These are the three questions I will endeavour to answer in this chapter. The answers to these three questions involves an argument made in two parts.

In the first part, I will concentrate on the production of commodities by means of the commodity of talent. Here, my main concern will be to highlight the growth of talent as a contemporary sigil of what constitutes a successful business and economy as the result of a redefinition of what constitutes labour, a sigil adding in to the notion of labour power all kinds of qualities which were formerly considered as outside its orbit, with the aim of 'developing the potential and realized capacities of individuals and groups and how they are organized, including those who are within the organization and those who might join the organization' (Boudreau and Ramstad 2007: 2). In other words, talent is about the development of potential, across the full spectrum of human capacities. The first section of the chapter also highlights the corresponding rise of an intermediary economy whose goal is to achieve a state in which the economy is being permanently re-organized and whose enabling discourse is precisely the potential for innovation and creativity shown by talented workers. Subsequently, I argue that the rise of an economy based on talent has all kinds of costs which need to be acknowledged – not as mere by-products but as central to the operation of the new form of capitalism. Specifically, a software-driven class of operatives has to be constructed whose purpose is, in part, to provide the space for the talented to function.

In the second part of the chapter, I will move to the consumption of commodities. Here I will argue that talent that lies outside the organization can be harnessed through the deployment of technologies of 'open innovation' which draw on consumer enthusiasms in order to produce a second string to innovation, so producing a perfect innovation engine in which all the energies of the population can, at least in principle, be pulled in to play in some fashion or the other. Here, my main concern will be to outline a 'flock and flow' economy (McCracken 2006) in which the passions of consumers become central as an inventive force, not least because it is becoming possible to construct 'worlds', rather than simple spaces of consumption. The construction of these worlds requires active intervention in order to produce spaces in which close relationships between corporations and consumers can thrive, narrative reworkings of space and time so that they will support the generation of individualized moments that can be taken up for profit because they act as a kind of space–time currency. These reworkings – what I will call worldings – do not just depend on raw data, though that is vital. They also depend on a constant recursive survey of spaces produced by a host of analytical methods for characterizing places and the people in them which produce a constant feedback about which of these moments will have bite where: they might be thought of as the latest interactive episode in a long history of survey (Igo 2007). In other words I will argue, in line with a number of recent thinkers, that capitalism's main project now is ontological: to invent numerous situations – worlds, if you like – in which it is possible to re-frame and juxtapose associations in order to produce new (and more profitable) inventive compositions. Finally, the conclusion summarises the main arguments and offers some thoughts on the political import of the developments I have outlined.

It is possible to interpret the chapter in three chief ways. First, it is an exercise in cultural political economy (Amin and Thrift 2004), in that it attempts to argue that, although capitalism is a loose formation that is jackdaw-like in its orientation, willing to profit from anything that will turn a profit, capitalists do, at times, tend to hit the same vein, and this is one of those times. That vein is what I will call the technology of cultural composition, in that it involves charging up the semiotic sphere in order to create and tap bodies of passion which display talent, although, as we shall see, what counts as the sign has changed in nature as the process of composition has become widespread. The result is clear at least: a vast human-made imagination machine, but a machine bent on directing imaginations in particular ways by multiplying promise and boosting potentiality. In particular, this charging up of the semiotic sphere can be seen as a search for new forms of animatedness brought about through the multiplication of institutions of public intimacy (or what is sometimes called 'extimacy', see Thrift [2008a]). In other words, this is the economy understood as a technically created entity but one that is rather different from the common understanding of this feat which tends to revolve around the creation of markets (e.g. Callon *et al.* 2007; Mackenzie *et al.* 2007).

Second, it is an attempt to sketch out what the new worlds of production and consumption created by a new technology of 'imaginnovation' look like, understood as a qualitative shift towards cultivating somatic attention (Thrift 2007). What might be called, following Sloterdijk (2004), the 'explicitation' of semiconscious thinking[2] takes place (quite literally) through the design of environments that can act as non-discursive lures pulling this kind of affective thinking into their orbit. This explicitation is, in other words, an attempt to define a new sense of affective touch, arising out of the prevalence of qualculative environments (Thrift 2005) and the new semiotic knowledges that have become available as a result. What is particularly interesting is that this sense of touch appeals to a full range of affects – including the so-called minor affects (Ngai 2005) – by broadening the spectrum of sensory practices that are considered as able to be brought into representation. We might call this state of affairs, after Thrailkill (2006), 'emotive realism'.

Finally, the chapter is a political intervention.[3] The technology of imaginnovation currently being created by capitalism – a technology replete with all manner of new forms of knowledge and skill – represents a different kind of politics from that which has been pursued before because it is focused on etching planes of experience which have often been thought to be opaque to manipulation. Thus any counter-politics, as I will outline in the conclusion, must be able to work in these planes. The first political act must be to understand that point and the different political resonances it makes possible. The second political act must be to widen out what is regarded as politics so it can take in this landscape. We are still only on the cusp of this second act.

One disclaimer is in order. It is important to note that capitalism encompasses a large number of things. All I can do in this chapter is to cover a few of them. So I start with a health warning. Though this is a synthetic and synoptic piece, arising from my continuing work on the practices of knowing capitalism (Thrift 2005), it is not a chapter that tries to cover each and every aspect of capitalism, not least because I think it could easily be argued that, contrary to those commentators who believe that the world is in thrall to but a few giant multinationals, capitalism is currently going through what might be termed a baroque phase of patterned complexity. Thus, the developments I will describe must be understood as going hand in hand with all manner of other forms of economic activity that will never exactly fit these developments and which have their own dynamic (for example, the importance of family lineages and firms, or the particular cultural forms of economic morality to be found in markets and homes, or the many current variants of kleptocracy such as the primitive accumulation found in oil states such as Nigeria), forms of economic activity that cannot be consigned to past forms of production and consumption, and that clearly do not represent the periphery of the economy (Bayart 2001, 2007).

Animating production

According to Michaels *et al.* (2001) there is a war for talent. Most companies are poor at talent management and need to embrace a talent mindset. They need to develop 'winning employee value propositions'. They need to affirm each employee but to invest differentially in them. They need proper talent review processes that will spot and develop talent. They need to hunt for talent all the time. Only then will they become 'talent pools'. At the same time, talent is a resource and 'the rising tide of talent is lifting all boats' (Michaels *et al.* 2001: 177). More talent is becoming available as more and more human resource is put into cultivation – but there will never, ever be enough. All this on the back of a definition of talent which is general, to put it but mildly: 'the sum of a person's abilities – his or her intrinsic gifts, skills, knowledge, experience, intelligence, judgement, attitude, character, and drive. It also includes her ability to learn and grow' (Michaels *et al.* 2001: xii). The resource is expanding, then, but it will always be in short supply. That is the rhetoric then; one which grew steadily through the 1990s and is now pervasive. But when we get closer to the quality called talent, what do we find? One might see the rise of an interest in 'obsessively identifying and multiplying talent' (Accenture 2007) as reflecting the nexus of a set of four different but related tendencies – talent as labour, as re-organization, as the work of others, and as class (Wooldridge 2006).

Talent as labour

The first and most important of these tendencies is in what counts as labour. Of course what counts as labour has constantly shifted through history (e.g. Robertson 2006). But the redescription of labour that is now going on still counts as significant. At the most transparent level, what is at issue is what skills are required in modern capitalism under the conditions of what is generally conceived of as a knowledge revolution in which the provisioning of firms with knowledge is thought of as a, and possibly the, crucial determinant of competitiveness. In particular, this provisioning is thought to require bringing into the knowledge base of capitalism not only boosted cognitive abilities but all manner of tacit skills and competences, largely intuitive skills of the kind necessary to conduct complex interactions in the more extensive and flexible work environments that characterize many modern jobs (which, at least in part, have become so in order to capture and capitalise on talent), that is the kinds of skills that are thought to underpin the rise in intangible assets as a proportion of the value of the market capitalisation of corporations. In other words, the goal is to *make the most of people*, as many management primers put it. Bryan and Joyce set out the goal straightforwardly, even brutally:

> Most companies today were designed for the twentieth century. By remaking them to mobilize the mind power of their 21st-century workforces, these companies will be able to tap into the presently underutilized talents, knowledge, relationships, and skills of their employees, which will open up to them not only new opportunities but also vast sources of wealth.
>
> (2007: 1)

Of course, the goal of tapping into the full range of talents of the workforce can be found throughout the history of capitalism (Thrift 2005). But it has become much more pronounced since the 1990s.

So what differentiates 'talent' from these earlier attempts to make the most of the labour force? One reason is a long-term fall in interaction costs,[4] driven by developments like the growth of information technology, which has greatly increased the value of intangible assets (talent, knowledge, reputation, relationships) relative to tangible assets such as labour and capital. Another reason is the growth of jobs which demand self-directed thought. During the twentieth century, the costs of co-ordinating their work across large companies was so large that mind power was trapped in small pockets of people scattered through each company. This no longer has to be the case. A further reason is the current general emphasis on creativity and innovation. The re-invention of invention as innovation (Thrift 2006) that has taken place over the last two decades or so has resulted from the increased pressure bearing down on many companies to improve their rate of inventiveness. This pressure demands, or so it is thought, more attention to nurturing disruptive agents who are able to make breakthroughs. A final reason, one to which I will devote considerable attention, is that business has increased the range of what it regards as thought, taking in all manner of aspects of thinking which had previously been seen as somewhat tangential.

The first and most straightforward attempt to broaden the spectrum of thought can be dated from the discovery of the importance of tacit skills. Although Polanyi's original work was carried out in the 1950s, it was not until the 1990s that these skills were generally acknowledged by business. Tacit skills underline the importance of what might be called semiconscious human assets that draw on the pre-personal register of sociality and require forms of intelligence that articulate human registers like feeling. Thus,

> [McKinsey] has divided American jobs into three categories: 'transforma-
> tional' (extracting raw materials or converting them into finished goods),
> 'transactional' (interactions that can easily be scripted or automated) and
> 'tacit' (complex interactions requiring a high level of judgement). The
> company argues that over the past six years the number of American jobs
> that emphasize 'tacit interactions' has grown two and a half times as fast as
> the number of transactional jobs and three times as fast as employment in
> general. These jobs now make up some 40% of the American labour market
> and account for 70% of the jobs created since 1998.
>
> (Wooldridge 2006: 4)

However, making visible and codifying tacit skills, yet alone deploying them in any systematic fashion, is difficult, not least because they arise not only from formal learning but also from the wellsprings of experience.

However, husbanding tacit skills has not proved to be the end of the matter. At about the same time, and partly related to the issue of the tacit nature of experience, the importance of what might be termed affective labour became apparent as a key moment in building competitive edge. I do not mean by this the increased attendance to emotional attunement which has now become commonplace in testing and training programmes in nearly every corporation, although this emphasis no doubt prepared the ground. Rather, I am pointing to what might be called the 'vitality' of workers, their passion for the job and their ability to order their passions in order to do the job well, and most especially the innovative energy that can be unlocked within and between them:

potential is redefined as emergent potentia and it is this potentia which is being bought and sold under the name of 'talent' (Clough *et al.* 2007). Mobilizing the passions has proved to be a considerable challenge, however. In particular, reproducibility has proved elusive: 'unlike processes, which can, with some effort be copied by competitors, passion is very difficult to duplicate' (Ready and Conger 2007: 75). However, through a combination of theory and experiment, this quality has now become both more visible and more able to be managed. What is clear is that business is trying to draw on the affective standing reserves of humanity without triggering negative tacit qualities like prejudice, poor practice, or uncritical or wayward intuition: qualities such as passion, energy and a kind of aesthetic judgement of the situation which is crucial to the conduct of economic life.[5]

Finally, cognition itself has come under further scrutiny, as a result of these redefinitions of labour. Innovative thinking began to be understood as relying on the ability to manipulate communities of practice which themselves can display the characteristic of talent. Body-as-organism, bounded and complete, is replaced by body as what Marx called 'social individual'. In other words, cognitive knowledge can be codified in new ways which, to an extent, rely on intangibles like networks of relationships which were previously thought to be epiphenomenal.

But the issue of talented labour does not end there. What is crucial to understand is that talent, howsoever manifested, has to be identified and husbanded by installing a functional kernel of processes which can produce 'the right people'. Thus, a whole series of actors have taken hold of the issue of 'talent' and attempted to systematize it, most notably the burgeoning human resources industry and management consultants of various kinds. In the process, the whys and wherefores of talent have widened: talent becomes equated with seeking out and nurturing 'pivotal people', it becomes a moment in the reorganization of the firm (so that, for example, the latent mind power that already exists in a workforce can be revealed and mobilized; see Bryan and Joyce [2007]), and it becomes a moment in strategic investment in 'talent pivot points' (Boudreau and Ramstad 2007). The result has been that 'talent' has become a vast technological infrastructure:[6] batteries of audits and tests;[7] the evolution of 'experts' and expertise, a development that is producing a new layer of consultants and managers who specialize in 'talent management'; and the evolution of 'talent marketplaces' in which talented workers can be exchanged. But the issue of talent does not end with its identification and systematization, for the process of identifying talent is about producing people who will 'produce disproportionate value from the resources their organizations make available to them' (Goffee and Jones 2007: 72). In other words, they will valorize their talent by becoming *more* creative. In turn, that requires the parallel production of situations in which this creativity can not only flourish but be boosted. That requires three things. First, it requires talent management strategies that will identify the talented and keep them happy, since their value means that they can easily steal away to other positions, if they are so minded (Goffee and Jones 2007). Second, as I have exemplified in some detail elsewhere (Thrift 2005, 2006), it requires the design of spaces which will produce the kind of intensity which will allow creativity to expand, whether that be at the scale of a room or a regional cluster. Third, it means adopting a flat model of organization which can allow the rapid construction and prototyping of ideas. There is a whole vocabulary of management that attests to this new set of facts – project working, collaborative innovation networks, and so on – all attesting to the need to produce high value cultures in which flows of talent can be visualized, controlled, and boosted. Indeed, so much has been written on these kinds of arrangement that I do not mean to go into them in any depth (cf. PricewaterhouseCoopers 2006 for a review). Rather, at least for now, I want to register the presence of these efforts, for they also signify the functioning of the extended enterprise.

Another take on labour

There is another deeper level at which labour is being redefined when the word 'talent' is mobilized. For, in a sense, the advent of a resource called talent represents a different understanding of labour from what has gone before. Certainly, it moves on from the idea that under capitalism labour is simply a source of labour power to a more general idea of labour as a distillate of all the powers of humanity: a new romance of labour, in other words, but taking a good part of that romance from the notion of romance espoused by the romantic poets – or indeed the younger Marx for whom labour was sensuous human activity – as a kaleidoscope of different powers. It would be possible to frame the history of how labour became reframed as a sensuous distillate in many different fields – in Marxian terms, as a part of the many debates about what constitutes labour in capitalist economies, spanning the debates on the labour process and to current debates on the multitude as a class analysis. In more general economic terms as part of a slow but sure move away from rational economic man, as indexed by developments such as the interest in behavioural economics, psychological testing, information economics, and so on. In business terms, as a part of the long march from a notion of the worker as simply something to be trained up to humanistic notions of the worker that began to become common in the 1950s and 1960s, which argued that work could be a fulfilling experience, to the worker of today, an element in a collaborative innovation network, no longer subject to central control but rather a creator, collaborator and communicator, fully committed and intrinsically motivated by the trust and ethical correlates established within a common, if distributed, culture (Thrift 2005). In more general social terms, these tendencies can also be seen as arising from the feminization of the workforce and the subsequent revaluation of what were once regarded as 'feminine' affective skills.

But there is more to talent than this. For talent also signifies a shift in the temporality of labour towards what might be called the 'to-come' (Negri 2005) which capitalism is intent on capturing and channelling as a modulation of futurity (Clough *et al.* 2007). The to-come can be understood as a general mobilization of process and neo-vitalist philosophies in practical form. The world is conceived – and practised – as always in motion and always productive. Each instant can be opened in a creative manner, indeed forms a creative opening, towards novelty (of form), driven, as in Deleuze, by the intensity of the virtual that is understood as a multiplicity of differences, or, as in Whitehead, by a set of interrelated becomings in which the process of becoming is more fundamental than the being that is achieved. Translated into the concreteness necessary to relate these philosophies to the lived social practice in which the economic takes place means thinking about an appetite for being which arises out of sociation and a corresponding thirst for the knowledge that comes out of the process of sociation, knowledge which cannot be known a priori.[8] The multiplicity of social practice is not based on individuals. Rather, human being is understood as a pre-personal relational essence of social life which is beyond subjective identity. The intention is to supplement Marx's economistic notion of morphogenesis (in the sense of successive modes of production) with a notion of morphogenesis which emphasizes continuous creativity and emergence and which is relatively emancipated from form. Or to put it another Whiteheadian way, there is no longer a procession of forms, only forms of process.

Labour plays a key part in the generation of intensity as a disruptive intensification that associates what has been considered unlike and thereby produces new combinations which are not attached to the past: in other words, talent is a solution to a problem which is often only imperfectly understood. It cannot be inferred from previous moves. It is about producing knowledge which cannot be known in advance, knowledge that arises from within the shared context of the situation. It might be thought of as calling on aspects of labour – all the powers of humanity – which were difficult to access when labour was understood as part of a dialectic between capital and labour, rather than as an immanent creative force which is being blocked by capital, a force of roiling innovation which can be channelled but cannot be undone.

But what are all the powers of humanity? Negri, Virno and other operaismo Marxists often have it that the distinguishing power of humanity is language and communication, although they often mean by this something closer to the kind of creative intersubjective accounting that would be found in ethnomethodology. But this is too narrow a compass. It tends to omit many of the other powers of embodiment. For example, it tends to omit much sense of the pre-personal relational essence of social life that is becoming a resource on which the economy increasingly draws, the affective flow, which Tarde was attempting to characterize in his economy of passions. But, more importantly, it could be accused of a certain residual humanism that it has been the job of many recent thinkers to attempt to erase in favour of a notion of the human as including all manner of things, held together in actor-networks of concernful being. In other words, labour can no longer be thought of as existing apart from all manner of material extensions, extensions that do not just provide physical extension but new means of thinking. Indeed, it could be argued that the emphasis now being put on mass intellectuality makes no sense without the vital more-than-intermediaries like the book and the web. As importantly, such a limited conception of labour also allows the stuff of humanity to be split apart from the goods that surround it in ways which go against all the theoretical developments and empirical studies of consumption of the past 20 years or so and are certainly at odds with the ethos of the contemporary arts of worlding that I will describe below.

Lazzarato is at his most instructive here in that he does not fall into these ways of thinking, the result of exposure to an odd but productive mixture of Foucault, Deleuze and Tarde. Lazzarato distinguishes between the planes of what he calls subjection and (rather too dramatically) machinic enslavement. For Lazzarato, like Virno, the subject is constituted through language and communication. The subject is an effect of the semiotics of the machine of communication. 'Believing itself to be a subject of enunciation, feeling itself to be the absolute, individual cause and origin of statements, whereas in reality it is the result of a machinery, no more than the end point in the process. Your words are folded over statements and modes of expression which are imposed on you and expected of you' (Lazzarato 2006: 2). So far, Lazzarato's account of the genesis of self-contained entities does not vary much from the Althusserian-derived account, which has become so common in cultural studies and other areas of the humanities and social sciences. Where Lazzarato becomes interesting is in his pulling into the account of the 'pre-individual, pre-cognitive and pre-verbal components of subjectivity' (Lazzarato 2006: 3), which access affects, percepts and sensations. In common with authors such as Agamben (and his account of bare life), Deleuze (and his account of a molecular economy of desire) and Thrift (2005, 2006) on non-representational economies, in considering this plane of existence, Lazzarato wants to make no distinction between the human and non-human, the subject and the object, and the sentient and the intelligible. Rather, individuals and all manner of machines become open multiplicities. They are sets of elements, affects, organs, flux and functions, all of which operate on the same level.[9]

> Thus, … 'subjectivity' finds itself simultaneously on the side of the subject and on the side of the object. Capitalism derives its great power from these two devices, which operate as two sides of the same coin. But it is machinic enslavement which endows capitalism with a sort of omnipotence, since it permeates the roles, functions and meanings by which individuals both recognise each other and are alienated from each other. It is through machinic enslavement that capital succeeds in activating the perceptual functions, the affects, the unconscious behaviours, the pre-verbal, pre-individual dynamic and its intensive, atemporal, aspatial, asignificant components. It is through these mechanisms that capital assumes control of the charge of desire carried by humanity. This aspect of the reality of capitalist 'production' remains invisible for the most part.
>
> (Lazzarato 2006: 4)

To summarise the argument so far, a new talented subject is being born. The armoury of the talented subject contains an array of particular and historically unusual (at least in the sense that they are for the first time being system-atized) skills and competences, and the talented worker will manifest these skills and competences or will not be worthy of that honorific. Thus, apart from high-level cognitive skills and competences, talent will manifest skills and competences which include increasingly quantified qualities like intuition, emotional intelligence, interpersonal skills, cultural empathy – the full armoury of the contemporary economy, in other words, that it is necessary to gird in order to be continuously innovative. To put it another way, talented subjects are required to have a stake in the plane of enslavement. They are able to tap into the prepersonal and mould it into something that they (and the corporation) own. In this, they are aided by all manner of technologies of visualization and training.

But we need to be careful about how we frame this subject. For, what is clear from recent work is that it does not consist just of the qualities of an embodied subject marked out by the boundary of the skin. Rather, the subject is a part of a material matrix that makes it more fitting to talk about an entity (or better, perhaps, infolding) which is a compound or zoon (Jones 2006), continuously linked to other talented workers by all kinds of technical prostheses which have become more than prostheses. It is too soon to talk about collective intelligence but if such a phrase is to be used in the modern world then it seems to me to apply to two main clumpings of socio-technical capacity – the talented worker and, as we shall see, the networked consumer.

Talent as re-organization

The second and related tendency that I want to examine is the re-organization of firms so that they are able to draw on all the powers of talented humanity, a process of so-called 'talent alignment'. That process requires a substantial upheaval in capitalist organization towards a model of an extended enterprise in which talent can be used optimally and which also gives talent the most advantageous terrain in which to work. As a result, haltingly, the enterprise is becoming something akin to a vital process, a condition created by inducing a state of permanent restructuring in which talent can thrive. This condition has become possible because of an industry made up of a cabal of actors including professional service firms, private equity, and the like, whose raison d'être is precisely permanent restructuring.

The permanent restructuring industry has three interlocking aspects. First, it has become an industrial sector in its own right. For example, the global revenue from professional service firms leapt from US$390 billion in 1990 to US$911 billion in 2000. Following a period of faltering growth after the dotcom bubble burst, the growth of this sector has now resumed. Second, the industry has been able to form and format an economy in which value arises out of permanent restructuring. As Folkman *et al.* (2007) point out, the greater intermediation provided by these kinds of firms has many and often contradictory goals but the net effect is clear: churn accompanied by the enrichment of the seniors of these firms, often to a point far above that enjoyed by the leaders of the firms who are the object of their attentions. As a result, just one form of investment (corporate mergers and acquisitions) has been responsible for 65–75 per cent of fixed investment in liberalized economies such as those of the US and the UK. Third, a massive discursive apparatus has grown up around animating the economy, based on the cultural circuit of capital (Thrift 2006), whose descriptions of the economy are increasingly correlated with what the economy becomes. The cultural circuit is dependent, in this case, on not just the mass media and its associated production of pithy phrases (for example, in the case of talent, 'It takes the best to make the best') and mellifluous (and generally meaningless) maxims which still have a certain force but also on a host of specialized outputs, in the form of myriad texts, numerous new methods and forms of measurement (such as various forms of questionnaire intended to measure qualities like emotional intelligence), and the collective discussions of professional service firms, business schools, human resource departments and an all-enveloping media apparatus. What has happened to this cultural circuit is that it has rapidly become not simply a discursive apparatus but, in concert with developments in finance (such as the rise of private equity firms), central to the economy of permanent restructuring. A particular set of discourses about management retailed by management consultants, advertising firms, and the like has become self-fulfilling as what were originally advisers have gradually taken on roles that move beyond inventing new management concepts, and giving advice on how to institute them, to becoming central players in restructuring whose words rapidly become dictates.[10] In other words, an economy that was regarded as derivative or even parasitic has become primary as these firms have increasingly produced means whereby they can call the shots, such as business process and other forms of value reengineering, the reworking of supply chains, various forms of subcontracting, means of drawing subcontractors not just into the supply of parts but also of ideas, and so on. In a sense, the business of production increasingly takes place through the remote control provided by what were formerly intermediaries. The movement of people from these firms into management and back again, coupled with the use of favoured specialist restructuring managers, often there to put a firm into shape to be sold on, means that what were formerly fairly rigid boundaries between management and consultant have become increasingly permeable.

In turn, a good part of recent management discourse has become based on the elite work experience suggested by the word talent, drawing on the experiences of managers and professionals for whom it is possible to declare an end to management and control in favour of a world of unfettered creativity. For the organizational communitarian, things are clear:

> What this means for those of you who have job titles such as 'director' or 'manager' or 'supervisor' is quite plain. You have to get used to being out of control. If you're a director, you don't direct anything (and in the modern world, you'd better learn to co-create with those outside, both clients and their customers and even your competitors …). If you're a manager, you don't manage anything either. You have to accept that your powers are strictly

limited and less important than the swirling seas of colleague-networks and customer interactions. If you're a supervisor, you should put away your stop watch and clipboard. And if you sit in the higher echelons of business (you have VP or SVP prefix on your business card, maybe) you'd better get used to the fact that you don't control anything outside the company.

No, the best we can hope to do is to cast a pebble on the water. Choose the pebble wisely. Choose how to throw it but once the stone leaves your hand we have to let go. Watch its flight, by all means, but then sit back and watch the ripples that it creates roll across the water.

(Earls 2007: 313)

Talent as the work of others

In direct contrast to this elite discourse of talent ascendant, the third tendency, a most important one given the fallout it produces in so many people's lives, is based on the fact that producing situations in which talent can be expressed requires a large amount of infrastructure which protects those who have been identified as talented from 'organizational rain'. All the distractions that the talented might suffer have to be worked on by others who get wet. In other words, the 'community' – in the much vaunted management idea of community of practice – has real limits. We therefore arrive at another aspect of modern day business, that part of it represented by practices like business process engineering, shared services, and other practices of administrative disintegration and reintegration, all of them aided by the advent of enterprise resource planning software which both formalizes and extends these practices in interesting ways (Head 2003). Thus, the rise of talent has also been paralleled by a rise in brutal, speeded-up administrative routine carried out in panoptic spaces of a very traditional kind. These routines attempt to winnow out any notion of individual initiative by using software as both script and prompt. Further, this routinized aspect of the landscape of work is probably moving up the hierarchy of skill as a result of the deskilling that this software makes possible of what were once thought of as sophisticated jobs carried out by talented people, most notably doctors and similar experts, by constructing simulations of judgement. Thus, in one management consultant's words 'we strive to create offices that function at unprecedented levels of ambulatory performance' (cited in Head 2003: 126). In other words, paralleling a fluid space of creativity, in which space itself is a part of the experiment, is a purposely deadened, robotic space in which everything turns up as expected, including intersubjective interaction. It is vital to remember the vast penumbra of jobs that explicitly or implicitly support the talented and which seem to run counter to so much of the prevailing management rhetoric of creativity. Thus we arrive at the chief paradox of modern capitalism: creativity is everywhere but only if large numbers of workers can be discounted as automatons with nothing to contribute but scripted responses which are a twisted simulation of intersubjectivity – and which often only work because those workers add back in their own intersubjective skills. At best, these workers are allowed to manifest degraded versions of tacit skills, masquerading as humanizing practices. At worst, not even that.

Talent as class

Finally, and relatedly, there is an obvious class dimension to all this, concerned with what kind of success is now sanctioned by social networks as a result of these changes. Paths to power have changed. Thus success is increasingly associated with new conduits of class mobility and, most especially, a move from personal networks associated with social affiliations like ethnicity and religion, which promoted narrow niches of opportunity, to screening that takes place through credentialized networks which are highly dependent upon higher education and the ways of thinking it promotes (Mayo *et al.* 2006). In turn, it is also associated with very large increases in pay for talent that capitalise on this education and the networks that it supports, with obvious consequences for income and social polarization. It is therefore, in certain senses at least, accurate to talk about a class of 'cultural creatives' (Ray and Anderson 2000), a class which wields the powers of innovation and creativity (both its own and those of the disenfranchized by proxy) as simultaneously economic and cultural capital in pursuit of its own enrichment. But this class is not as benign as it is often painted. In particular, it can be counted as a new form of meritocracy, with all of the negative as well as positive resonances that word enjoys.

More generally, the above four different but related tendencies can be understood as moments in the construction of a new form of what might be called companion capitalism, one that is much closer to lived social practice. But that requires radical changes to the organization of firms so that they can dip into the flow of social process, vital forms of organization which are plastic, fast-moving and continuous and which, ideally, can achieve a kind of perfect pitch in which they are able to resonate with the world around them and turn it to their advantage. In turn, these changes require the construction of new forms of organizational spatiality and temporality that allow enterprises to nestle alongside consumers as they go about practising everyday life. That these changes have occurred can be counted as an achievement of the numerous intermediaries from the cultural circuit of capital that have become involved in organizational change, and the consequent growth of extended enterprises that sustain innovation via networked organizational forms, collaborative innovation networks and the ability to visualize the *flow* of knowledge and passions (Gloor 2006). These intermediaries have produced a new current of management thinking which emphasizes swarm creativity, network intelligence, herd intelligence, crowds and tribes, collaborative intelligence, and other such phrases: what is being retailed is an attempt to understand economies as imitative affective flows a la Tarde, and to intervene much more systematically in these flows. The mission statements of firms increasingly reflect this manner of thinking. For example, Yahoo's mission is 'To connect people to their passions ...' and 'To create unique experiences ...' (see also Ouellet, Chapter 8, this volume).

Animating consumption

To understand the full import of these kinds of shifts means turning to the sphere of consumption. For one of the purposes of the kinds of corporate reorganization that is now taking place is to bring enterprises closer to consumers, so as to be able to tap into the talent of consumers as well as formal employees. Enterprises will act not so much as traps for consumer passions as continuous companions, able to intervene in opportune ways, to identify and bring on consumer talents. That requires both new means of linking to consumers and new understandings of what the commodity is and what it stands for.

Distributing talent

It would be quite possible to argue at this point in the chapter that the world of talent was something of an illusion, restricted to the few and highly dependent upon the ministrations of a legion of people who never get any opportunity to display talent and indeed are actively dissuaded from doing so. But what is interesting about the current juncture is that the talent of both the skilled and the deskilled can be called up by corporations outside the workplace by other means, chiefly by linking into their activities as consumers and co-creating with them – innovation and marketing becomes 'everybody's job' (McCracken 2006). Co-creation and open innovation are currently, like talent, key managerial buzzwords, signifying the way that firms increasingly draw on innovation that is not generated within the firm and lies outside the boundaries of the firm as conceived before the extended enterprise became an aspiration, but they nevertheless have real import as a way of pointing to how useful knowledge is increasingly understood to be widely distributed so that even the margins can create innovation.[11] As McCracken (2006: 10) puts it, 'the right to be a producer of innovation is assumed by more parties. Younger generations believe it is their right to rework existing inventions and create new ones. In sum, the right, the willingness, the means, and the opportunity to produce invention has expanded in the last few decades'.

One of the reasons for the current reorganization of capitalism is the need to tune into the *vital conversation* of consumers so as to pick up on the latest enthusiasms, some of which may lead to innovations, but also so as to enter into interactive relationships which make it possible to tap into consumers' innovative powers through co-creation, in a time when the barriers to entering at least some markets have fallen. This vital conversation has been given a massive boost by the emerging culture of conversation on the web, not least because that culture gives people new means of making their culture writable, allowing them to mix and match in many new ways. In particular, a new stream of reactions to goods has been made possible by the Internet which arises from consumers' many involvements with them and which provides a medium that allows the vital conversation to go on continuously and allows it to coalesce, usually only in a transient fashion, in the form of consumer communities. Further, increasingly the conversation can go on one-to-one with individuals. In turn, the range of what can be represented as formal data by corporations has been extended, as has their capability to track and trace and trace and analyse that data (Thrift 2007).

This vital conversation can be seen as the latest manifestation of a process of subjectification which has been going on since the 1970s. That is the hastening of a process of 'mass' individualization which supports a new form of psychological individuality and self-determination (Zuboff and Maxmin 2002). The desire to be understood and treated as an individual is now more or less constantly expressed, in particular through the medium of a re-invented consumption that can satisfy three values: sanctuary from the pressures of the working world, various forms of giving voice to self-expression, and social connection. 'In the standard enterprise logic of managerial capitalism, people must adapt to the terms and conditions of consumption set by producers. But the real essence of the individuation of consumption is an inversion of that logic. It requires the agents of commerce to operate in individual space. There they form a relationship with the individual ...' (Zuboff and Maxmin 2002: 171–2). That is the real import of current managerial buzzwords like long tail, co-creation, wikinomics and the like (Thrift 2006). It requires that enterprises know much more about their customers and strive to enter into an individualized relationship with them: it requires, in other words, nearly continuous survey and interrogation which, in part, is possible because customers now expect to be surveyed in polls and samples and focus groups. For example, 'Americans today are accustomed to a seemingly endless stream of questions from survey researchers, political pollsters, marketers, and census takers' (Igo 2007: 3). Indeed, as subjects, people have in part come to understand themselves precisely as a result of survey. Survey is a good part of what they know and how they know as well as how they are known, underwriting categories as different as 'the average citizen' and the sexual self and providing a good part of the information that people have on the other: 'not sure of the information we come by – where it comes from, how to verify or challenge it – we nonetheless do live by it' (Igo 2007: 298). Survey, in other words, is now a key part of the consciousness industry, creating new tribes and lifestyles rather than simply passively attending to their creation. But these surveys are now becoming more active, since the Internet increasingly allows individuals to be followed. The goal is to create and direct attention, and increasingly this means putting a whole battery of techniques together that record and ponder desire. For example, Yahoo has created so-called tag maps whose goal is to produce a means of gathering individual photographic records of attention and the more general formation of subjectivity, using the slogan 'you are where you are'.[12] The more general aim of developments like these is to create so-called 'extimacy', a new condition of pleasure arising from a constructed public intimacy.

The net result is clear in any case: economies 'flock and flow'; they become akin to weather systems (McCracken 2006). Tarde's economy of passions is operationalized as the passions of individual consumers are aggregated in all manner of temporary constellations of want to which corporations can play and which they can sometimes influence. Consumer economies come to resemble swarms or crowds in which value comes from a process of relentless reshuffling, rather than established principles. Demand comes from multiplicity, from oscillation and difference, and the potential for invention that arises from them. In principle, it therefore becomes possible to trigger new economic wants through the modulation of swarms and crowds, but in practice a much more haphazard process occurs in which corporations are as often chasing desire as creating it which is why it is so crucial that they re-organize so as to remain constantly immersed in the flow of social process. To an extent, the 'flock and flow' model has always existed in capitalism but what has changed is the ability to aggregate desires in so many different ways, reaching out to so many different forms of community, some formal, some informal, some permanent, some fleeting.

Boosting the allure of commodities

The continuing development of the tendency to mass individualization, and its amplification of all kinds of currents of desire, goes hand in hand with a shift in what the enterprise is selling to consumers, which is no longer consumer goods *sensu strictu* but rather, born out of a long history of involvement with manipulating experience, what I will call *worlds*. Helped in particular by the good offices of information technology, modern business has moved on from a focus on producing objects to a focus on producing worlds which must also inevitably be spaces. 'Worlds' are not necessarily totally constructed stages through which each moment plays. More usually, they are temporary constellations, brief real-isations which contain enough relevant signs to direct affect in particular ways. At a minimum, the aim of the corporation is to chime with consumer desires; at times, the corporation will be able to direct or even create that desire. In other words, the business enterprise no longer aims to create its object but the world within which the object exists. As a corollary, the business enterprise does not aim to create subjects (as happened in the older disciplinary regimens) but the world within which the subject exists. Thus, as Lazzarato puts it:

> The company produces a world. In its logic, the service or the product, just as the consumer or the worker, must correspond to this world; and this world in its turn has to be inscribed in the souls and bodies of consumers and workers. This inscription takes place through techniques that are no longer exclusively disciplinary. Within contemporary capitalism the company does not exist outside the producers or consumers who express it. Its world, its objectivity, its reality, merges with the relationships enterprises, workers and consumers have with each other. Thus the company, like God in the philosophy of Leibniz, seeks to construct a correspondence, an interlacing, a chiasm between the monad (consumer and worker) and the world (the company). The expression and effectuation of the world and the subjectivities included in there, that is, the creation and realization of the sensible (desires, beliefs, intelligence) precedes economic production. The economic war currently played out on a planetary scale is indeed an 'aesthetic war' ...
>
> (2004: 188)

Constructing these worlds has become possible because of a series of four linked developments. One has been the importation of performance knowledges from the performing arts into capitalism, a development that first took place via the media (as in work on advertisements and especially brands, whose aim is to provoke a semiconscious reaction) and then through the growth of the so-called experience economy in the 1990s, a developing set of practices concerned with how to apply performance in business that began its course in obvious arenas like tourism and retailing but has now become general, not least because digital and mobile technologies make it possible to combine media and actual situations in hitherto impossible ways. What was important about this importation was the way that it demonstrated business's increasing ability to prime environments, in particular by concentrating on the full range of senses in order to produce all manner of affective effects. A second development has been the growth of information technology which provided a means of producing interactivity and feedback in a detailed way. Information is no longer an object; it is a continuing process which allows mass customization to occur. A third development, which is important enough to separate out from the previous development, has been the growth of locative technologies. These technologies have made it possible to build what might be called *inhabitable maps* in which space itself becomes a means of conveying information and communication, rather than simply a material template through which information and communication must be conveyed. Space becomes a mass of quantitative and qualitative *signs*, what I have called elsewhere 'movement-space' (Thrift 2005). Thus, space no longer needs to be overcome. Rather it needs to be designed, prototyped, and rolled out, rather like a semiotic carpet. Increasingly, therefore, space is not enclosed in the same way. It is no longer an ensemble of enclosed communities. Rather it is becoming a spatialized matrix. It is making the move from a means of providing enclosure and material consistency, to the spatialization of different moments in a matrix. It has become a spatialization of time. Fourth, and in turn, design has become central, understood as a means of squeezing maximum affective response from objects and environments by producing *knowledges of arrangement and disposition*. These knowledges were first integral to the practices of theatre, landscape gardening, and the like. Now, powered up by performance and locative technologies, they allow new kinds of cultivation to take place based on the invention of new conjunctive relations, new forms of near.

What becomes clear is that, as a result of these four developments, space and time are themselves becoming not so much wrappings around the objects of consumption as integral elements in the generation of an individualized mass consumption that revolves around more than the simple commodity: the object is but a part of a larger ensemble, a world that is perhaps best understood as a semiotically enhanced space which allows individualized relationships to thrive. This is a world perfused with signs sent and read because each environmental niche is always also a semiotic niche. Space and time are no longer something external but a key moment in the design of these myriad semiotically enhanced worlds and this requires a recursive envelope that can transmit sensation as much as information. Thus place can now be understood as both deeper than what came before in that it is loaded up with all manner of signs, and shallower in that it depends on the central control (or, at least modulation) of the sensation and information they impart. But what is clear is that these places are meant to be more responsive – thinking spaces of a kind. They are semiotic machines; crucial elements of a new world-modelling system that can invite, capture, guide and monetise attention.

In turn, attention can be captured and guided by a whole set of affective devices that are now able to be introduced into these worlds in ways that would have been difficult before – new kinds of cultural nerve, if you like, which build extra facets of 'you' (Terada 2001). The invention of melodrama in the nineteenth century (Thrift 2007), the re-invention of the decisive moment as a result of photography and cinema in the early twentieth century (Thrift 2008a), the allure of the extreme in the early twentieth century (Hampton 2007), all come to mind as examples of ways in which a *narrative intelligence* has gradually been developed which allows the passions to be deployed to economic advantage, by allowing consumer situations to be ' "moved" in the dual sense of emotionally engaged *and* repositioned with respect to the world' (Thrailkill 2006: 366). The restlessness of attention becomes an asset that can be valorized through this emotive realism.

In practice, under capitalism the production of space means the deployment of a narrative intelligence that can use affective devices such as those discussed above to make everyday life into a cavalcade of semiotically charged and rapidly changing moments that can be used for profit. The rise of this narrative intelligence has become possible because of the accompanying rise of non-discursive systems of communication which allow spaces to become continuously (inter)active (see Thrift 2009). The result of the genesis of this new kind of modular 'writing' is that space is able to be more and more carefully designed – to elicit particular affective responses, to unleash speculation and creativity, to amplify what counts as the object of desire.

It is important to remember here my initial comments about worlding: what is actually being produced, consumed and distributed is multiple ontologies, and this process of 'facting' brings aesthetics to the fore since what is being produced can best be understood via Baumgarten's (1986[1750]) original formulation of the field of aesthetics as 'the science of how things are known via the senses' and clearly involves the construction of sensori-emotional values which *make things feel real*, the production of a sensuous certainty.[13] In other words the goal is to mass produce real fictions which stimulate affective responses.[14] What is important to note here is that these ontologies have constituent power (Negri 2005); they have force – force which is designed, at least in part.

Another way of understanding these developments is as the project of phenomenology becoming incorporated into capitalism, in that capitalism now strives to attain 'the simple nearness of an unobtrusive prevailing' (Malpas 2006: 306). What we are faced with is an industrialized phenomenology produced out of the ability to manage the whole sensory range of the encounter in order to attain a kind of mass primordiality. Take the case of Heidegger. In certain ways, Heidegger's rethinking of thinking, and of modernity might be understood as a primer for modern capitalism, as in his writings on the attentiveness of what might be thought of as the tacit skills of comportment, on the unitary, holistic environment, on things as gatherings, and on place understood as that within which we find ourselves given over to the world and as an unfolding, as a continuous happening (Malpas 2006). Ironically, the Heideggerian corpus can be seen as a creator of the world we now inhabit, rather than simply making a claim on the nature of reality. However, this is a calculated and calculative form of the poetics of dwelling, a closeness that has been achieved through the intervention of information technology, not huts. In other words, this is a presentness, which carefully refuses aesthetic or instrumental determination, and instead just is. It is this 'isness' that is now seen as susceptible to mass reproduction, a kind of homecoming to the world but one born out of a systematized public intimacy, so-called 'extimacy'.

There is an almost routine way of reading this condition, typified by Peter Sloterdijk's recent work.[15] In Sloterdijk's reading of the modern world, a third wave of globalisation based on rapid communication is 'joining the nervous systems of inhabitants in a coherent space' (Sloterdijk 2004: 226). But, in doing so, it is producing a global provincialism of 'connected isolations', of microclimates in which 'communicative relations are replaced by the inter-autistic and mimetic relations, a world that is constructed "polyspherically and interidiotically"' (Funcke 2005: 5); that is, quite literally, taken in. A certain kind of being-togetherness is threatened by this inter-passivity. Thus,

> At the centre of the third volume [of *Spheres*] is an immunological theory of architecture, because I maintain that houses are built immune systems. I thus provide on the one hand an interpretation of modern habitat, and on the other a new view of the mass container. But when I highlight the apartment and the sports stadium as the most important architectural innovations of the modern, it isn't out of art- or cultural-historical interest. Instead my aim is to give a new account of the history of atmospheres, and in my view, the apartment and the sports stadium are important primarily as atmospheric installations. They play a central role in the development of abundance, which defines the open secret of the modern.
>
> (Funcke 2005: 5)

For Sloterdijk, in other words, the modern world has become a foam made up of a series of consumerist phenomenologies, bubble-like monads cut off from each other, which constantly, even manically, invent new responses, decisive moments that in truth decide little at all and make us immune to many forms of shared understanding and human flourishing.[16] We are not condemned to freedom but to frivolity (Van Tuinen 2006).

However, this account is too gloomy: in particular, it ignores the vast archive of empirical work on consumption, which shows some very different practices occurring from those that theorists in their eyries suppose must exist and, in general, exaggerates the current mediatized situation. But it does have grip in the sense that it shows the shape of the perfect innovation engine that business might like to achieve and is attempting to achieve by animating both production and consumption: a predictable world fuelled by the talents of talent.

Conclusion

In this chapter, I have tried to set out why there is a bright new sign in the capitalist zodiac – talent – and what it portends. In particular, I have argued that this sign suggests that capitalism is increasingly able to tap in to the pre-personal as a means of further valorizing both the worker and the consumer. The pre-personal functions as a resource that is able to be harvested. But for this to happen the pre-personal has to be stabilized as an economic form so that it can routinely be called into existence. That requires the production of non-discursive languages which can literally write the pre-personal into being so that it can be operated on. In turn, that means the production of semiotically rich environments which can act as lenses for affect and as lures (Thrift 2006). The inspiration for these environments – the proto-language of worlding – might be understood as phenomenology. But, in turn, the multiplication of the tenets of phenomenology in practical form produces millions of little bubbles of absorption which are, as Sloterdijk puts it, 'interidiotically' stable – the monad in its modern form – and which, because they are stable, can be marketed.

How might it be possible to understand the significance of these developments? In four ways, perhaps. First, and most simply, they might be seen as the addition of a further factor of production to the standard triptych of land, labour and capital – namely, invention, understood as the germination of new ideas. Capital is born in the associations made by an inventive mind and not as a copy of laborious activities. This is the association first made by Tarde and subsequently taken forward in reduced form by economists like Schumpeter. Second, they might be seen as a turn to trying to understand the stretching of the present and the ability to harness the energy of the future through the power of ideas, rather than simply through the secular collaboration of labour. This has not, of course, been so far from the interests of many economists – the Austrian economists come to mind, so too does the work of Shackle, and so on. Then, third, these developments might be seen as the manifestation of an economy of passions. Most often associated with the work of Gabriel Tarde but now resurrected by many authors, economies are seen as being concerned with the association of isolated and dispersed forces that suddenly gather momentum, turning into semiconscious flows of new ideas/passions/wants. Finally, it is possible to argue that what is being constructed, as a result of technological change, is a collective intelligence. Care needs to be taken with these kinds of statements for fear that they stray into simplistic hyperbole. Progress is slow and stuttering. But, what seems clear is that the knowledge base that can now be found is not only much more extensive and complex than before but continually modulates not just in response to cognitive imperatives but increasingly to precognitive ones too, as a result of a new form of socio-technical mix.

A more general way of summarising what these developments portend would be the reaching of an era of the real subsumption of labour in which capitalism is so dominant that there is no longer an outside, an option that the operaismo Marxists take. Capitalism has become parasitic on the total social process and sucks its lifeblood. Equally, there are linked accounts in which capitalism has become immanent – nothing is left outside of the vitalist flow.

I think these kinds of 'nothing but' accounts are too easy. There are four main problems. First, they give capital powers it struggles to maintain and overestimate the degree of consent that its agents manifest. As Ehrenreich (2006) has documented, the stress, overwork and general uncertainty of corporate managerial life is manifest for those who are not deemed to be talented, and no doubt some of those that are. Second, they make much too clear a distinction between market and non-market relations. But in most societies the economic has always been entangled with the social and cultural in ways which must make this distinction problematic, whether that be in the realm of money or intimacy (Zelizer 1995, 2005).

Third, they allow a Manichean account to be developed by the back door, in which capitalism blocks off the real talents of the multitude. This seems to me to overbalance the books. Finally, it also seems to me that such accounts misunderstand the mixed and messy nature of reality, in that all manner of things are able to thrive under the new form of capitalism, not all of which are necessarily detrimental. So, for example, returning to my second problem, the extension of marketized relations that I have described which is involved in the process of worlding is being accompanied by an equal spread of non-marketized relations. For the spread of new forms of community promoted by the web has produced a substantial sector of non-market and peer production that can be understood as 'a major new source of defining widely transmissible statements and conversations about the meaning of the culture we share, mak[ing] culture substantially more transparent and available for reflection, and therefore for revision' (Benkler 2006: 293). In effect, as Benkler (2006) goes on to point out, a 'high production value folk culture' is coming into being.

The issue then becomes to what extent this new resource can declare independence, producing its own worlds, and to what extent business can infiltrate and choreograph this new culture, producing worlds which are highly scripted. It is a complex problem on both sides. For those on the left it may seem obvious that what is needed are several non-market fortresses, but this would probably mean losing many resources. For those in business, it may well be that controlling this culture would ultimately lead to a loss of inspiration and the vacating of new sources of revenue that come from 'off-field'.

In any case, what seems to me equally remarkable about the present time are the numerous attempts to begin to forge a counter-politics of the awakening of both bodily intelligence and environmental semiosis, which rely on enlarging the bestiary of affects that count. That requires consideration of a series of different registers that can enliven and stimulate responses by introducing forms of creative hesitation that in turn can induce transformative behaviour: in other words, what is being developed is a politics of animatedness that can produce contrary motions that hint at other possible worlds. But that is the subject of another chapter (see Thrift 2009).

Notes

1   I would like to thank the three anonymous referees for the journal *Distinktion: Scandinavian Journal of Social Theory*, for their helpful comments. This chapter has also been presented to audiences from the Sociology Department at the University of Essex and Jawaharlal Nehru University, Delhi. The comments received have equally helped to hone the arguments in the chapter.
2   Following Tarde, semiconscious thinking differs from both conscious acts of cognition and automatic neural firing; it can therefore be directed but only through particular kinds of interventions, most notably those based around mimesis.
3   My critical stance is straightforward. I am convinced that there are better ways of living but, at the same time, I am not someone who believes that it is possible or desirable to act as a theoretical terrorist, as Sloterdijk puts it, using theory as a fixed standpoint from which to dispense righteous wrath, whether prophetic or apostolic. Rather theory must necessarily foster a multiplicity of attachments (Mialet 2003).
4   Interaction costs can be defined as 'the costs of parties with dependent economic interests working together within the same economic entity (that is the costs of organizing people working together within a firm)' (Bryan and Joyce 2007: 49).
5   Indeed, it may be that capitalism is also trying to draw in negative qualities too. Thus both Virno (2004) and Negri (2005) argue that the incorporation of so-called minor affects like envy or irritation are a vital part of how capitalism now functions.
6   Indeed, 'talent technology' software is rapidly becoming a category in its own right (cf. Media Planet 2008).
7   Throughout, as in previous papers, I will want to argue that the developments I am describing cannot be divorced from the development of a quantitative background. A war of analytics is part and parcel of these developments, in the assessment of labour, in the tracking of consumer appetites, in the making of decisions. Quantitative and qualitative are not opposed, they are part of a seamless 'qualculative' whole (Thrift 2005).
8   One might think of Tarde's monads unfolding their appetite for being along the dimension of sociation or Simmel's quanta of affective energy driven by intersubjective pulsion.
9   I should add that although this account strikes me as right in its essentials, it has some problems. In trying to describe a plane, Lazzarato, like others, tends to gloss over the way in which capitalism is coming to understand this plane, by making it visible, and by thereby making it the subject of spatial and temporal variation. Again, too dramatically perhaps, Lazzarato, like Virno and Negri, insists that the plane of machinic enslavement is immeasurable. But this is not the case. It might be more accurate to say that it has been immeasurable but that it is becoming more measurable over time. With the advent of a world encased in numbers in which everything counts and is counted, in which quantification has become qualculation (Thrift 2005), in which many insights are numerical, even by proxy, it is no surprise that the plane of the pre-personal is increasingly measured. No doubt many of the measurements are dubious but their very existence points to a project which is ongoing and which will allow affect and other such qualities to be technologized.
10   The case of management consultancy is particularly instructive. Consultants are now the world's pre-eminent business knowledge brokers (McKenna 2006), extending the

knowledge and abilities available to enterprises by constantly topping up a wasting asset. They have something approaching jurisdictional power over business knowledge.

11 The exact extent of co-creation and open innovation systems remains to be established. Most studies are of high-tech industries and it is unclear how far it spreads outside these (Chesbrough *et al.* 2006).

12 The computational model is based on diacritics.

13 However, this is an everyday aesthetics, which does not conform to the canons of art (Saito 2007).

14 It is always worth remembering that many of the same centres of the brain fire off whether a situation is real or imagined.

15 In his *Sphären* trilogy, Sloterdijk takes Heidegger on dwelling as a root point of reference but then spatializes his thinking by posing the question of being as the question of being-together: 'one is never alone only with oneself, but also with other people, with things and circumstances; thus beyond oneself and in an environment' (Sloterdijk 2004). 'Being-a-pair' or a couple precedes all encounters. In other words, Sphären is concerned with the dynamic of spaces of co-existence, spaces which are commonly overlooked, for the simple reason that 'human existence … is anchored in an insurmountable spatiality' (Sloterdijk 2004: 229).

16 This is a familiar plaint in accounts provided by left thinkers: think of Zizek's notion of 'shared, collective privacy', for example.

Bibliography

Accenture (2007) 'Outlook' *The Economist*, 24 March, Advertising Supplement.

Amin, Ash and N. J. Thrift (2004) *Blackwell Cultural Economy Reader*, Oxford: WileyBlackwell.

Bayart, F. (2001) 'The paradoxical invention of economic modernity', in A. Appadurai (ed.) *Globalization*, Durham, NC: Duke University Press, pp. 307–34.

Bayart, F. (2007) *Global Subjects*, Cambridge: Polity Press.

Benkler, Y. (2006) *The Wealth of Networks. How Social Production Transforms Markets and Freedom*, New Haven, CT: Yale University Press.

Baumgarten, A. G. (1986[1750]) *Aesthetica*, 1750. Hildesheim: G. Olms.

Boudreau, J. W. and P. M. Ramstad (2007) *Beyond HR. The New Science of Human Capital*, Boston, MA: Harvard Business School Press.

Bryan, L. L. and C. I. Joyce (2007) *Mobilizing Minds. Creating Wealth From Talent in the 21st-Century Organization*, New York: McGraw-Hill.

Callon, M., Y. Millo and F. Muniesa (eds) (2007) *Market Devices*, Oxford: Blackwell.

Chesbrough, H., W. Vanhaverbeke and J. West (eds) (2006) *Open Innovation. Researching a New Paradigm*, Oxford: Oxford University Press.

Clough, P.T., G. Goldberg, R. Schiff, A. Weeks and C. Willse (2007) 'Notes towards a theory of affect itself', *Ephemera*, 7(1): 61–77.

Earls, M. (2007) *Herd. How to Change Mass Behaviour By Harnessing Our True Nature*, Chichester: John Wiley.

Ehrenreich, B. (2006) *Bait and Switch. The Futile Pursuit of the Corporate Dream*, London: Granta.

Folkman, P., J. Froud, S. Johal and K. Williams (2007) 'Working for themselves? Capital market intermediaries and present day capitalism', *Business History*, 49(4): 552–72.

Funcke, R. (2005) 'Interview with Peter Sloterdijk', *Bookforum*, February/March, available at http://www.bookforum.com/archive/feb_05/funcke.html

Gloor, P. A. (2006) *Swarm Creativity. Competitive Advantage Through Collaborative Innovation Networks*, Oxford: Oxford University Press.

Goffee, R. G. and Jones (2007) 'Leading clever people', *Harvard Business Review*, March: 72–9.

Hampton, H. (2007) *Born in Flames. Termite Dreams, Dialectical Fairy Tales, and Pop Apocalypses*, Cambridge, MA: Harvard University Press.

Head, S. (2003) *The New Ruthless Economy. Work and Power in the Digital Age*, New York: Oxford University Press.

Igo, S. E. (2007) *The Averaged American. Surveys, Citizens, and the Making of a Mass Public*, Cambridge, MA: Harvard University Press.

Jones, C. A. (ed.) (2006) *Sensorium. Embodied Experience, Technology, and Contemporary Art*, Cambridge, MA: MIT Press.

Lazzarato, M. (2004) 'From capital-labour to capital-life', *Ephemera*, 4(3), 187–208.

—— (2006) 'The machine', available at http://transform.eipcp.net/transversal/1106/lazzarato/en

Mackenzie, D., F. Muniesa and L. Siu (eds) (2007) *Do Economists Make Markets? On the Performativity of Economics*, Princeton, NJ: Princeton University Press.

Malpas, J. (2006) *Heidegger's Topology. Being, Place, World*, Cambridge, MA: MIT Press.

Mayo, A. J., N. Nohria and L. G. Singleton (2006) *Paths to Power. How Insiders and Outsiders Shaped American Business Leadership*, Boston, MA: Harvard Business School Press.

McCracken, G. D. (2006) *Flock and Flow. Predicting and Managing Change in the Marketplace*, Bloomington, IN: Indiana University Press.

McKenna, C. D. (2006) *The World's Newest Profession. Management Consulting in the Twentieth Century*, New York: Cambridge University Press.

Media Planet (2008) 'Talent technology', *The Times*, 10 March, supplement.

Mialet, H. (2003) 'The righteous wrath of Pierre Bourdieu', *Social Studies of Science*, 33(4): 613–21.

Michaels, E., H. Handfield-Jones and B. Axelrod (2001) *The War for Talent*, Boston, MA: Harvard Business School Press.

Negri, A. (2005) *Time for Revolution*, London: Continuum.

Ngai, S. (2005) *Ugly Feelings*, Cambridge, MA: Harvard University Press.

PricewaterhouseCoopers (2006) *Successful Strategies for Technology Management*, Technology Executive Connections, Vol. 3, London: PwC.

Ray, P. H. and S. R. Anderson (2000) *The Cultural Creatives*, New York: Three Rivers Press.

Ready, D. A. and J. A. Conger (2007) 'Make your company a talent factory', *Harvard Business Review*, June: 69–77.

Robertson, K. (2006) *The Laborer's Two Bodies. Labor and the 'Work' of the Text in Medieval Britain, 1350–1500*, New York: Palgrave Macmillan.

Saito, Y. (2007) *Everyday Aesthetics*, Oxford: Oxford University Press.

Sloterdijk, P. (2004) *Sphären III Schäume*, Frankfurt: Suhrkamp Verlag.

Terada, R. (2001) *Feeling in Theory. Emotion After the Death of the Subject*, Cambridge, MA: Harvard University Press.

The Economist (2006) 'The search for talent', *The Economist*, 7 October: 14.

Thrailkill, J. F. (2006) 'Emotive realism', *JNT: Journal of Narrative Theory*, 36(3): 365–88.

Thrift, N. J. (2005) *Knowing Capitalism*, London: Sage.

Thrift, N. J. (2006) 'The reinvention of invention: new tendencies in capitalist commodification', *Economy and Society*, 35(2): 279–306.

Thrift, N. J. (2007) *Non-Representational Theory. Space, Politics, Affect*, London: Routledge.

Thrift, N. J. (2008) 'The material practices of glamour', *Journal of Cultural Economy*, 1(1): 9–23.

Thrift, N. J. (2009) 'Halos: making more room in the world for new political orders', in B. Braun and S. J. Whatmore (eds) *The Stuff of Politics*, Minneapolis, MN: University of Minnesota Press.

Van Tuinen, S. (2006) 'The obscene voice: terrorism, politics and the end of representation in the works of Baudrillard, Zizek and Sloterdijk', *Pli. The Warwick Journal of Philosophy*, 17: 38–60.

Virno, P. A. (2004) *Grammar of the Multitude*, New York: Seminotext(e).

Wooldridge, A. (2006) 'The battle for brainpower', *The Economist*, 7 October, available at http://www.economist.com/surveys/displaystory.cfm?story_id=7961894

Zelizer, V. (1995) *The Social Meaning of Money: Pin Money, Paychecks, Poor Relief and Other Currencies*, New York: Basic.

Zelizer, V. (2005) *The Purchase of Intimacy*, Princeton, NJ: Princeton University Press.

Zuboff, S. and J. Maxmin (2002) *The Support Economy: Why Corporations are Failing Individuals and the Next Episode of Capitalism*, New York: Penguin.

Part 5
Conclusions/provocations

Conclusion
Cultural, political, economy

R. B. J. Walker

Who could now doubt that all three of the terms that are of most pressing concern in this collection of essays are indispensable for any useful analysis of what we have become and what we now do as human beings constituted by and enmeshed in diverse forms of collective existence? Perhaps reductionist appeals to a biology, psychology or instrumental rationality retain an appeal in some places. Perhaps a few intrepid scholars have been convinced that some teleological logic of universalization lurks somewhere behind the particularizing categories deployed by the modern scholarly disciplines. Perhaps the disciplinary structures of the contemporary academy are quite perfectly aligned with the phenomena they seek to engage. Perhaps it is still too soon to tell, and in any case events move very rapidly. For the most part, however, and as the essays in this book demonstrate in an impressive array of contexts, it is really very difficult to think of anything that is simply economic, or political or cultural, at least in the way these concepts have been shaped by and continue to express our most basic assumptions about what it means to claim knowledge about the collective existence of contemporary human beings. This book thus affirms what should be a fairly uncontentious common sense. It is a common sense that must seem especially uncontentious insofar as the apparent complexity of emerging forms of collective existence makes any appeal to concepts predicated on the possibility of distinguishing the cultural, the political and the economic as autonomous spheres of human activity seem touchingly archaic; as indeed they are.

At the same time, few would also doubt that prevailing forms of scholarly practice remain indebted to intellectual traditions and institutional forms that can scarcely work without treating these three concepts as expressions of distinct and even autonomous realms. Academic disciplines such as economics, political science and cultural studies have forged distinctive identities and professionalized status, and such identities and such status are often more persuasive indicators of the way knowledge is produced and legitimized than the stories we are usually told about the appropriate conditions and procedures of a properly cumulative scholarship. Academic disciplines are often prone to universalize their specific ambitions and to marginalize the relevance of other disciplines, and other ambitions. In any case, most of us have a fairly strong sense of knowing what we mean when we refer to something as cultural, political or economic, even if we might struggle to say exactly what this something is or suspect that whatever these terms refer to is neither some thing nor subject to identical interpretations in different intellectual traditions and scholarly communities. It is in this sense that the overt concern of this book to develop a cultural political economy expresses a difficult struggle to engage with what might otherwise seem entirely unremarkable. For although it may be the case that it would be unwise to object to claims that scholarly credibility in many contexts demand attention to practices that are at once cultural, political and economic, it is not so obvious that these three concepts can be brought together without engaging with the conditions under which they have been used both to refer to identifiable but distinct phenomena and to sustain – cultivate and authorize – carefully differentiated forms of scholarly knowledge about these apparently distinct phenomena.

In seeking to open out what might be at stake in this doubled form of common sense, I would like to pick up on three themes that have been developed earlier in this book about three concepts. First, much of the force of the preceding chapters derives from a desire to engage with practices that are understood simultaneously as cultural, political and economic without lapsing into theoretical and methodological routines that privilege any of these terms as somehow prior, ultimate or foundational. Nevertheless, second, the sequence in which these terms are typically deployed works to remind us of the many ways in which some sort of economy has been treated as determinate while a political or a cultural have been relegated to mere effects or some other ephemeral or even adjectival status. Third, and as Jacqueline Best and Matthew Paterson rightly note in their Introduction, the distinctions between these concepts and the possibility of both affirming and destabilizing them are themselves part of the practices of cultural political economy that are in need of more extensive analysis.

It is the third point that I would especially like to affirm here and to explore a little further by pushing at what I take to be a productive tension between the appeal to simultaneity and the legacy of a specific sequence. These three concepts have been produced historically, in ways that invite analyses of the cultural, political and economic conditions under which this production has been enabled, shaped, reproduced and transformed. As concepts with a history, indeed with multiple and still actively contested histories, the commonsensical call for all three terms runs up against the conditions under which they have already been distinguished, authorized, appropriated, subordinated, reified, destabilized and restabilized as categories of authoritative scholarly analysis. In these brief remarks, therefore, I would like to raise a few questions about what might be at stake in bringing these three concepts together, without in any way pretending to provide anything like the genealogical account of how these three terms have been used to identify distinct phenomena that would be necessary to engage with contemporary skepticisms about the distinctions they express.

Cutting what ought to be a long story very short, my basic argument will be that it is futile to expect the imminent arrival of a cultural political economy in any cohesive or integrated sense, for two basic reasons. One is that each of these terms already imply versions of the others. Indeed, each term already includes the others in some way, so that any attempt to pursue a strategy of inclusion will be thwarted by the various ways in which specific forms of inclusion and exclusion have already been achieved through the production of each concept and the relations between them. The other, conversely, is that these terms imply claims about value that are in profound contradiction with one another. Despite the degree to which each of these terms already includes the others, each also works to affirm autonomy from the others. A much broader pattern is at work in this respect, to which I can only allude rather cryptically: a pattern that expresses the characteristically contradictory and aporetic constitution of what we have come to know as the modern (cultural, political and economic) subject (for more sustained discussion, see Walker 2010).

It is especially worth noting that similar and equally important problems would arise if the present list of concepts were extended to include, for example, society, community, gender or ethics, concepts that are invoked at various points in the book and indeed must be invoked once concepts such as culture, politics and economy are brought into play. Much of the discursive form of contemporary scholarly analysis has been shaped by the delineation of concepts that respond to shared questions about foundational principles (and not least about the sources, sites and agents of ultimate authority) while expressing very different answers to these questions and radicalizing these differences as responses to apparently different phenomena in ways that minimize the initial conflict over common problems of principle. In very general terms, that is, it is often possible to identify shifts from historical conditions characterized by struggles to articulate and pose questions about foundational values of some (ontological, epistemological, aesthetic, axiological or even theological) kind to a differentiation of categories expressing competing answers to such questions. In this sense, it is not difficult to see how all three of the concepts at issue here have been significantly shaped as competing responses to the multiple crises of authority accompanying various challenges to theological, feudal and imperial hierarchies in early-modern Europe. Indeed, where most of the conceptual genealogies invoked in the preceding chapters tend to draw attention to moments and texts from the late eighteenth-century onward, my own sense is that much earlier struggles over the authorization of foundational values offers an even more important context in which to understand what might be at stake in contemporary attempts to place the concepts of culture, politics and economy into some kind of conjunction.

One exemplary case in this respect has been the conversion of the agonistic relationship between an ethics appropriate for the salvation of souls and an ethics suitable for the liberty of political communities (a relationship perhaps identified most famously by Niccolò Machiavelli) into a profoundly disabling distinction between ethics and politics. Calls to add ethics to the kind of power politics celebrated by the forms of political realism that are said to have dominated the study of international relations often seem to have a familiar commonsensical and even progressive quality, at least until it is remembered that the sovereign states engaging in such forms of power politics are precisely the expressions of ethical possibility celebrating claims about identity, liberty and self-determination that have been held up as the crucial normative project distinguishing modern liberal orders from all their others. Attempts to simply add ethics, rather than to engage with competing or even incompatible forms of ethics, are thus not especially helpful despite their initial plausibility. The seductive possibilities produced by the proliferation of terms works primarily to obscure much of the profoundly aporetic character of competing claims about ultimate value, to the extent that it is still scarcely possible to engage in a discussion of future political possibilities without playing out some version of the claim that we need to move from a world of power politics to something more soothingly ethical. Concepts of culture, politics and economy share at least equally complicated and consequential histories of mutual implication and antagonism. As with many other calls to add or bring something back in, it is thus necessary to think about prior patterns of inclusion and exclusion enabling the patterns of inclusion and exclusion that now seem so problematic.

To seek to add gender to analyses of an international order, for example, is to confront the degree to which the exclusion of gender is already enabled by the inclusion of gendered accounts of what it means to be a (universal, but presumptively male) subject who might be included or excluded from modern political life. To seek to add culture to analyses of an international order is to confront the historical expression of culture as national identity, an expression that has often been reduced in turn to simple affirmation of value among competing values at play in relations of power between states. To seek to add environment to analyses of an international order is perhaps even more difficult, for it is to confront the constitutive exclusion of nature that was the primary condition under which it has been to possible imagine modern political subjects and citizens seeking to become free from hierarchical forms of authority invoking natural law while simultaneously reconstructing specifically modern accounts of nature informed by a supposedly sovereign reason and its authorized methodologies; and thus to imagine forms of culture, politics and economy that are precisely not natural while depending on constitutive accounts of what nature must be. Similar problems arise in relation to the sharp distinctions between secular and sacred or civilized and barbarian. There are many contexts other than the immediate one involving culture, politics and economy in which a demand to add may make perfect sense, but many of these suggest that prior patterns of subtraction, and many complex authorizations of distinctions and conceptual boundaries, enable commonsensical calls for greater inclusiveness to be countered with an even more commonsensical insistence on the necessity of distinct categories, and characteristic valorizations of their necessary relationship.

The Introduction by Best and Paterson advances a number of arguments for the development of a more cultural political economy. Similar arguments have been made in many different ways in different contexts, and versions of them are at work in many of the subsequent chapters. For the most part I find these arguments to be persuasive. However, the most striking characteristic of that introductory statement of the problem to be addressed is its pervasive ambivalence as to what the key problem in fact is. On the one hand, it articulates an ambition 'to combine culture with political economy' so as to contribute to 'the revitalization of political economy itself', and thus in effect to give a more cultural cast to the forms of political economy that have managed to find some purchase in the contemporary Anglo-American social sciences. On the other hand, there is the ambition to stimulate a more ambitious reopening of the meanings expressed by all three terms over a considerable longer period. Both ambitions seem reasonable, although I would say that the second is likely to have fairly significant implications for the first, perhaps to the extent of calling into question many of the most cherished assumptions, and canonical texts, that have enabled political economy to find a modest purchase in the modern academy.

In either case, the range of more specific ambitions is very wide. Some speak to the conditions appropriate for adequate 'understanding' or even 'explanation', and have a primarily epistemological character. Some speak to more ontological questions about what culture, politics and economy are or do, sometimes so as to pose questions about the role and functions of various practices and sometimes so as to transform established (and perhaps especially Gramscian) accounts of what a (cultural) political economy should be and do. Some speak to very specific phenomena, like the conditions under which marketing strategies become intelligible, the commodification of identity and difference, the production of and investment in specific meanings, the shaping of specific subjectivities, novel practices of calculability and governmentality, the effects of specific media, orchestrations of spatiotemporalities and scalar relations, and so on. Some speak to a capacity to interpret contemporary historical/transformations, especially in relation to claims about globalization, on the one hand, and about the increasingly cultural character of political economy, on the other. Nevertheless, the final sentence of the introductory chapter reins in the ambition considerably. 'In short', Best and Paterson say, 'a focus on cultural political economy not only enables us to better understand new patterns of activity and to attend to different sites of economic importance, but also contributes to our understanding of the core questions of political economy: the nature of production, trade and finance, the global patterns of distribution and inequality, and the power relations that sustain and constrain them all.' This is undoubtedly the case. Still, much of what is said throughout both their Introduction and the book as a whole suggests that the most important promise advanced by placing the terms cultural political economy together lies less in the possibility of adding culture to an already established political economy than in drawing attention to what is at stake in the deployment of all three terms, whether singly or in combination, sequentially or simultaneously.

Each of the three terms currently in play here is both massively contested and subject to cliché, caricature and reification. They are concepts after all, not things. The relationship between each concept and its supposed referents is enormously complicated. More to the point here, and as I have sought to intimate already, the relationship between these concepts is also complex, and subject to two contradictory dynamics.

On the one hand, it is not so difficult to make any one of the terms do the work of the other two. This is partly why the familiar reductionisms have become possible. In the final instance it is always possible to invoke the determinations of capitalism, or the supreme authority of the state, or various manifestations of some essentialized logic of modernity. It is *all* culturally constructed, as one might say to recent absurd claims about 'constructivism' in what are after all the social and thus historical sciences. Yes, there is relative autonomy, but only relative autonomy. Machiavelli worked out an economy of violence, but the term invokes another sense of economy than the one we are supposed to be thinking about. Hobbes *produces* his story, which works as a topology of sovereign authorization prioritizing space over time while Locke, Hegel and Marx *produce* variations on the same basic theme that prioritize time over space; stories about the sovereignty of the state are not so far removed from stories about the sovereignty of capital, narratives about the territorial state work through much the same logic as narratives about property and the constitution of the modern subject – and so on. Each of these three terms in some sense assumes and includes the others (and they arguably work, formally, as variations of a similar logic of unity–diversity, identity–difference and space–time).

On the other hand, these three terms have come to specify incompatible understandings of ultimate value: crudely, the value of a sovereign authority split between the sovereign state, the system of sovereign states and the sovereign subject–people; the value established by property and the market; and the value of identities and differences structured between potentially autonomous subjects–nations and potentially collective communities. This is why the familiar reductionisms generate complaints. Push reductionism too far, and aporias are broached. Relations between capital and the state have to be mediated; hence social democracy and Keynes, for example. Push the state too far and both subjects and markets will be in danger. Push subjects and markets, under the banner of ethics or cosmopolitanism, for example, and the political will shrivel. In this context, what is of interest is neither politics, economics or culture, but the relations and the boundaries between them, and the negotiations and struggles that have resulted in our sense that there can be something we call 'the political,' or 'the economic' or 'the cultural'. These terms, and the relations between them that we have come to take for granted are the expression of a specific historical/structural formation: symptoms or expressions of what needs to be explained/understood as well as dense strategies through which we have come to believe that explanation/understanding can occur. Buy into an assumption that there are practices we can identify as *the* cultural, *the* political or *the* economic and any chance of engaging with the production of specific forms of culture, politics or economy is considerably reduced.

The force of the claim by Best and Paterson that a more cultural political economy 'contributes to our understanding of the core questions of political economy: the nature of production, trade and finance, the global patterns of distribution and inequality, and the power relations that sustain and constrain them all' is nevertheless not trivial. In the background lies an implicit narrative about the bad old days in which forces of economy could be treated as primary in some way (as the most real, or material, or determinate) and both the political and cultural could be treated as secondary (as mere consequences or epiphenomena). Part of this background relates to the highly contested legacies of thinkers such as Marx who were acutely aware of the social complexity of economic practices and the struggle to recover their contributions to a sophisticated political and cultural analysis of capitalism. Part relates to the extraordinary influence of very specific (neoliberal) accounts of capitalist economies on most of the Anglo-American social sciences since the mid-1970s or so. Much of the immediate impetus for working towards a cultural political economy now comes from the tendency for very specific forms of economic analysis to invoke scholarly authority well beyond their sphere of competence, with predictable consequences for the credibility of scholarly pretension in many contexts. Nevertheless, it seems that a more properly political economy has attained or re-attained some degree of credibility. Economic reductionisms have been dismissed in favor of far more complex ontologies and causalities. Legitimations, regulative capacities, governmentalities, genders, subjectivities and consumers have come into play. As politics has itself been understood as a more diverse and complicated arena than some accounts of the state and its administrative practices sometimes suggest, so there have been many calls to add a more cultural sensibility to the mix.

Not the least difficulty here, of course, is that the standard terms through which we are encouraged to identify the broader context in which to understand the relations between these three terms have long become code-words signifying claims about the priority of one of the three terms over the other two. Capitalism has become the choice of those favoring the term economy, at least in the famous final instance. Modernity is the code-word for those with a more cultural bent, with Weber as grand alternative to Marx among the gods trying to explain the peculiarities of 'the West,' or 'the culture of subjectivity' or 'the culture of disenchantment.' Not so long ago, Marx and Weber were the two figures around which the terms culture, politics and economy might be organized and valorized, though both have receded from view as utilitarian accounts of decision in a competitive market have gained so much ground as a universal code through which to understand culture, politics and economies as variations upon a common cultural, political and economic conceit.

Leaving aside all the damage done to Marx, Weber and many others in the over-coding and conflation of terms like capitalism and modernity, they clearly signal huge controversies about what kind of phenomena we think we are dealing with, how they are to be known, and how we ought to be responding to them. Capitalism signals not only economy, but specific forms of property relation, a labor theory of value, conceptions of self-interest and the generalized circulation of money: the kind of world sketched in John Locke's startling chapter on property in the late seventeenth century and celebrated by Adam Smith and others a few generations later. Modernity signals the rise of the modern subject, scientific knowledge, secularization and the sovereign state. Chicken and egg questions ensue, and keep going round the requisite circles. Competing sovereignties also ensue as claims about the origins and limits of authority are traced to the foundational value of price in a self-regulating market or to the foundational value of law in a self-constituting state; although in this context, curiously enough, the term economy often signals a specific array of primordial causal determinations and authorizations of authority to which the term sovereignty is only rarely applied.

Perhaps even more is at stake in this respect than in the struggle to evade the economic reductionisms that played such a crucial role in twentieth-century scholarly life. Much of the early-modern European period is conventionally understood as a complex and highly uneven array of attempts to resist the claims to authority affirming hierarchically organized theological, imperial and feudal orders in the name of liberty and equality. This is a name that has come to have many conflicting meanings depending on whether the stories about the transformations of early-modern Europe affirm the centrality of Roman/Italian republicanisms, contracts between free and equal individuals, a duty to improve the earth that was given in common and the rewards of property and money that follow from its fulfillment, the sovereignty of reason that enables the possibility of universality within particular subjects and of particular subjects within a universalizing order, or the unfolding of all such potentials within the limits of a progressive or tragic history. If modern forms of sovereignty are understood, as I think they must be, in relation to the authorization of claims about the beginning and ending of things, about the authoritative founding and delimitation of authority and thus what comes in between as a relation between norm and exception, limit or margin, then it is difficult to see how the kind of story about the legitimacy of private property told by Locke is any less important for understanding contemporary practices of sovereignty than the story told by Hobbes about the contractual state. Crucially, it is not the same form of sovereignty, and the multiple conflicts between the sites of foundational value expressed in these two stories about property and the circulation of money on the one hand and the liberty of subjects within and under the jurisdiction of a sovereign state, on the other, have played a rather significant role in the constitution of the forms of life we identify through terms like culture, economy and politics ever since. In this context, while there are certainly many good reasons to insist that the term economy be accompanied by the term political, there is perhaps even more to be said to the need to think about the ways in which the term economy has come to express one of the key articulations of political authority while seeming to be a source of authority that is somehow different from or even prior to political authority. Read in relation to the framing of contemporary accounts of liberty and sovereignty, at least, there is reason to suspect that the supposed relation between economy and politics might be better understood as an aporetic relation between two competing forms of politics, and thus some reason to feel some sympathy for those who have discovered that bringing the terms politics and economy together is more difficult that it might seem if we take these terms on what has become face value.

Moreover, it might also be said that the term culture tells us less about how we might identify a field of phenomena that might be studied, one that is somehow different from the fields identified by concepts of politics and economics, than about the specific practices that helped shape what we now identify as politics and economics. It is a term, after all, that works to affirm presumed oppositions between matter and consciousness/idea/ideal, between particular cultures and more general or even universal civilizations, and between some (essential, achieved, spatialized) condition of being and a (temporal, productive, constitutive) process of cultivation: oppositions that are worked out in different ways in the constitutive spatiotemporalities expressed in various accounts of what we mean by politics and economics.

If we want to make some sense – explain, understand – much that is going on under contemporary conditions, adding culture to a political economy holds considerable short-term promise. What is most disconcerting, in fact, is that is that this remains a project that needs to be engaged. It is nevertheless a project that is necessarily pluralistic, one that reads phenomena in (at least) three ways; though in my view three is rarely enough. Yet hopes for a more cultural political economy must eventually draw attention to the difficulties of engaging with phenomena that already find expression in the relations and antagonisms at work in the terms cultural, political and economy. There can be no pretence that the antagonistic claims to value and authority expressed in these concepts can be transcended within some grand synthesis. Each of these terms encourages a discourse of either/or, but they express a condition of multiple contradiction. I would thus not put my own hopes in the creation of a cultural political economy as such. I would look, instead, to those sites at which the boundaries of these reified claims about ultimate value are being shifted, substituted and rearticulated thereby giving rise not least to struggles over what counts as legitimate authority. Claims about 'the economic,' 'the cultural' and 'the political' often tend work very effectively to depoliticize what has to be politicized, and the most urgent tasks for contemporary practices of politicization occur on the boundaries, borders and limits of hegemonic concepts quite as much as in any practices to which we assume such concepts must refer. It is in this sense that this book might be read less as an attempt to construct something that might be called a cultural political economy than as an expression of the practices of politicization, depoliticization and thus politicization that are at work whenever claims about a politics reach their limits, including limits that have been defined as economic or cultural.

Bibliography

Walker, R. B. J. (2010) *After the Globe, Before the World*, London: Routledge.

Index

An environmentally friendly book printed and bound in England by www.printondemand-worldwide.com

PEFC Certified

This product is
from sustainably
managed forests
and controlled
sources

www.pefc.org

This book is made entirely of sustainable materials; FSC paper for the cover and PEFC paper for the text pages.

#0383 - 010915 - C0 - 234/156/14 - PB - 9780415489324